Handbook on Land Survey in India

Edited by

Anandhi
Snehasis Mishra

B.N. Yugandhar Centre for Rural Studies
Lal Bahadur Shastri National Academy of Administration
Mussoorie

(First Published in India in 2022)

Rs 1250

ISBN: 978-93-91978-05-1

2026 Imp., PoD

Handbook on Land Survey in India

Published by:
SHIPRA PUBLICATIONS
LG 18-19, Pankaj Central Market
I.P. Ext., Patparganj, Delhi 110092, India
+91 11 47322068; 96500 28065, 9810522367
info@shiprapublication.com
www.shiprapublication.com

श्रीनिवास आर कटिकिथाला, भाप्रसे
निदेशक
Srinivas R Katikithala, IAS
Director

Foreword

Agriculture is still the principal source of livelihood for the bulk of population in rural areas. Ownership of land and its access are therefore essential for individual and societal development. Immediately after Independence, India's land policy was dominated by the Kumarappa Committee's recommendations on comprehensive agrarian reform measures which were largely based on four principles i.e. tenancy reforms, celling of surplus land, consolidation and abolition of intermediaries. Clarity in land records and strengthening revenue administration were mostly ignored in that period. The paradigm of India's land policy had shifted towards improving land revenue administration since 1995 onwards.

In India, cadastral survey and land settlements followed different methodologies in different state/territories due to historical reasons. Apart from that, 'maintenance of land records, survey for revenue purposes and records of rights' comes under State list in the Seventh Schedule of the Constitution, and therefore, there is no national level or standard methodology for land survey and preparation of land records. Some States have modernized their survey techniques and updated their records bringing down the possibilities of error and litigation while some others are still in the process of this upgradation. Apart from technology, there is also a lot of dissimilarities in the methods, processes applied by different States and many have tried to improve these from time to time.

This handbook is therefore, an attempt to bring to one source, the many technologies, methods, rules, processes followed for survey across the country. It also captures some of the experiments attempted by some states in improving

their existing system and its results. Therefore, this handbook would be useful as an introduction to survey methods for Officer Trainees as well as for officers of various States, working in the Survey & Settlement sector as it also covers the practices of 12 states, their state specific rules of survey and settlement, practices of surveying, issues, challenges and initiative and future plans. The selected states are significant not only because they together cover more than 55 per cent of national land area but also because their practices are largely followed by their neighbouring states as well, thereby covering almost all forms of survey practices in the country.

The importance of accurate land records and survey cannot be overemphasized in a country like ours where land matters affect nearly every person directly or indirectly. This is foremost responsibility of Officers dealing with land management across the nation and I am certain that this handbook will be of great service to them and will also attract and prove useful to readers interested in the field of land revenue survey and mapping.

Mussoorie
18th May 2022

(Srinivas R. Katikithala)
Director & Chairman
B.N. Yugandhar Centre for Rural Studies

A Message from the Editors

The basic objective of the handbook is to develop a resource on land survey by bringing different state practices of land surveying and recording practices, rules, historical perspective and applications of modern survey techniques, which can be used as a guide for the field practitioners. This handbook includes 12 state chapters, covers almost all the major zones of India in north, south, east, west, centre and north-east. Each of state chapters covers their historical and contemporary land recording practices, deficiency and challenges of the existing system and future initiatives towards modern survey.

We are grateful to all the contributors and their institution for their efforts to make this handbook a useful document for the practitioners to not only to understand the methods used for land survey in the state, but also helps to learn the intricacies of land survey mechanisms followed by the other states. For the convenience of the readers this handbook also discusses the modern methods of land surveying to understand the advantages and disadvantages of the modern techniques.

We are sure that this handbook will help to recognize the genesis of land survey, its challenges that are faced by the respective state by following contemporary methods and invite attention to the practitioners to take measures to establish comprehensive-accurate-real-time land records by using modern land survey techniques.

Anandhi, IAS
Snehasis Mishra

Acknowledgements

The Handbook on Land Survey in India is an endeavour to understand the different state practices followed in survey operations and the book holds a discussion about available modern techniques which could be a solution for the states to implement as per their capacity. Moreover, this handbook is also a collaborative effort of many individuals who have contributed and cooperated at various stages in its completion. First of all, we would like to express our gratitude to Shri Ajay Tirkey (IAS), Secretary, Department of Land Resources, Shri Hukum Singh Meena (IAS), Additional Secretary, Department of Land Resources and Shri Sonmoni Borah (IAS), Department of Land Resources, Ministry of Rural Devolvement, Government of India for providing financial assistance for publishing the handbook. We would also like to express our sincere thanks to Shri Srinivas R. Katikithala (IAS), Director, Lal Bahadur Shastri National Academy of Administration, Mussoorie who has always been very supportive to and encouraging in the endeavour to bring out this handbook.

We convey our grateful thanks to Shri C. Sridhar and Shri N.K. Sudhansu, the former Centre Directors, of B.N. Yugandhar Centre for Rural Studies, Lal Bahadur Shastri National Academy of Administration, Mussoorie, for their guidance. We are also thankful to Abhiram G. Sankar, Deputy Director, Lal Bahadur Shastri National Academy of Administration, Mussoorie for his support. We are extremely thankful and express our heartiest gratitude to Dr. R. Kannan, IAS, Former Additional Chief Secretary to Government of Tamil Nadu, Tourism, Culture and Religious Endowment Department for his support and cooperation. We express our sincere gratitude to Dr. D. Sajith Babu, IAS (Kerala) for providing expert inputs for the Handbook at initial stages.

We would also like to acknowledge the contribution of Lt. General Girish Kumar, VSM, (Retd.) Former Surveyor General of India, for his keen interest in this topic and for providing all the necessary inputs and sharing valuable insights. He has continued his support even after retirement. The Authors of the state chapters have cooperated beyond their limitations and take out time from their busy schedules. They deserve our grateful appreciation. In addition, we would like to express our sincere gratitude to Shri S. Chockalingam, Director General, YASHADA, Pune; Shri Lalit Gogoi, IAS, Director of Land Records & Surveys, Assam; Shri J.S.V. Prasad, IAS, Director General, APHRD Institute, Andhra Pradesh; Shri K. Jayakumar, IAS (Retd.), Director, Institute of Management in Government,

Kerala; Shri Rohit Gupta, IAS, Settlement Commissioner, Rajasthan; Shri Jai Singh, IAS, Director, Land Records and Survey, Bihar; Shri Pramod Chaturvedi, Officer-in-charge (Training), RCVP Noronha, Academy of Administration & Management, Madhya Pradesh; Ms. Surina Rajan, IAS, Director General, Haryana Institute of Public Administration, Haryana; Ms. Manisha Trighatia, Secretary & Commissioner, Revenue Department, Uttar Pradesh; Shri Kaushik Bhimajiyani, Settlement Commissioner & Director of Land Records, Gujarat; and Smt. V. Manjula, IAS, Director General, Administrative Training Institute, Karnataka for nominating their best persons from their respective states and encouraged them to write the state chapters. We express our sincere thanks to Shri Chittaranjan Das, IAS (Rtd), Former Member, Land Reforms & Tenancy Tribunal, West Bengal for his valuable suggestions, help and advice.

Our grateful thanks are also due to all our colleagues of the B.N. Yugandhar Centre for Rural Studies, Lal Bahadur Shastri National Academy of Administration, Mussoorie for their support and assistance.

Editors

Contents

Abbreviations

APSBA	Andhra Pradesh Survey & Boundary Act
AT	Aerial Triangulation
BC	Before Christ
BTAD	Bodoland Territorial Areas District
CAD	Computer Aided Design
CGS	Centimetre Gram Second System
COGO	Coordinate Geometry
CORS	Continuously Operating Reference Stations
CSIS	City Survey Information System
D&O	Digital & Offset
DD	Deputy Director (Land Records)
DEM	Digital Elevation Model
DGCA	Director General of Civil Aviation
DGPS	Differential Global Positioning System
DILR	District Inspector of Land Records
DILRMP	Digital India Land Records Modernization Programme
DMRS	Document Management Retrieval System
DRO	District Revenue Officer
DSO	District Survey Office
DTDB	Digital Topographic Data Base
DTM	Digital Terrain Model
EDM	Electronic Distance Meter
ETS	Electric Total Station
FE	Feature Extraction
FMB	Field Measurement Book
FPS	Foot Pound Second System
FRS	Functional Requirement Specifications
GCN	Ground Control Network
GCNS	Ground Control Network Software
GCP	Ground Control Points
GIS	Geographical Information System
GNSS	Global Navigation System Satellite
GoI	Government of India
GPDP	Gram Panchayat Development Plan
GPS	Global Positioning System

GSD	Ground Sample Distance
GT	Great Trigonometric
GTS	Great Triangulation Station
HARSAC	Haryana Space Application Centre
HRSI	High Resolution Satellite Imagery
IEC	Information Education & Communication
IGS	International Geodetic Survey
ILR	Inspector Land Record
IMU	Inertial Measurement Unit
IORA	Integrated Online Revenue Administration
ISRO	Indian Space Reasearch Organisation
KJP	Kami Jashti Patrak (Survey Collection)
KMC	Kolkata Municipal Corporation
LPM	Land Parcel Map
LRA	Land Reforms Act
MISS	Management Information System Software
MoD	Ministry of Defence
MLM	Missing Line Measurement
MT	Mainline Traverse
NC	Non-Cadastral
NCM	New Cadastral Map
NIC	National Informatics Centre
NLRMP	National Land Records Modernization Programme
NNRMS	National Natural Resources Management System
NRIS	National Record Information System
NSDB	National Spatial Data Base
NSDI	National Spatial Data Infrastructure
OCM	Old Cadastral Map
OMOK	One-Man-One-Khatian
ORI	Ortho Rectified Image
PCP	Primary Control Points
PDE	Public Data Entry
PPK	Post Process Kinematic
PPP	Public Private Partnership
PSP	Private Service Provider
PT	Plane Table
PTCL	Prohibition of Transfer Certain Land
RDM	Remote Distance Measurement
REM	Remove Elevation Measurement
RLR	Rajasthan Land Revenue
RGB	Red Green Blue
RoR	Records of Rights

RPC	Rational Polynomial Coefficients
RPOR	Rural Property Ownership Records
RTC	Record of Tenancy and Crops
RTCs	Records of Rights, Tenancy & Crops
RTK	Real Time Kinematic
SCDLR	Settlement Commissioner & Director of Land Records
SCP	Secondary Control Points
SDC	State Data Centre
SDO	Sub Divisional Officer
SEZ	Special Economic Zone
SLR	Superintendent of Land Records
SoI	Survey of India
SRA&ULR	Strengthening Revenue Administration & Updation of Land Records
SSLR	Survey Settlement Land Records
ST	Secondary Line Traverse
TCP	Tertiary Control Points
TSP	Technical Service Provider
UAV	Unmanned Aerial Vehicle
ULPIN	Unique Land Parcel Identification Number
UPOR	Urban Property Ownership Records
WBEAA	West Bengal Estate Acquisition Act
WV	World View

1

Introduction
Land Survey in India

Anandhi, IAS and Snehasis Mishra

Introduction

The predecessor of the modern human race never migrated and therefore did not have food surplus to survive, when nature turned hostile and they became extinct. The modern human race always migrated in search of food and stored the surplus that enabled longer life expectancy. This enabled them to have few natural catastrophes and have larger populations. As population increased, they organized themselves into tribes of nomads. There was no settlement and accumulation was in the form of livestock like cattle. In course of time, they learnt the arts of agriculture. Later as they settled down for longer periods, they started cultivation for one season and then moving on to another place. Finally, they settled down in fertile places like valleys or near to rivers and as an outcome, land became an important item of wealth. The human race understood the value of land and due to that, groups of peoples or tribes or community gradually delineate their land by making physical boundaries. In due course of time, peoples among the groups, tribes or communities have divided the land into privately owned land.

Land administration in India witnessed different rules such as community ownership, emperorships of different dynasties especially Mughals, Presidency rules under British, now it is managed through the federal structure of state and Government of India. But, it has been observed that under any of the structure, protecting property rights of citizens is one of the fundamental duties of the government. Therefore, to secure property rights; record preparation by a conducting survey was felt necessary from time immemorial.

Surveying is defined as "Surveying is the art of making such measurements of the relative positions of points on the surface of the earth that, on drawing them down to scale, natural and artificial features of the surface (i.e. land) may be exhibited in their correct horizontal or vertical relationship, on a sheet of paper, i.e. a map". (David Clarke).

The prime objectives of survey are to collect field data, based on the field data to prepare a map, analyses and calculate revenue and for setting out future plan.

Based on the purpose (for which surveying is being conducted), surveying has been classified into:

a. *Control survey*: To establish horizontal and vertical positions of control points.

b. *Land survey*: To determine the boundaries and areas of parcels of land, also known as property survey, boundary survey or cadastral survey. (Figure-1B)

c. *Topographic survey*: To prepare a plan/ map of a region that includes natural as well as man-made features including elevation. (Figure-1A)

d. *Engineering survey*: To collect requisite data for planning, design and execution of engineering projects. Three broad steps are:
   - Reconnaissance survey: To explore site conditions and availability of infrastructures.
   - Preliminary survey: To collect adequate data to prepare a plan/map of the area to be used for planning and design.
   - Location survey: To set out work on the ground for actual construction/ execution of the project.

e. *Route survey*: To plan, design and laying out routes such as highways, railways, canals, pipelines, and other linear projects.

f. *Construction surveys*: Surveys which are required for the establishment of points, lines, grades, and for staking out engineering works (after the plans have been prepared and the structural design has been done).

g. *Astronomic surveys*: To determine the latitude, longitude (of the observation station) and azimuth (of a line through the observation station) from astronomical observation.

h. *Mine surveys*: To carry out surveying specific for opencast and underground mining purposes.

In India, land revenue survey can be divided into three broad categories, based on time, methodology and area it covers. These are as follows:

i. *Cadastral survey*: The term cadastral comes from the Latin base term *'Cadastre'*, referring to a registry of lands using a cadastral survey or cadastral map. The Cadastral Survey is a field by field survey of a Revenue Village or an estate undertaken by Government, to ascertain the position of boundaries, area and quality of each field. It provides the data for the Settlement of Land Revenue and the preparation and maintenance of Record of Rights (R.G. Gordon, 1974). A cadastral survey is a comprehensive land recording of the land and real estate by metes-and-bounds of a country. Therefore, cadastral surveying is executed to determine and define the land ownership and boundaries. Cadastral surveys deal with one of the oldest and most fundamental aspect of human society i.e. ownership of the land. These are the surveys that create, mark, define, retrace or re-establish the boundaries and sub-division of public land. This survey will be

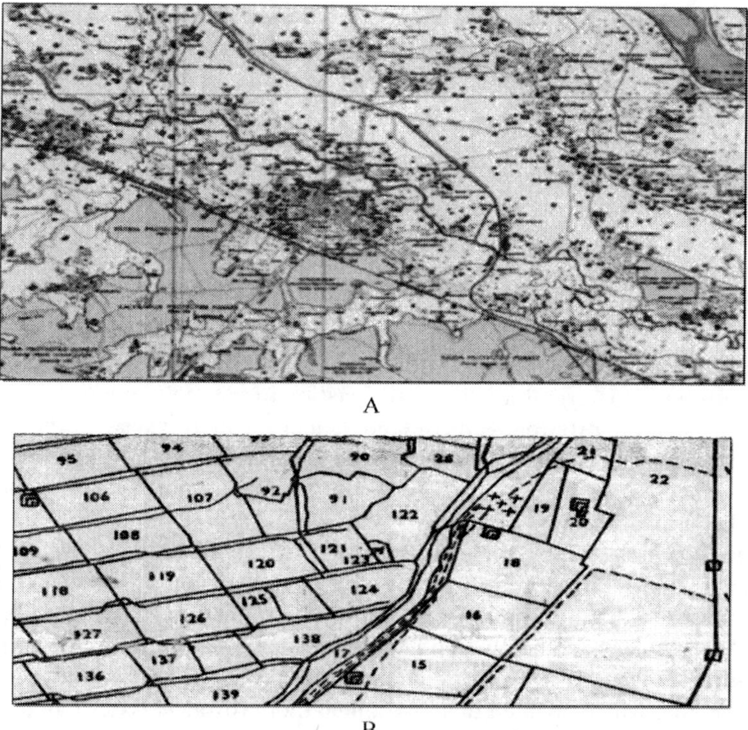

Figure 1 *A-Topographical Survey, B-Cadastral Survey*

authenticated by a government agency and is the central repository of information for other departmental users for their operational management. Necessity of Cadastral Survey

- A cadastral survey is necessary to determine the boundaries of the field area, ownership of each holding. Measurement and assessment on a piece of land proportional to its area is collected direct from the person, in whose name the land is registered in the revenue record.
- It helps the government to safeguard the community or government lands from encroachment and also helps the government to settle boundary disputes.
- Cadastral survey done for the first time is called initial cadastral survey or original survey. Those done subsequently for the second time or third time are called resurvey confined to the area originally surveyed. A resurvey is done when the changes in occupation and in the boundaries of the field are numerous or when the previous survey is considered defective. During the British time it was done once in every 30 years interval.

The Cadastral systems in India were designed initially to earn revenue through the collection of taxes on the property. Cadastral surveys are important because invariably these surveys are linked with ownership of the property. The cadastral systems support the legal ownership of the land, depiction of legal and topographical aspects including area and parcel boundaries. Depiction of legal and topographical aspects of the land becomes more important if it pertain to urban/town property. Due to fast developmental activities, the system plays important role in land administration activities by policymakers, resource planners and administrators who make decision about the land. They need more detailed land information than has been traditionally available. The general scale of the Cadastral Survey is 1: 4,000 (formerly 16 inches to a mile in the F.P.S. System). However, there is great variation in the scales adopted by various states and in different belts of land. Under the metric system, the areas are calculated in hectares (one hundredth part of a square kilometers).

ii. *Revisional survey*: It means survey operations initiated and conducted on the basis of the blue print map of the cadastral survey in order to update the lord records (Bihar Special Survey and Settlement Act, 2011). When there is addition to territory or un-surveyed land, change in land classification from forest to agricultural or from rural to urban, resurveys become necessary. The British government had resurveys done every thirty years so that the effect of the increase in production and productivity is reflected in land records, which enabled them to collect more revenue. After independence, many states of India had resurveyed their land parcels, but there were so many districts and areas left, where no revisional survey was carried out. Therefore, revenue records and map records are mismatched in almost every corner of India. It happened because of so many reasons, as revenue collection was not such a priority of the government, they become reluctant for periodical resurvey. As a result, village accountant who were responsible to maintain updated land records, have been deployed into some other works and land records maintenance was neglected. In recent times, under the DILRMP or state programmes, some states (Kerala, Gujarat, Haryana, Madhya Pradesh, Himachal Pradesh, Jharkhand, West Bengal, Tripura, Nagaland) have initiated resurvey and preparing new land records.

iii. *Updation of the survey*: Updation is a half way measure between no resurvey and full resurvey. When it is felt that the changes are not so huge as to necessitate the expenses, labour and time consumed for a resurvey, the records are updated so that all changes on ground are reflected in the records. In India, state level cadastral survey was conducted during British time, though some districts were not covered during the survey due to many reasons. After the Independence, some states had conducted revisional surveys to record the field level changes and updating records. Due to the dynamic nature of land transactions, the survey of land should be conducted in regular intervals, most of the states did not conduct the periodical land survey. As a result, records and maps are out-dated and do not reflect the ground reality. Therefore, updating survey records by doing the survey of land parcels at regular intervals is necessary.

Basic Principles of Survey

In course of survey work, errors may creep in at various stages, making the survey inaccurate and distorted. In all survey work, the aim should be to keep the errors to a minimum and to maintain a uniform standard of accuracy throughout the survey. For achieving this, the following guiding principles are followed:

(i) Working from whole to part,
(ii) Economy of accuracy,
(iii) Consistency of accuracy, and
(iv) Independent check.

The above mentioned principles are explained as follows:

(i) *Working from whole to part*: This is a basic principle that is followed in all types of survey work. To survey a fairly extensive area, a network of control points is first established around the periphery of the area to be surveyed. The positions of those points, fixed on the ground with a high degree of accuracy, form a closed polygon around the area under survey. As such, the whole periphery is surveyed with high accuracy at first. Next, the polygon is divided into a number of parts or quadrilaterals (known as murabbas, khandams etc.). Survey of internal details of the area is then taken up by less accurate and less expensive methods in each quadrilateral separately, the idea of working in this way is to prevent accumulation of errors and contain the errors in a limited area, so that the errors can easily identified and rectified.
On the other hand, if the reverse process is followed, that is, the survey is made to expand outwards, minor errors get added and the total error becomes unbound at the end.

(ii) *Economy of accuracy*: There are different methods, procedures and instruments for different types of survey, depending on the purposes of survey and the accuracy required. There are certain purposes of survey, requiring a high degree of accuracy, and in such cases, procedures and instruments used are elaborate, expensive and time-consuming. But, for purposes like cadastral etc. highly accurate methods are not necessary. If such methods are applied, where they are not necessary, it would be wastage of labour and money. In other words, there should not be any needless refinement.

(iii) *Consistency of accuracy*: In extensive surveys where different portions of the survey have to be done by different surveyors or at different times, a uniform standard of accuracy should be maintained. Similar procedure

should be followed and instruments used should be similar in all such cases so that the whole survey can be treated as one and corresponds to the same specifications throughout.

(iv) Independent check: An independent check on the survey work done by a cadastral surveyor (known as Survey Kanungo or Lekhpal, Amin etc.) must always be done by a superior official to ensure that the work is of required accuracy. Suitable provisions for independent checks should be included in the procedures to be adopted for all types of standard survey work.

History of Cadastral/ Revenue Survey in India

The origin of Cadastral Survey in India can be traced to the pre-Mauryan and Mauryan period circa 3rd Century BCE. Cartography or the science of survey and map making has a 2000-year written history from the time of Plato in the Western world. In India, there is a reference to maps and diagrams even from the days of the Mahabharata circa 3100 B.C. The Chakras are intricate geometric diagrams inscribed usually on copper plates to attract cosmic energies. The whole universe as per the Bhagavata is depicted on a cloth diagram in a manuscript kept at the Maharaja Vijai Singh Library, Jodhpur (Kannan, Dr. R., 2009).

Historically, way back even by First Century B.C., the institution of a village accountant known as Gopa who was answerable to the next tier of administration of the district, had come into being. "He looked into the accounts and statistics of a group of villages. He recorded and numbered plots of grounds, both cultivated and uncultivated, plains, marshy lands, gardens, vegetable gardens, forests, altars, temples of gods, irrigation works, cremation grounds, feeding houses, places where water was freely supplied to travellers, places of pilgrimage, pasture grounds, and roads within his jurisdiction. He fixed the boundary of villages, fields, forests, roads, and registered gifts, sales, charities and remission of taxes regarding fields." (Col. G.C. Agarwal).

In the historical period, i.e. the period from which written records were prepared, Survey of Land and Revenue Settlement is usually dated to Sher Shah Suri (1472-1545 A.D.) though the Arthasastra of Kautilya shows the use of maps to show the extent of the Mauryan Empire as well as its use in warfare. Raja Todarmal, the Finance Minister of Emperor Akbar established the village level revenue officials in-charge like Lekhpal, the Village Accountant. The Khasra system of survey in North India owes its origin to Raja Todarmal.

After 1757, the British rule was imposed in the vast territory of Bengal, then without delay, they started scientific survey to assess the various resources in the country for the purpose of their own revenue generation. Different surveys were initated such as topographical survey, marine survey, route survey, revenue survey, military survey, trigonometrical survey, geographical survey, etc. The Britishers started collecting land revenue based on the system that had been created by the Mughal emperor. They found that the territory was divided into provinces (*subhas*), districts *(sarkar)* and sub-districts *(parganas)* along with other sub-divisions like *mauzas, chaklas, tarafs, tappas*, etc. without any accurate boundary maps and records. Based on that scenario, Britishers were committed to establishing a robust revenue administartion by starting revenue survey, settle the land with the owners, preparation of maps and records, etc. to omit the uneven nature of information about property rights and to increase the land revenue. Revenue survey was conducted in different phases in the three major presidencies namely; Bengal, Madras and Bombay and other provinces. To get the maximum land revenue, the entire territory of British India was divided into three types of land revenue systems:

i) The East India Company for the ease of collection after getting the Diwani (in reality rulership) of Bengal, Bihar and Orissa by the Treaty of Allahabad, settled on a few large assessees whom they made Zamindars and for long terms – the Permanent Settlement. Zamindari system means there is one person, an individual or a legal body, that is between the actual co-sharer or the soil worker, and the State (B.H. Baden Powell). Landlord systems were established mainly in Bengal, Bihar, Orissa, the Central Provinces (modern Madhya Pradesh state) and some parts of Madras Presidency (modern Tamil Nadu and Andhra Pradesh states). In some of these areas, the Zamindars were declared as landlords under the "Permanent Settlement" of 1793, the British administration had no direct dealings with the cultivating peasants. In some other areas, a "temporary" settlement was implemented whereby the revenue was fixed for a certain number of years, after which it was subject to revision.
ii) The second type of revenue-system i.e. individual cultivator based systems or Ryotwari which prevailed in most areas of Madras and Bombay Presidencies and also in Assam. In the Ryotwari land tenure system every registered holder of land is recognized as its proprietor, and pays land revenue directly to the Government. Under the revenue system Settlement Officer was appointed and given the duties to prepare a new record of rights, surveying of lands etc.
iii) 'Mahalwari' or the mahal-village based system of land revenue was practised in Central Province, North-West Frontier, Agra, Punjab, Gangetic Valley. The Mahalwari system was introduced by 1822 with the estate or mahals proprietary bodies where lands belonged jointly to the village community technically called the body of co-shares. The Lambardar or village headman has to apportion the tax among the farmers and collect it and then pay to Tahsildar. In this system, settlement operations were carried out after doing the cadastral survey of villages. Settlement Officers, Assistant Settlement Officers and Tehsildars were bound to exercise the survey and settlement operations and update records of rights.

As different revenue systems were introduced by the British rulers in the three Presidencies (Bengal, Madras and Bombay) in India, the methods of cadastral mapping also differed according to the units of assessment of land revenue.

The revenue officials of the Bengal Presidency, where 'Permanent Settlement' was imposed, realized that due to the improper records, revenue collection was not adequate and felt the necessity of carrying out a detailed cadastral survey. Finally, the East India Company decided to break this impasse, and on 7 August 1822 it issued Regulation 7 instructing its officials in the Bengal Presidency and North West Provinces to commence detailed cadastral surveys, on which all future land settlements were to be concluded (Bernardo A. Michael). In the Bengal Presidency area, the revenue assessment units were whole mauzas or revenue villages, which were components of individual estates, under proprietary ownership of intermediaries or Zamindars as per the Permanent Settlement Regulation, 1793. As such, for accurate assessment of revenue for each revenue village, which was normally much larger in area than individual holdings or parcels of land, scientific method of survey in the form of theodolite traverse surveying was started, for preparation of map in a particular scale and accurate measurement of area of each village. The area of an estate was calculated by summing up the areas of all villages included in that estate, which facilitated correct assessment of revenue to be paid by the estate to the Government. This was the object for conducting Revenue Survey (1835-1877) in the permanently settled areas.

But in other Presidencies, like Madras Presidency or Bombay Presidency, it was mostly Ryotwari system, where the ryots were direct tenants under the Government, with no intermediaries like zamindars or talukdars in between. As the ryots were holders of individual parcels of land, which were much smaller in area than a village, it was sufficient to take linear measurements of the sides of the parcel of land and prepare a sketch map or an unscaled plan, showing the dimensions or lengths of each side from pillar to pillar of the land. Sometimes such field measurements are plotted in a convenient scale also. Diagonal lengths are also measured and shown on the map, where possible. A number is given on the land as depicted on the map for its identification and the parcel of land is then identified as a survey number. Similarly, when subinfeudation of a survey number is required due to partition or any other ground, it is divided into subdivisions by measurement on the field and shown on the map. Each subdivision is also given a separate number for identification. Maps of this kind are commonly known as Tippons or FMBs. Field measurement details are noted in the FMBs or Field Measurement Books. For measurement of areas of such survey numbers or subdivision numbers, the land parcel is divided into geometrical figures like triangles, (sometimes right-angled triangles), trapeziums, rectangles, squares etc. as per convenience and then areas of each such geometrical components are calculated by applying appropriate formulae and the summation of the areas gives the area of the survey or subdivision number. Ownership details and other relevant information are noted in the associated records. The survey methodology used was mainly chain survey, using chain and cross stuff.

By mosaicking the adjoining survey numbers, a village map is prepared. However, from such village maps, prepared by following "part to whole" (reverse of the scientific survey principle of "whole to part"), accuracy of village area is difficult to be ensured.

In those areas of "Mahalwari" revenue system, maps were prepared for individual parcels of land for assessment of revenue like that of ryotwari system, but revenue was assessed for the entire village or Mahal by adding the revenue of all land parcels of the Mahal, which was collected by the village head or any other person engaged by the government. In some places, system of traverse survey for mapping of a village or Mahal was also adopted for assessment of revenue.

A few words on the scientific surveys initiated by the British in the 18th and 19th century in India:

i) **Rennell's Survey:** Modern surveying was initiated by the Britishers in this country in 1760s. The pioneer of modern surveying in India was James Rennell, who started his work in Bengal. His earliest works were entirely connected with river surveys for preparation of river maps for trading routes in Bengal Presidency. Later he conducted upland surveys also to produce general maps of the Province. He used an angle-measuring instrument called Quadrant and a chain for his survey work initially, but afterwards he used theodolite. His maps lacked the accuracy of modern maps, yet they possess valuable information about the rivers of his time. His original maps are preserved in the Survey of India archives and one copy at Survey Building, Kolkata.

ii) **Great Trigonometrical Survey:** The Great Trigonometrical Survey was started by William Lambton, a British Army Officer, under the aegis of the Survey of India on the 10 April 1802 at Mount St. Thomas near Madras and continued for over 60 years. The main aim of the survey was to establish a network of permanent stations on the ground. The positions of these stations were calculated with the highest degree of accuracy in terms of latitude, longitude and height above the Mean Sea Level. These stations are called G.T. Survey bench marks or stations. They cover the whole of India and act as control points for Topographical Survey in any part of the country. Cadastral surveys are also sometimes connected with available GTS stations for checking their accuracy. The procedure was to build up a series of triangles with sides about 7 to 8 miles long starting from an initial base line and closing on another base line, the lengths of which were measured with extreme accuracy. As it is easier to attain a high degree of accuracy in angular measurement than to attain the same by linear measurement, the lengths of the other two sides of the triangle were very accurately computed by "solution of triangle", using the linear measurement of the base line and the two observed angles by theodolite. Then the latitude and longitude of one Station were determined accurately from astronomical observations; the latitudes and longitudes of a series of stations connected by a chain of triangles were deduced there-from, on the basis of the known angles and lengths of the lines joining them. The latitude and longitude of a far-off station, so deduced were checked against the observed latitude and longitude of that Station, thus the difficult task of determining accurately the latitude and longitude of each station was obviated. The geographical coordinates of each GTS station in terms of latitude and longitude was thus computed with a high degree of precision.

Objective of the Handbook

The objective of the handbook on the land survey in India is to develop a resource on cadastral survey and resurvey, which can be referred to as a guide for the use of grassroot level revenue officials at different level. This handbook of research on survey is useful as a textbook on survey and mapping techniques for new learners for the coming years. It is a collaborative effort of experts and covered a wide range of potential research areas, including methodology of survey, land survey scenarios across the country, science and its applications, scenario of land records, identify potentiality of cadastral survey and its effect of land administration etc. The handbook brought available practices on a land survey in the country including modern methods of surveying. This handbook is to improve the understanding of scientific analysis and promote evidence based policy formulation in the regional and local levels.

Definition of Different Terms with reference to Land Survey

- *Basic Tax Register*: This is a subset of Settlement Register which primarily contains the details of the landholders who are supposed to pay the land tax to Government, arranged on survey/resurvey number basis. This register also contains the details of Government lands which are interspersed between the above survey numbers. This register is a permanent register that cannot be altered.
- *Bi-junction*: While taking offset from G line to the bent points, if the distance is more, then a bent point would be taken temporarily, intermediary junction called bi-junction.
- *Check line or Diagonal lines*: The lines which are being drawn from one tri-junction to alternate opposite tri-junctions towards making the survey field into triangles pursuant to formation of G lines. Offset is to be taken from these check lines for subdivision bends and junctions. The check lines should neither be broken nor crossed while doing triangulation of the survey field
- *Connecting lines*: These are the lines which are drawn from the boundary points to fix a minor survey field within a survey field.
- *Constant Azimuth*: It is an imaginary line that intersects each meridian at some angle. This is also called Rhumb line or Loxodrome. All meridians have a constant azimuth of 00 North or 1800 South and equator and other parallels have a constant azimuth of 900 East and 2700 West.
- *Cut measurements*: The distance between two bent points while doing the survey of fields characterized by narrow width and high length. For example while doing the survey of roads, streams etc. cut measurements are necessary
- *District map*: The unscaled map shows the details of all taluks in a district. This necessarily contains all the topographical details present in the taluks. The total area of the district will be written over the top of the map.

- *Double line boundary*: When there is a stream demarcating two villages, taluks or districts, then theodolite survey is done through the boundaries of streams on both banks. This is called double line boundary and the imaginary line connecting the midpoint at the centre of the stream is called the Midline boundary.
- *F line or Field Boundary line*: The side measurements are taken from the side boundary lines of survey/sub-division fields
- *Field Measurement Sketch*: For each survey number there will be sketch clearly showing the sub-divisions and side measurements of each line in the sketch in a scaled manner. Since these sketches show all the measurements taken from the field, it is called Field Measurement Sketch. The bound volume such sketches in the form of the book is called the Field Measurement Book.
- *G line or Ground line*: This is the line which joins one tri-junction with another tri-junction.
- *Geodesy*: A branch of applied mathematics and earth sciences that deals with the measurement and representation of the Earth, including its gravitational field, in a three-dimensional time varying space.
- *Geographic Co-ordinate System:* It is system of defining places on earth by using angular units of measurement using latitude and longitude.
- *Government/Sirkar land*: The land which is recorded as Government or the land which is not settled/recorded against anybody's name as private property.
- *Great Trigonometric Station/GT Station*: The Survey of India has divided the entire geographical area of the country into great triangles by a process called major triangulation, towards facilitating triangulation survey. The tamper-proof permanent identification marks at the corners of these triangles are called GT stations. The latitude, longitude and height of the station would be measured and kept as a permanent record.
- *Intermediate junction*: This is a sub-division bent point taken temporarily as intermediary junction towards drawing G line from one tri-junction to another tri-junction. This is done when there is no scope for creating a bi-junction.
- *Junction*: The point at which two or more lines join is called a junction point.
- *Key map*: This is a draft sketch prepared by the village level official to indicate the position of land at the reporting period.
- *Khandam*: To correct errors in the survey process and to help in map plotting, each village is divided into parcels containing sizes of 25-50 hectares and a traverse survey is being done with theodolite. The above parcels are called Khandams.
- *Land Acquisition*: Land acquisition refers to the process by which government compulsorily acquires private property for public purpose. There is a heightened public concern on land acquisition issues in India.

Despite many amendments, over the years, to India's Land Acquisition Act of 1894, there was an absence of a cohesive national law that may address fair compensation when private land is acquired for public use, and fair rehabilitation of Landowners and those directly affected from loss of livelihoods. Land acquisition in India is currently governed by The Right to Fair Compensation and Transparency in Land Acquisition, Rehabilitation and Resettlement Act, 2013 (RFCTLARR Act, 2013) which came into force from 1 January 2014 after the replacement of Land Acquisition Act of 1894.

- *Litho map*: For the routine usage of village and/or block map, the same is printed either in paper or cloth in a concise manner, for easy handing. Such maps are called litho maps.
- *Main circuit*: While surveying large villages/Blocks intermediary survey fields measuring 150 to 200 km^2 are created for making the survey process easy and accurate and also to check and correct the discrepancies locally. Such large survey fields which mostly are iso-terminous with either village or block boundary are called the main circuit. Usually main circuits are surveyed using theodolites.
- *Map projection*: This technique comprises of processes like mathematical, graphical and geometrical methods to accommodate the spherical shape of earth in a plain surface.
- *Minor circuit*: In circumstances wherein surveying process is to be carried out in large extent of land as single units like rivers, lakes, backwaters, rocky tracts and if the extent of land in possession of private persons exceeds 4.00 hectares, the surveying process can be carried out only using Theodolites. Such large land masses are called minor circuits.
- *Offset:* This is the shortest distance from either G line or check line to a particular point.
- *Original survey*: This survey process is for the purpose of collecting tax from a piece of land which has recently been brought under assessment and revenue administration.
- *Part measurement*: If a boundary line is fragmented by incorporating various points in that line then that line is called a fragmented line. Each measurement between the adjoining points is part measurements which are recorded inside the line at the corresponding place and the total length of line is recorded outside the line usually at the centre point.
- *Quadra-junction*: This is the meeting point of four survey fields or four villages or four blocks.
- *Register for Transfer of Registry*: The Transfer of Registry/Mutation is a process which should happen subsequent to deed transactions as per Registration Act, 1908. The register, which contains such changes, is called the Register for Transfer of Registry.
- *Revenue field*: A group of adjoining revenue numbers gives rise to a revenue field.

- *Revenue list*: This a list prepared from Basic Tax Register by the survey officials before the actual field survey begins in the field. This contains the details of landholders, extent of land possessed, survey number, boundaries etc.
- *Revenue number*: The temporary number which is assigned by the revenue authorities to a fragmented or a consolidated piece of land based on possession is called revenue number. Revenue number will be replaced by the subdivision or resurvey number once updation survey or resurvey process is completed.
- *Settlement Register*: The register which is prepared as part of the settlement process and which contains the details like survey number, resurvey number, name of the holder, extent, type, tenure, details of boundaries, tax due etc. are entered in a systematic manner. This covers the entire area in a village including unassessed portions within the village limits. This is permanent register which should not be altered under any circumstances.
- *Settlement*: It is one of the important aspects of survey primarily to assess the extent, type, tenure and the name of possessor of a parcel of land.
- *Single line and double offset system:* While doing the survey of narrow fields like roads, streams etc. instead of triangulation; after a line is drawn from one tri-junction to another tri-junction, offsets are taken from this line to boundary points towards preparing the field book. This system is called single line and double offset system.
- *State map*: The unscaled map shows the details of all districts in a state. This necessarily contains all the topographical details present in the districts. The total area of the state will be written over the top.
- *Subdivision Number*: To accommodate the fragmentation in a survey number after the updation survey a new survey number is assigned called the subdivision number.
- *Supplementary Basic Tax Register*: This is a register which is similar in character as Basic Tax Register, but prepared as a supplement to Basic Tax Register prepared originally. This is prepared to include the changes happening in the field pursuant to changes in possession of land.
- *Survey field*: This sketch is basically prepared to accommodate the changes in possession of lands. The extents are either consolidated or subdivided subsequent to land transactions and during the updation survey process is being carried out to accommodate these changes and new survey numbers are given starting from the last allotted survey number.
- *Survey Number*: Each survey field is assigned with a particular number which would remain the same till there is a resurvey or updation survey. This number is called survey number which may be started from the North-western corner and proceeding to South-eastern corner of a survey field only at the time of creation of fresh survey field.

- *Taluk map*: The unscaled map which shows the details of all villages/blocks in a taluk. This necessarily contains all the topographical details present in the villages. The total area of the taluk will be written over the top.
- *Tie line*: Line measuring not less than three jaribs and not more than seven jaribs taken for ascertaining a mustakil (fixed traverse points on tri-junction established in fields as well as map).
- *Topographical details*: Natural as well as manmade objects like roads, streams/rivers, hillocks, graveyard, well, buildings, forest, railway, religious structures etc. on a map/sketch.
- *Topographical survey*: This survey is being carried out by the Survey of India towards preparing topographical maps. This is basically done to have an assessment of the intensity of roads, the height of hillocks, width and spread of rivers etc.
- *Traverse survey*: A series of connected survey lines of known lengths and directions is called traverse. Traverse survey is of two types: i) closed traverse, in which a complete circuit is made i.e., when it starts and ends at the same point, forming a closed polygon, and ii) open traverse, in which it does not form a closed polygon, but it consists of a series of survey lines extending in the same general direction and not returning to the starting point. Traverse survey is conducted when a map of higher accuracy is required to be prepared for a large area, like an entire village or a cluster of villages.
- *Triangulation*: It is a method used in survey process to calculate the area on enclosed triangles within a surveyed field.
- *Tri-junction*: This is the meeting point of three survey fields or three villages or three blocks
- *Village map and Block map*: This is a map prepared in so many interconnected sheets, prepared in 1 cm = 50 m scale and showing the entire survey numbers in a village or block. Though this may not contain individual measurements, the topographical details with standard index are correctly entered in this map without fail. The total area of the village will be written over the top of this map.
- *WGS - 84*: The World Geodetic System (WGS) is not referenced to a single datum point. It represents an ellipsoid whose placement, orientation, and dimensions best fit the Earth's equipotential surface which coincides with the geoid. The system was developed from a worldwide distribution of terrestrial gravity measurements and geodetic satellite observations.

References

1. B.H. Baden Powell: *The Land Systems of British India* – Vol, II – The System of Village or Mahal Settlements. Published by Oxford
2. B.H. Baden Powell (M DCCC XCII – 1892) *The Land Systems of British India* – Vol, III – The Ryotwari and Allied Systems Published by Macmillan & Co, Oxford; Printed at the Clarendon Press, Horace Hart, Printer to the University.

3. Bernardo A. Michael (2007) *Making Territory Visible: The Revenue Surveys of Colonial South Asia in Imago Mundi*, Vol. 59, No. 1 (2007), pp. 78-95 (20 pages).
4. Bernardo A. Michael: *Making Territory Visible: The Revenue Surveys Of Colonial South Asia* Source: Imago Mundi, 2007, Vol. 59, No. 1 (2007), Pp. 78-95 Published by: Imago Mundi, Ltd. Stable URL: https://www.Jstor.Org/Stable/40234068
5. Clements R. Markham: *Memoir on The Indian Surveys*: W.H. Allen and Co. 13, Waterloo Place. 1871
6. COL. G.C. Agarwal: Cadastral Surveys in India: https://www.isprs.org/proceedings/XXIII/congress/part11/196_XXIII-B11.pdf
7. Dr. R. Kannan (2012): *The Tamil Nadu Survey Manual*, Volume IV, II Edition Fully Revised, 2012 Dealing With Electronic Survey For Modern Survey Using Global Positioning Systems (GPS) And Electronic Total Stations (ETS), Published Chennai: Department of Survey and Land Records, Government of Tamil Nadu, Survey House, Chepauk, Chennai – 600 005.
8. Dr. R. Kannan, (2009): *Unravelling the Mysterious Diagram in the Form of Chakras (Sacred Circles) in Mehrangarh Fort, Jodhpur*, Maharaja Man Singh Pustak Prakash Research Centre.
9. Dr. Vijender Singh: Akbar's Land Revenue System, *International Journal of Engineering, Management, Humanities and Social Sciences Paradigms* (IJEMHS) (Volume 19, Issue 01) Publishing Month: March 2016 ISSN: 2347-601X
10. Nilmani Mukherjee (1962) *The Ryotwari System in Madras 1792-1827*, Publisher Calcutta: Firma L.K. Muhopadhyay.
11. R. G. Gordon, I.C.S: *Manual of Land Surveying* (Revised in Metric System And Corrected Up To 29-7-72) Government Central Press, Bombay, 1974
12. Rama Deb Roy: The Great Trigonometrical Survey Of India- In A Historical Perspective: *Indian Journal of History of Science*, 21 (1): 22-32 (1986)
13. S.S. Khera (1964) *District Administration in India*, Published Delhi: Asia Publishing House.
14. *Tamil Nadu Survey Manuals*, Vols-I to III, Published by Dept. of Survey and Land Records, Govt. of Tamil Nadu, Survey house, Chepauk, Chennai-600005.

2

Existing Practices of Land Surveying and Recording Systems in States

Land surveying and recording practices in India are largely varied from state to state and sometimes in intra-state situation. Political or administrative boundary of state that are supposed to be the actual divisions, were non-existent when the first phase of cadastral survey and records preparation was started. It is already discussed that, in past, records were kept with the officials of Zamindars or Emperors or the British rulers, and then land revenue system was

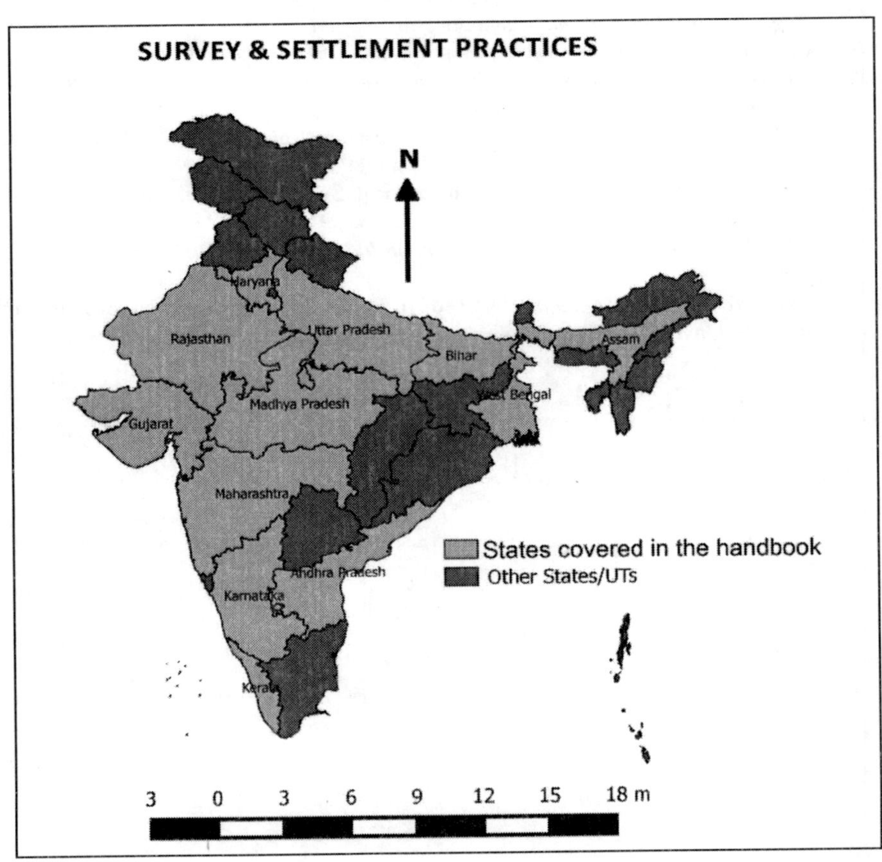

designed based on their territory. Not only the practices, but also the language written on records, units and scale of measurement, etc. are completely different in states. Topographical variations were also impacted largely on the survey practices.

The practices of land survey and record preparation are different in different states because of the different revenue structures. Therefore, to bring the essence of land surveying practices in India, 12 states were selected based on different geographical regions and administered under different revenue systems in the past, to assess the variations of land surveying and recording practices. From the northern zone, two states are selected namely; Haryana and Rajasthan, Uttar Pradesh and Madhya Pradesh are selected from the Central India. Similarly, two states from Eastern region such as; West Bengal and Bihar, and Assam from North-east region are selected. Gujarat and Maharashtra are selected from the Western India and from the Southern India; Andhra Pradesh, Karnataka and Kerala are selected.

The state-chapters attempt to address various point of land surveying; historical perspectives, how modern techniques change the scope of land surveying and record preparation, existing practices, problems faced at the field level and the future initiatives.

2.1

Andhra Pradesh

Siddharth Jain, IAS

Survey, Settlement and Land Records in Andhra Pradesh – An Overview

Land is the most basic and precious resource to the mankind. Ever since man had learnt agricultural practices and settled down for production of agricultural wealth for sustenance, right to landed property too evolved gradually. Ownership of land is, perhaps, as ancient as the unique Indian tribal settlements which gradually came to be known as villages. The only difference between the present landholder and his earliest companion is that in those ages there was more land than people could own, manage and cultivate.

An Indian village is typically a geographic tract of country with a fixed habitation and hundreds of acres of arable and wasteland. It forms the most basic administrative unit. In the olden days, it was generally owned either by the Government (or the King or Emperor who himself was the Government) or by a middleman subordinate to Government or King/ Emperor. The middleman, who held an intermediary tenure on the villages, was often called Zamindar, Jagirdar, Palegar etc., and used to enjoy the income derived from the lands in the form of land tax. Fixation of land tax was approximate and at times even arbitrary. Naturally, there was scope for coercion, exploitation and harassment of the farmer. It has been chronicled that the landholders in Government villages enjoyed relatively more freedom in agricultural practices, lower land taxes and better irrigation facilities as compared with their counterparts in Zamindary or Muttadar or Mokhasa[1] villages etc. Resistance, protests and upraising of the farmers against tyrannical collection of exorbitantly high land taxes in non-Governmental villages have gradually forced the Government to regulate both possession of land as well as payment of rent. On one side, Government introduced regulatory legislations and on the other, sought to make permanent settlement more scientific and universal. Permanent settlement itself had not been

[1] The consequence of the Agency rule was the strengthened of various revenue officials in the society such as Zamindars, Munsabdars, Muttadars etc. their main duty was to collect revenue and favour the government. The Muttadari system played an important role in the tribal area of Andhra Pradesh

a sudden development but had evolved over a period of time owing to variety of circumstances, the most important among them being the awareness that dawned on the tiller-farmer about his legitimate rights. It helped, no doubt, in formulating a systematic procedure of levying land revenue, which in those days, happened to be a major source of income to Government.

The earliest landmark legislation towards recognition of farmers' rights in land was the Madras Land Regulation, 1802, promulgated in the then Presidency of Madras. It provided for registration of landed estates by paying certain revenue to Government. Subsequently, Inam lands[2] were regulated by introducing the Madras Enfranchised Inams Act, 1862 and later the Madras Enfranchised Inams Act, 1869.

However, the very first attempt towards genuine regulation of rights of tenants and landholders was made by enacting the Madras Estates Land Act, 1908. In order to ameliorate themilitant unrest among the farmers of the Presidency, the Estates Land (Reduction of Rent) Act, 1947 was later brought in. It sought to bring down the rates of rent obtaining in the Estates on par with the neighboring Government (ryotwari) villages. Ultimately, the inevitable happened and all estates were abolished by enacting the Madras Estates (Abolition and Conversion into Ryotwari) Act, 1948.

Consequently, all estate lands automatically stood converted into ryotwari lands i.e., lands directly held by the farmers under the Government on condition of paying land revenue. Inams too were abolished by introducing the Andhra Pradesh Inams (Abolition and Conversion into Ryotwari) Act, 1956.

In the Telangana region of the State too, all intermediary tenures such as Surf-e-Khas (crown lands across the princely state of Hyderabad belonging to the Nizam family), Jagirs, Inams etc., were abolished by promulgating the Surf-e-Khas (merger) Regulation, 1358 Fasli, the Hyderabad (Abolition of Jagirs) Regulation; 1359 Fasli and A.P. (Telangana Area) Abolition of Inams Act, 1955. Thus, all intermediary tenures in Andhra Pradesh stood abolished within a decade of our country becoming independent and the landholders in all the villages of the State started enjoying equal rights and were subject to uniform taxation.

Permanent settlement, by now, evolved into a fairly scientific procedure involving measurement of land holdings, estimating their fertility and fixing assessment for irrigated wet and dry lands besides settling the title in land and conferring pattadar rights on the landholders. Thousands of Government villages were permanently settled by conducting large-scale survey and settlement operations. Provincial Government of the then Madras Presidency and Hyderabad

---

[2] An Inam is a gift of land or land revenue. The origin of the Inam can be traced back to the times of Hindu, Mohammadan periods of rule. Parcels of lands were granted by the Hindu and Mohammadan Rulers to persons for services rendered by such persons or the services to be rendered by such persons in future.

State had well-organized Survey and Settlement Department which undertook survey and settlement operations in Estates/Jagirs also, of course, for a prescribed fee to be paid by the Estate – holder or Jagirdar. Elaborate system of maintaining Land Records too had been devised and introduced with the objective of keeping title in land up to date at any given point of time. Andhra Pradesh State, with minor modifications, still continues the Land Records System introduced in its predecessor provinces about 80 years ago.

Land Assets of Andhra Pradesh

S. No.	*Type/ Item*	*Extent of Land*
1.	Total geographic area	4,02,72,000 Acres
2.	Forest reserves	95,87,689 Acres
3.	Barren and uncultivable land	33,23,567 Acres
4.	Land put to non-agricultural uses	50,85,429 Acres
5.	Cultivable waste	10,18,074 Acres
6.	Gross cropped area	89,82,281 Acres

Source: Socio Economic Survey of Andhra Pradesh, 2018-19.

System of Land Records

The system of land records in the State consists of the following ingredients:

- Preparation of field (land holding) maps depicting measurements and boundaries and compilation of village maps from these data;
- Settlement of revenue assessment on lands based on soil classification and conferment of title on landholders; compilation of revenue registers showing title, extent, assessment etc;
- Creation of readily identifiable field boundary framework on ground by erecting designated boundary marks on land holding junctions – fixation of responsibility on the pattadars for its maintenance;
- Updating the land maps and land registers by promptly incorporating new field boundaries and the corresponding title;
- Redressal of grievances of landholders by showing obliterated boundaries, resolving boundary disputes and safeguarding their titles, besides arresting encroachments on Government owned land and lands earmarked for communal purposes; and
- Revision or repreparation on a large scale of fresh land records if changes on ground are too numerous to keep pace with.

Cadastral Survey and Settlement Operation: At a Glance

All procedures involved in the measurement and mapping of land holdings go by the name Cadastral Survey (Cadastre: Public record of rights in land) or Revenue Survey. Cadastral Surveys are a State subject and fall within the scope of the 45th entry of the State List in the Seventh Schedule to the Constitution, along with record of rights and maintenance of land records. They are different from other types of surveys such as topographical surveys, oceanic surveys, geological surveys etc., which are conducted and controlled by the Union Government. Survey of India is a Government of India organization which conducts topographical surveys of our country and prepares the topographical maps. Survey Settlement and Land Records Department of A.P. Government, which functions under the direction of Revenue Ministry, attends to revenue survey operations in the State.

Experimental revenue surveys were made by Madras Government from 1853 onwards in South Arcot district. Revenue surveys of the Presidency, on a regular basis, were commenced in 1858. Several methods were employed while conducting the surveys with the sole objective of identifying and adopting the best method. Some of the methods employed were:

Khasra Method	*(followed from 1862 to 1874)* Fields were measured either as quadrilaterals or triangles; only sides of fields were measured.
Triangles Method	*(followed from 1876 to 1888)* Each field was divided into triangles and all sides were measured.
Plane Table Method	*(followed from 1887 to 1891)* Field junctions were measured by Offsetting them from the sides of triangles formed by connecting traverse stations.
Block Map Method	*(followed from 1891 to 1896)* Village was divided into traversed blocks, each consisting of about 160 acres. These blocks were divided into larger triangles boundaries of survey fields were offset from the sides of the triangles.
Punganur Method	*(followed from 1914 to 1916)* its name was derived from the Estate in Chittoor district which was first surveyed using this method. A single diagonal line was run across each field and all field bends were offset on this line.
Diagonal and Offset Method	*(followed from 1900 onwards)* Whole village was traversed, divided into khandams which were also traversed and each survey field (generally a group of revenue fields) was triangulated. Bends of the field were offset on the nearest diagonal lines.

Only three simple instruments viz., chain, cross staff and theodolite are used in all these methods. The last designated method i.e., D&O system is found to be the most ideal method from the point of view of convenience, accuracy and cost and time effectiveness and it is still being used without any changes. Most districts of Madras Presidency were surveyed during the period from 1858 to 1928.
The following record was prepared:

A. *Village map* in the scale of 1 cm=2.5 chains showing the boundaries of groups of individual holdings is called survey fields and the more important topographical details.

B. *Large-scale plans* of survey fields are called field measurement sketches showing the boundaries of each holding, topographical details and all measurements.

C. *Land register* giving the number, tenure, area, assessment and reputed ownership of each holding.

The survey of a village (Revenue survey or Cadastral survey) consists of two principal activities. They are:

i) Physical survey of boundaries of the village and all land parcels within the village.
ii) Settlement (procedure involving classification of lands, their assessment and conferment of ownership).

Process involved in Cadastral Survey

Technically, these processes are denoted by alphabets A to H as follows

A work	Village/ khandam[3] boundary demarcation
B work	Village/ khandam boundary traversing
C work	Traverse computation
D work	Traverse plotting
E work	Field demarcation
F work	Field measurement
G work	Village map plotting
H work	Village map finalization for printing

The survey of a village is conducted on the principle called "whole to part". It means that first the village boundary is demarcated and surveyed, thereby delimiting the outer boundary of the village. Then the boundaries of all land parcels within that village are surveyed and plotted in the village traverse skeleton, which ensures accuracy of survey. As already mentioned, a village is the basic unit for revenue surveys. Survey of a village is done in a sequential manner, as follows:

- Demarcation[4] of village boundary and its traversing.
- Division of the village into appropriate number of khandams (100 to 250 acres each) demarcation of khandam boundaries and their traversing.
- Identification, demarcation and recording of revenue field/survey field boundaries; local enquiry is conducted to identify enjoyment limits (location sketch[5] is prepared).
- Measurement of fields by running diagonals and offsetting all major bends, noting of topographic details, with measurements, if needed.
- Plotting of field sketches.
- Plotting of village/khandam traverse and finally arriving at or developing the village map.

[3] Khandam: a sub-unit of village, generally created for ease of measurement and reduction of errors in field measurement and plotting.

[4] Demarcation: Identification and recording of a boundary, be it of village, khandam, survey filed or revenue filed

[5] Location sketch: a rough drawing made by surveyor indicating measurable field units, their shapes and relative locations

Details of actual procedures to be followed are compiled in the form of Departmental Rules. The following manuals are referred to by the departmental staff and officers for guidance:

1. *A.P Survey Manual of Departmental Rules: Vol-I : Measurement, Inspection, Town Survey, Boundary Disputes, S&B Act and Rules: Vol-I-II : Duties of officers/ staff, survey instruments, traversing, printing of maps, trigonometric solutions of survey problems'-III : All Departmental Forms*
2. *Chain Survey Manual for Village Administrative Officers and Revenue Subordinates*

Settlement has two components. The first one is the settlement of soil fertility and the second one is the settlement of reputed ownership and conferment of title. Conferment of title has always been a revenue function. An elaborate procedure of classification of the soils is followed to arrive at its fertility as follows in the Andhra region:

- general soil classification into series, classes and sorts;
- valuation of soils;
- grouping of villages for dry cultivation;
- classification of irrigation sources;
- determination of money rates applicable to different classes and sorts of soils;
- Working out assessment.

Like survey, settlement of soil fertility too is a time-consuming activity, which lays scientific foundation to land revenue assessment. Once settlement work is completed, land revenue payable by each landholder is worked out based on the extent and fertility of the soil of holding.

The land register built up during survey operations will get finalized by the settlement officials by filling in the relevant particulars. This finalized register is variously called Permanent Village Register Manuscript Diglott, Manuscript Diglott Register, RSR (Permanent Settlement register for Government villages), Fair Adangal (Permanent Settlement register for Estate and Inam villages) etc. If it is printed, it is called printed 'Diglott Register' (i.e. a register which has entries in two languages, English and the Vernacular). For all Government villages in Andhra area, printed Diglott Register or printed Resettlement Registers are available. For ex-estate and ex-inam villages of Andhra region, manuscript Diglott Registers have been prepared. They are presently being printed for supply to Collectors. Thus, on surveying and settling a village, the following Land Records[6] are prepared and made over to the District Revenue Administration for maintenance:

[6] There are several other subsidiary records but the above are the most important. These are all permanent records which are replaced by a fresh set of records only when a village is put to resurvey. Hence, they can appropriately be termed as Basic Land Records. Basing on

1. Village Map
2. Field Measurement Book (FMB)
3. Permanent Settlement Register or Fair Adangal
4. Correlation Statement.

Maintenance of Land Records

Any system, to render optimum service, requires to be maintained. The system of Land Records is no exception. Unless land records are maintained and updated, the titles and boundaries recorded therein tend to become outdated and after considerable time, become totally irrelevant. Several changes that occur in title and consequently in land holding boundaries on a day-to-day basis must, therefore, be promptly incorporated into the land records so as to enable them to serve the farmers and Government alike. Thus, the primary object of maintenance of land records is to keep the permanent records handed over by the Survey and Settlement Department up-to-date and useful in the day-to-day revenue administration.

Changes in title and field boundaries occur due to the following reasons:

- Assignment of Government land to landless poor, acquisition for land-based development activities, and assignment of surplus land surrendered under agricultural land ceiling law;
- Relinquishment, transfer of registry on account of sale, gift, partition etc.;
- Change in land classification such as wet to dry or dry to wet, assessed waste to poramboke or vice versa etc.

Such changes necessitate correction of permanent records by incorporating the resultant new titles and new boundaries. The records so maintained are:

- The permanent village register;
- The atlas of field maps i.e. FMB;
- Village map.

In Andhra region, new titles are incorporated into the permanent village register and new sub- divisions in the FMB. Likewise, changes due to clubbing of survey fields or splitting of big blocks and major topographic alternations are incorporated in the village map. Title and its physical boundary on ground are

---

these records, certain special registers are prepared for day-to-day revenue administration, as part of village accounts. Adangal in Andhra and Pahani in Telenganais is one such register. Recently, village accounts in both the regions of the State have been integrated. The new village account No.3 is now termed as Adangal-Pahani. This account, unlike the permanent records, is updated and re-written once every year. Some tend to further classify the basic land records into two groups; the 'graphic land records' consisting of map and field sketch (graphic=pictorial) and the 'descriptive land records' consisting of fair adangal, Permanent Settlement Register etc.

complementary to each other. It is difficult to safeguard or maintain the one without the other. So, an up-to-date/correct title must correspond to a distinct and readily identifiable boundary on ground. For property boundaries to be readily identified and maintained, the original 'survey framework' of a village has to remain intact. A deficient framework is detrimental for proper maintenance of land records. Survey framework of a village comprises survey marks or stones planted on the village boundary, khandam boundaries and field junction points which are all interconnected through precisely measured straight lines. With the help of the recorded measurements, missing survey marks can be got replanted at correct positions, provided the number is not quite high. Periodic inspection and renewal of missing survey marks are very important aspects of Land records maintenance. Any neglect leads to total collapse of the framework necessitating resurveys. If that happens, the elaborate descriptive register and revenue accounts of a village become practically worthless.

The A.P. Survey & Boundary Act and the L.R. Act have provided for maintenance of survey marks. Under these statutes, every registered holder is bound to maintain, renew and repair all survey marks on the boundaries of his holding. If he fails to do so, repair or renewal can be done at Government's cost, which is later recoverable from the landholder as arrears of land revenue. Detailed office and field procedures[7] involved in the maintenance of:

- Survey framework, and
- Revenue records and registration.

Necessity of Resurvey

The Government of Andhra Pradesh envisioned the introduction of Title registration system instead of the prevailing presumptive title and deed registration system in Andhra Pradesh, to transform the rights of the Landowners on immovable properties to next level, by conducting resurvey. Therefore, the Andhra Pradesh Land Titling Act, 2019 is enacted to introduce title registration system to ensure title security to Landowners of all immovable properties not only agricultural lands in rural tracts, but also in rural/urban habitations.

a. Deficiency in the existing system

I. Four different standalone systems/departments deal with the rights on land viz; instrument registration by Registration Department, mutation in revenue accounts by Revenue Department, conducting field survey by Survey Department, and land usage/development by the Town and Country Planning Department. Therefore, it became very difficult not only for a common man, but also for an educated person to get the required full-fledged and secured rights over a piece of land and it takes six to nine months on an average.

---

[7] Andhra Pradesh Revenue Board Standing Orders, 34-A, B, C and D.

II. The existing survey records are century old records which were prepared during the survey conducted from the years 1880 to 1910 and subsequently in 1960-1980. There are 49 lakh Field Sketches consisting of 156 lakh subdivisions covering 1.22 lakh sq.km. There are approximately 236 lakh land holdings recorded in Adangal and out of which 15% are still not assigned regular khata numbers due to lack of proper adjudication. Thus, there is huge gap between ground truth to Adangal entries and FMBs. Further, there are 1.20 lakh FMBs which are either missing or in brittle/torn/faded condition and which need to be rebuilt by conducting field survey only. There are too many obliterations of boundaries within a short time due to the sudden development of the area as a result of conversion of dry lands into wetlands and also too many transfers of holdings, which are not being incorporated simultaneously in all land records. The records are not updated to reflect the ground truth.

III. Due to the complexities involved in the registration process and updating records with various other departments, many (poor) people often do not register property transactions. In the present system of deeds registration, the Registration department has no mandate to ensure that only legal owners do the transactions on the property. It is the responsibility of the buyer to verify the veracity of the seller and his legal right to sell. If any dispute arises, the Landowners are compelled to approach the Civil Court which becomes burden to Courts and the Landowners in terms of physical, mental, financial and sometimes lead to unrest and law and order problems.

IV. Further, the Agricultural Department, and various other financial institutions in service sector are using the land records data for their planning and promoting projects and schemes for which the truthful land information is not available at a glance.

The solution for all the above deficiencies is resurvey, which is long overdue. The resurvey of all land parcels in the State will facilitate the digital transformation and urbanization by creating an Integrated Land Information Database System and pave a path to introduce an infallible or efficacious Title Registration system easily to assure title security to the Landowners. Therefore, a project to conduct resurvey of all lands including land properties in rural and urban tracts is proposed.

b. Salient features of the proposed new system

An Integrated Land Information System with Title Registration provision by following three principles viz; mirror, curtain and insurance principles, will be introduced, to overcome all the existing problems. The new system will facilitate to create, administer, organize and manage all aspects of land – information, management, control, usage; in a unified manner which is the need of the day. The fundamental change envisaged in this system would be the paradigm shift from the department centric approach to the service-centric approach, which would be characterized by an integrated system for capturing, storing, checking, integrating, analyzing and displaying data about land property and its use, ownership and development. The system shall deliver the service to its users through a unified interface.

The proposed system would immensely benefit people of all strata especially those living in the rural areas. The Title Registration system provides security of title to the owners by way of issue of conclusive title, eliminates the land litigations, in turn reducing the burden on judiciary. It facilitates quick and secure land based marketing, speedy and secure land transactions, resulting in the opening up of the land market. It provides reliable and real-time land information to the government. Continuously updating land records results in assured supply of capital that would boost the confidence of farming community and help them make investments on higher crop yielding varieties etc. In urban areas, this will bring transparency and predictability to the property tax values.

c. Vision of the proposed project

The resurvey aims to update the land records and record of rights to purify the land records and facilitate to introduce the Title registration system. The vision of the proposed project is to establish and manage a comprehensive and sustainable Land Information Management System, which serves as a record of conclusive Title of all land parcels and provides related services in an integrated, efficient and cost effective manner.

d. Objectives of the proposed system

The key objectives of the project are –

- Resurvey of every square inch of land
    1. CORS Network will be established
    2. Flying of Drones and Processing the Data
    3. Creation of Ortho rectified village Map
    4. Land parcel Map preparation with Geo Codes
    5. Integration of both textual and spatial data using GIS Platform
    6. Entire process through online
    7. Conclusive boundaries.
- Title Registration System
    1. Administer a system of recording conclusive Title, which is secure and enjoys public confidence
    2. Indemnity of title of land property
    3. Issue of Title Smart Card to Titleholders
- To establish Land Authority
- Provide integrated land related services
    - Through a unified interface
    - With efficiency and easy accessibility
    - In a cost effective manner
    - Services to people through online only

- Implement a transparent system of property valuation
- Develop and maintain a Geodetic Control Network for referencing maps
- Maintain all records in integrated digital form in a central repository
- Implement systems and processes for maintenance and auto-updation of data
    - Establish a sustainable operating model
    - Provide Value-added Services in areas like
        - Development planning
        - Welfare schemes
        - Land related taxes Proposed Surveying technology.

e. Proposed surveying technology

A) Earlier, initial as well as resurveys were conducted using Chain & Cross Staff for linear measurements and Theodolite machine for angular measurement (village and khandam traverse[8]). The simple triangulation and Diagonal & Offset systems were the survey methodologies adopted. The Diagonal & Offset system survey methodology is a superior one in quality of measurements, mapping and for relaying the measured boundaries on ground.

B) As per BSO, there is mechanism to update these records at village and Mandal levels as per the changes occurred in boundaries and classification. Practically it is not taking place as there is shift in priorities of Revenue department these days. Many records have not been updated for fragmentation on ground, while implementing the RoR Act during 1990s as the surveying in traditional method is tedious, time consuming and requires lot of human resources. Further, while mutating patta transfer cases or ownership change in revenue records, RoR/Land Acquisition cases, subdivisions were not implemented and hence huge number of newly created boundaries i.e. boundaries of revenue holdings within Sy. No. have not been reflected in survey records. The spatial data i.e. survey records cannot be put aside for updation on par with RoR as the location and measurement of revenue fields are very much essential to maintain spatial data in consonance with RoR.

Today, it is an international standard that every spatial data is being described in Geo-coordinates of WGS84 datum. Therefore, the Geo-coordinates of all vertices of the land parcels in a village will be recorded in a database.

There are various state-of-the-art technologies like Aerial photography, Digital photogrammetry, Electronic Total Stations, GPS/DGPS and CORS (Continuously Operating Reference Station) Network available. In view of the terrain model, size of the land holdings, man power availability, time factor and future maintenance, it is proposed to establish the CORS Network, the

[8] Angular Circuit formed for part of a village.

state-of-the art technology which is now being used in all advanced countries and every country is trying to move towards adopting this technology. As part of this infrastructure, about 70 permanent Base Stations in network format with an average 60 to 70 km trilateration will be erected at permanent Government office buildings. The Government of Andhra Pradesh has entered into an MOU with Survey of India, which is a National premier mapping agency. As a part of the Agreement, the SOI will fly drones and supply ortho-rectified village maps for ground truthig. Every Surveyor involved in resurvey will verify the ortho images in the presence of farmers and validate the boundaries, and simultaneously update field attributes with reference to Purified RoR data. The entire data is uploaded to GIS database.

Using this technology, Geo-coordinates of each vertex of land parcels will be recorded and a unique ID will be assigned. Every land parcel will be protected by introducing geo-fencing concept and by the technology advancement in future, every individual landholder will be able to demarcate his/her land parcel at their own by using the recorded Geo-cods. All relevant attributes of each and every land parcel will be recorded in a GIS application software which was developed as per designed Functional Requirement Specifications (FRS) with maximum automation and minimum human intervention. Every land parcel having a unique ID shall be notified under Survey & Boundaries Act, 1923 and under the A.P. Land Titling Act, 2019 as per appropriate provisions.

f. Evolution of Surveying Technology

The land survey based on two basic principles –

i) Whole to the part, and
ii) Any point shall be determined with reference to at least two known points.

Accordingly, different survey systems were experimented since 1858 A.D. with an object of evolving a cost effective and scientifically accurate survey method. Finally, the Diagonal & Offset system was found to be more scientific and cost effective method in 1900 A.D. and it was adopted in erstwhile Madras Presidency in British India. Chain, Cross staff and Theodolite are the instruments used for measurement in field survey. The comprehensive survey of a village was divided into "A" to "H" Processes for better planning, work distribution, skill development and separation of functions. It was a very successful method and the survey was completed in all villages by 1930. After converting the Estate and Inam villages into Ryotwari villages under A.P. Estate Abolition (Conversion into Ryotwari) Act, 1948 and A.P. Inam Abolition (Conversion into Ryotwari) Act, 1956, surveys were conducted from 1960 to 1980.

The proposed resurveys in AP, which will be conducted now onwards nearly after 100 years, has been named "Geo-Coordinate" system of survey using more advanced technology.

Case study of the Pilot Project of Resurvey: Success, Challenges and Way Ahead

(A Report on Resurvey pilot project in Takkellapadu Village, Jaggayyapeta Mandal, Krishna District, Andhra Pradesh)

A resurvey pilot project has been taken up in Takkellapadu Village, Jaggayyapeta Mandal, Krishna District, Andhra Pradesh to study the feasibility of employing highest precision GNSS Rovers with reference to Continuously Operating Reference Stations (CORS) Network comprising five Base Stations in network form with 70 km diameter separation and to evaluate the proof of concept for conducting cadastral resurvey.

Resurvey Methodology (Pre-Survey)

The survey records in vogue were prepared using Chain & Cross staff and Theodolite instruments in Diagonal & Offset system of survey which was the proven, accurate and feasible method for cadastral survey by 1900 A.D. Since three decades several state-of-the art technologies have been evolved in IT environment viz; Digital photogrammetry, Total Station, HRSI, GPS/DGPS, Drone (UAV) and CORS Network etc. In the pilot project Takkellapadu village has been surveyed using GNSS Rovers with reference to CORS Network.

The cadastral survey/resurveys in Andhra Pradesh are taken up under the provisions of A.P.

Survey & Boundary Act, 1923 and the survey methodology prescribed under survey manuals.

a) Any Cadastral Survey, whatever may be the technology used, the following activities are mandatory apart from the statutory process under Survey & Boundary Act, 1923:
    1. Boundary demarcation on ground in presence of landholders which is now coined ground truthing
    2. Plantation of survey stones
    3. Refixation Government land boundaries with reference to existing records
    4. Measurement of demarcated boundaries or data collection
    5. Mapping
    6. Preparation of Field or Land Register
    7. Quality check/over check of boundary demarcation and Land Register
    8. Preparation of final records viz; Land Parcel Maps (LPMs), Village Map and Land Register.

b) The resurvey methodology using CORS Network broadly is carried out in the following steps.
    1. Ground truthing: Data collection using GNSS Network Rover (RTK)
        a. Survey team was provided GNSS Rovers
        b. Time of observation of each point is not more than 01 minute.

   c. Online data export to selected GIS software
   d. Writing the Field Register.
2. Data processing:
   a. Mapping in any CAD based software
   b. Export to indigenously developed GIS Application software
   c. Field register data entry and integration of each land holding entry with the corresponding LPM.
3. Generation of records, notices in the GIS software.
4. Statutory protocol:
   a. A statutory notice has been issued to every individual landholder with resurvey schedule to attend and show their land parcel boundaries.
   b. After conducting field survey and generation of draft records, a notice has been issued along with sketch to every individual landholder to call for appeals within 30 days, if any.
   c. The Appeals received were disposed of within 60 days.
   d. A final notification u/s 13 was published to conclude the resurvey operations.
   e. The notified resurvey records will be promulgated under RoR Act or A.P. Titling Act.

All other mandatory activities viz; stone plantation, Government land re-fixation, quality check/over check, scrutiny of records, are conducted as per standard norms.

Takkellapadu Resurvey Data Analysis (GNSS Rovers): Post Survey

A) Survey Profile:

Sl. No.	*Survey details in Ac.cts*	*Revision survey in 1932*	*Resurvey in 2020*
1	Total village extent	1539	1533.56
2	Total extent as per Adangal	1573.36	–
3	Total Sy.Nos./LPMs	150	631
4	Original land holdings as per RSR	182	–
5	Total land parcels as per Adangal	801	631
6	Extent of Govt. lands (86 parcels)	272.52	272.23
7	Extent of Forest land	144.63	144.94
8	Avg. extent of land holding	8.46	2.43

Observations

1. Variation in total village extent of revision survey (1932) and resurvey (2020) is Ac.5.44 (0.35%), which is very negligible and it is evident that the revision survey as well as resurvey are accurate.
2. Variation in total village extent of revision survey (1932) and Adangal is Ac.34.36(2.235), which is evident that there is considerable variation due to poor maintenance of revenue accounts.

3. All the Government lands, forest lands are intact on ground and area exactly tallied.

B) Extent Analysis

Extent variation of Sy. Nos. FMB (182) *Recorded vs Computed* from digitized FMB

% Variation (Nos.)		*Extent wise (Nos.)*	
Total Sy.Nos./subdivisions: 182			
No variation : 11			
% of No variation	6.04	< 2 cents	45
< 2%	118	2–5 cents	39
2% - 5%	33	5–10 cents	48
>5%	20	>10 cents	49
Lesser extent Sy.Nos/subdivs. : 43			
More extent Sy.Nos/subdivs. :128			
Highest variation : Ac. -2.10 cts			
Lowest variation : Ac. - 0.01 cts			

Observations

1. The measurements were closed within allowances and area was calculated using Area Square Paper on plotted FMBs to scale, in which there is scope for measurement, scale and human errors which are compensatory in nature.
2. When the FMBs are digitized, the polygon is closed by adjusting the errors in measurements and area is meticulously calculated, hence the variation arises, but the mathematically computed areas from digitized FMBs are correct.

C) Resurvey vs Adangal (existing)

Extent of land parcels vs extent recorded in Adangal (most of the land parcel are with unsurveyed extents). Adangal is a current Land Register of the year showing the reputed owner, extent, Sy./ Subdivision No. etc.

% Variation (Nos.)		*Extent wise (Nos.)*	
Total Sy.Nos./ Subdivisions	631 (Adangal:801)		
No variation	71		
% of No variation	11.25		
< 2%	138	< 2 cents	103
2% - 5%	132	2 – 5 cents	93
5% - 10%	117	5 – 10 cents	124
>10%	173	>10 cents	240
Lesser extent Sy.Nos/subdivs.: 43			
More extent Sy.Nos/subdivs.:128			
Highest variation	Ac. -3.73 cts		
Lowest variation	Ac. 0.01 cts		
No. of land parcels differed with Pattadar name in Adangal:17			

Observations:
Areas calculated using Area Square Paper were recorded and maintained in the existing revenue accounts.

Critical Analysis of Resurvey using CORS Network

a) The DILRMP guidelines of 2008-09, combination of TS+DGPS was preferred for survey in all conditions. The CORS is nothing but the upgraded DGPS method. The CORS method was not conceptualized in India while the guidelines were prepared in 2008-09. The CORS Network is upgraded architecture of DGPS method.
b) The positional accuracy obtained using CORS Network is time tested and internationally accepted one and proved precise in the pilot project.
c) The variation in extents recorded in Adangal and resurvey is unavoidable as the area recorded in Adangal is unsurveyed and the FMB original recorded extents varied with the computer generated extents.
d) When two technologies or methods having different levels of accuracy are compared, the variation in measurement exists. The extents arrived at using instruments and methods of highest accuracy shall be taken into account.

Recommendations

a) By conducting resurvey, the land records will be purified, updated and upgraded to create a comprehensive land information system with single source of truth. This database ease for digital transformation to render hassle free and deliver all land related service through single window with less human intervention.
b) The CORS Network, which will be a spatial infrastructure for Andhra Pradesh may be adopted to conduct resurvey of entire state.
c) The Geo-Coordinate system of survey, the next generation of Diagonal & Offset system of survey method may be adopted.

Resurvey Project Undertaken in Andhra Pradesh: Success, Challenges and Way Ahead

The state government as part of implementing" NAVARATNALU" (assurances given by Sri Y.S Jagan Mohan Reddy during Padayatra) has taken up prestigious programme titling as "వై.యస్.ఆర్. జగనన్నశాశ్వత భూహక్కు మరియు భూరక్షపధకం" **(YSR Jagananna Saswatha Bhoo Hakku Mariyu Bhoo Raksha Padhakam)** from 21 December 2020 to conduct total Resurvey of Agricultural lands, habitations and Urban areas throughout state after a period of 100 years.

The Nation's premier mapping agency Survey of India has come forward to extend its support to the state government to take up Resurvey project using hybrid technology with combination of CORS Network and DRONE Imagery.

Scope of the Programme

Total Area	1.26 Lakh Sq. KMs (Covering All Agriculture Land, Habitation and Urban Areas)
Villages	17,460 Phase–I 5,000 I Phase–II 6,500 I Phase–III 5,500
Habitations	47,861
Urban Local Bodies	About 3345.93 Sq. Kms. 10 lakhs open plots, 40 lakhs assessments and Population 1.5 crores
In Agriculture Land	90 Lakh Pattadars covering an extent of 2.26 Crores Acres

Salient Features of Resurvey

a) 4500 village Survey Teams (consisting of Village Surveyor, Village Revenue Officer/Village.
b) Revenue Assistant are formed, Mobile Magistrate in each Mandal/Tahsil.
c) Resurvey operations are proposed to be conduct in three phases, Phase I – 5000 Villages, Phase II- 6,500 Villages, Phase III – 5,500.
d) Resurvey operations are being taken up with the coordination of Revenue, Survey Panchayat and Municipal Departments.
e) After completion of Resurvey, Village Secretariats will function as Registration offices to carryout transactions of immovable properties.
f) Resurvey survey records will be generated in digital form.
g) Budget for Resurvey 1000 Crores (600 Crores for Stone plantation – The stone cost will be borne by the Government)
h) 90 Lakh Pattadars, 2.26 crores Acres of Agricultural lands.
i) 85 Lakh properties in 13,371 Panchayats.
j) 40 Lakh Assesments, 10 lakh plots in 110 Municipal areas.
k) It will be completed by January 2023.
l) Andhra Pradesh consists of 13 Districts, 51 Divisions, 679 Mandals, 17,461 Villages, 1.26 lakh Square Kilometres of area.
m) New Survey and Revenue records will be in Digital form – 1) LPM (Land Parcel Map) for each individual holding, 2) Village Map, 3) Resurvey land register, 4) 1B Register (Reference of title granted to a registered landholder under RoR Act),

Permanent Land Property Card

Micro Pilot project has been taken up in 51 villages by selecting one village from each Revenue Division. The criteria for selecting these villages is taken up keeping in view the availability of records, fewer land disputes, lesser extents, easy access to the villages for inspections and monitoring the survey activities etc.

Various stages involved in resurvey:

- Statutory procedure
- Refixing of village boundary, Government lands-survey of habitation boundary-data generation

- Drone flying-image capture
- Ortho Rectified Image (ORI) generation
- ORI quality check
- Ground truthing – undisputed & disputed boundaries – LPM marking on ORI + Writing of Field Register
- Additional and missing data collection-integration with ground truthing data
- LPMs generation by vectorisation
- Integration of village boundary, habitation boundary data to ground truthing data
- Seamless data generation by data processing-Software
- Field Register entry and spatial and textual data integration-software
- QC of generated data
- Draft record preparation (Field Register + LPMs + Village Map)
- Validation of data where Adangal & Resurvey Data is inconsistent.
- Issue 9(2) notices and 10(2) orders to landholders (Notices issued for decision made to determine undisputed and disputed boundaries respectively at the time of survey as enunciate in Survey and Boundaries Act).
- Appeal receiving-disposal-incorporation
- Final resurvey records (Land Register + LPMs + Village Map)
- 13 notification publication
- Promulgation under RoR or Titling Act.

An Overview of Existing and New System of Survey Records

Existing Survey Records	*New Survey Records after Resurvey*
1) Field Measurement Book	1) Digitized & Geo referenced Land Parcel Map (LPM)
2) Village Map (with Angular data)	2) Digitized & Geo referenced Village Map (with Coordinate data)
3) Land Register	3) Digitized Land Register
4) Correlation Map	4) Digitized & Geo referenced Correlation Map
5) Correlation Statement	5) Digitized Correlation Statement
6) Demarcation Sketch	6) GCPs Map with Coordinates data
7) Stone Registers (A & B)	

List of Manuals and Acts

- Board of Standing Orders 34(A)
- Board of Standing Orders 34(B)
- Board of Standing Orders 34(D)
- Andhra Pradesh Survey & Boundaries Act,1923
- Andhra Pradesh Survey Manual: Vol- I
- Andhra Pradesh Survey Manual: Vol- II
- Andhra Pradesh Survey Manual: Vol- III
- Hand book on Survey, Settlements and Land Records in Andhra Pradesh by Sri P. Kasturi Reddy, Former Director of Survey, Settlements & Land Records
- Lectures in Survey & Maintenance by N.C. Alley.

2.2

Assam

Indrajit Das and Manoranjan Ray

Brief History of Land Survey and Settlement in Assam

Before the annexation of Assam by the British, the greater part of Brahmaputra Valley was under the Ahom[9] rule. The Ahom rulers who had entered Assam as conquerors, wanted to establish their right not only over a portion of the produced as revenue, but also in the soil and the subjects. Though the rulers were owners of the soil, they remain satisfied with poll tax or plough tax. The land as it was cultivated by the first settlers was considered joint property of the group or *khel* who occupied it. In special cases, land was settled either free of revenue or a very low rate of revenue.

The land tenures evolved in the early British period might be said to be mere by-products of various kind of settlements made from time to time for the purpose of revenue collection from land. The British administrators first introduced poll tax in place of personal services to the ruler. Each district was divided into several blocks called *Mouza*. A local influential man was appointed as *Mouzadar* in its Mouza and was entrusted with the work of collecting the poll tax as commission agent. Later on, the poll tax was abolished and regular land revenue was introduced. Assessment was made on the basis of the category of land viz. *basti* (homestead land), *rupit* (paddy land) and *faringati* (high land growing inferior crops).

In the nineteenth century there was abundant supply of fertile land in the Brahmaputra Valley and the cultivator preferred annual leases to periodic leases. In order to encourage cultivators to take periodic leases, the government declared in 1870 that the right of the periodic lease holders will be heritable and transferable. In 1883, a system of 10 years of settlement was introduced in the temporary settled districts. The Assam Land and Revenue Regulation, 1886 conferred a permanent, heritable and transferable right to persons holding land under decennial leases. The holders of annual leases were not given any such right.

---

[9] The Ahom's entered Assam fully assimilated and ruled Assam for nearly six hundred years. The period of Ahom rule is a glorious chapter in the history of Assam. The Ahom dynasty was established by Sukaphaa, a Shan prince of Mong Mao who came to Assam after crossing the Patkai Mountains. (Assam State Portal).

From 1902, a system of 20 years of settlement was introduced and from 1927 a system of 30 years of settlement was introduced, which is still going on. Until the introduction of 10 years of settlement in 1883, government started the work on land measurement with some developed technologies by then some revenue commission agent like *Mouzadar, Chaudhury, Kakati* and Recorders (*Mandals*) for fixation and collection of land revenue. Government of India introduced Survey in 1882 under guidance of Sir Charles Elliot. Error was detected in survey and land classification by the *Mauzadar* and Recorders. The basic aim of carrying out survey works precisely was to classify the land, demarcation of village boundary and erection of boundary pillars and to check whether the revenue was collected as per Land Settlement Rule,1870 or not. However, a Professional Survey Party had already progressed in survey work. On the other hand, Sub Deputy Collector was ordered for conduction extension survey in assistance with *Mandals* (Recorders) under direct supervision of Director of Land Records and it was seen that the work was identical with the survey work of Professional Survey Party.

In 1898 Professional Survey Party left Assam and then a Party of Survey of India under the guidance of Director of land Records started survey partially. In 1909, the Party was brought completely under the Director of Land Records. Assam Survey and Drawing office was established in 1915 and Superintendent of Survey of India was given officer in charge of the office. In 1933, this office was upgraded to the office of the Assistant Director of Survey, Assam and Director of Land Records also became the Director of the office. Since the establishment of Assam Survey in 1915, this team started survey work systematically.

Presently Director of Land Records is also the Director of Survey. Apart from this BTAD (Bodoland Territorial Areas District) and Karbi Anglong Autonomous Council has separate office of the Assistant Director of Survey. Now the office of the Joint Director of Surveys erstwhile Assam Survey prepare the polygons or framework of Non-cadastral villages of Assam, demarcate the Inter State Boundary, Inter District boundary and international boundary contiguous to Assam.

Government of Assam has taken initiative for computerization of land records and digitization of cadastral map. The land records are incorporated with the cadastral map using the software Bhu-Naksha. Now people can easily access their land record through the web site www.revenueassam.nic.in.

Evolution of Technology for Cadastral Survey

a. Traditionally, survey operations were carried out using plane table survey, the traverse method, the chain survey method etc. In these methods, the distances were measured using metal chains; and angles were measured using the theodolite instruments. These methods required greater resources in terms of time, cost and manpower. Moreover, they were prone to both systemic as well as random human errors besides the fact that possibility of manipulation of measurements due to various pressures was omnipresent.

b. With the advent of newer technologies like Electronic Total Station, Differential Global Positioning System, Satellite Imagery and Internet etc., it has now become technically and financially feasible to generate highly precise and accurate maps with improved accuracies with an error ranging from 1 to 40 cm. Modern maps are geo-referenced and contain a lot more information than the traditional cadastral maps.

Procedure of Cadastral Survey (Settlement Operation) by Conventional Methods

The cadastral survey means the preparation of map on the basis of right and possession of land by individuals as well as classification of land making a detailed land census of the village. The main purpose of making cadastral survey is to access and collect land revenue. Besides it also helps finding the extent of land occupied by an individual as well as the revenue thereof he has to pay. The cadastral survey carries out in two processes namely Settlement operation and Resettlement operation. Now, Assam has 34 Districts and 155 revenue circles.

The Non-Cadastral (NC) villages of Assam are surveyed through the following procedure:

I. *Declaration of Cadastral Survey*: For cadastral survey of a particular NC village, Deputy Commissioner will approch to the Government of Assam. As per requisition of the Deputy Commissioner, Government of Assam will declare for cadastral survey of a particular village as per Assam Land and Revenue Rule, 1886.

II. Before Survey of the NC Villages, recorders or *mandals* along with Surveyor should visit the surrounding area of the village to be surveyed and select the stations in such a way that
   - The stations should not be more than 2½ chains away that both inside and outside from the boundary of the village.
   - The chain distance between two consecutive stations should not be more than 20 chains.
   - The two consecutive stations should be chainable and inter visible.

III. *Preparation of Traverse Polygon*: Conventionally, traverse polygon which controls the framework of cadastral survey is prepared with the help of theodolite traversing by the office of the Director of Land Records and Surveys erstwhile Assam Survey. However, in present days due to advancement of science and technology in the field of surveying Total station and Differential Global positioning system is being used. The polygon prepared is sent to the concerned Deputy Commissioner along with *Khaka* and UT area for detail survey. If it is not provided by the said office, the Recorders of LR staffs have to prepare the traverse polygon with the help of Plane Table applying Traversing method.

IV. *Preparation of Khaka*: The Traverse polygon of a cadastral village is roughly or exactly drawn in brown paper (other paper may also be used) and is called Khaka. Generally, Office of the Director of Survey provides *Khaka* to LR staff, if not provided then LR staff have to prepare the khaka.

V. *Survey of Boundary of the village*: LR staff should keep the plot sheet in the office and take the khaka to the village and start the boundary survey from any of the traverse station by keeping the village left hand side to the surveyor. During this time surveyor should use chain, optical square, poles, flags etc. for taking the offsets, katans etc. of the boundary of the village. For doing this survey, the surveyor uses the khaka as field book to survey the boundary of the village.

VI. *Base Line*: The surveyor will divide the village into some quadrilaterals by some chain lines called base line which joins the stations situated breadth wise of the village. This makes the survey process easier. The surveyor will mark the points both on the field in the *khaka* where the base line cuts field boundaries, roads, canals etc. these points are known as katans. The distances of the *katans* are to be noted on the *khaka*. Some convenient *katans* of the base line marked as sub stations, from that further quadrilateral and the triangles can be formed.

VII. *Murrabba Line:* Now the surveyor will select substation as mentioned above so that the distance between two consecutive substations should be as follows:

In 16” = 1 mile (1:3960) - 10 to 14 chains
In 32” = 1 mile (1:1980) - 5 to 7 chains
In 64” = 1 mile (1:1000) - 3 to 5 chains

Subject to the above conditions some triangles and quadrilaterals are to be formed by dividing the village into even more smaller units by chain lines between –

a) Two substations for opposite baseline.
b) A substations and a boundary station.

The line by which quadrilaterals and triangles are formed are called *murrabba* line and the divisions are called *murrabba* division. Only the *katans* of the *murrabba* lines are to be noted on *khaka* and the marks of *katans* are mark on the ground by spade.

VIII. *Plotting*: In the office, the surveyor has to perform plotting on the traverse sheet from the details which are recorded on the *khaka* as per scale.

IX. *Sikimi Line and internal survey*: After dividing the village into some *murrabba* division, each of the *murrabba* division is to be surveyed separately for recording the details or *dags* of the village. Now surveyor of recorder should proceed to the field with the traverse sheet which is mounted on the P.T. and along with other survey instruments.

To record all the details or *dags* of a *murrabba* division some subsidiary chain lines are to be taken both on the ground and on the traverse sheet. These subsidiary lines are called *sikimi* lines.

The following points are to be taken into account for the *sikimi* lines –

- Sikimi lines should run by joining either two katans on the opposite *murrabba* lines or a katan on a *murrabba* line and a *katan* on a boundary line.
- The interval of the *sikimi* lines should not be more than three chains.
- In a murrabba division two *sikimi* lines should not cut each other.

The surveyor by using chain optical square and other chain survey instrument has to survey along the *sikimi* line and take the offsets, *katan* etc. Also the surveyor should plot the offset points, *katans* etc. and join them by seeing the size of the *dags* on the traverse sheet. During this survey, permanent features like kilometre post, pillar, road, river, rail line etc. are to be recorded and are to be plotted on the map.

In a densely populated area where the *sikimi* lines are not possible, measurements should be taken by pole from corner to corner of a dag. In this case the surveyor may also take the help of different methods of P.T. survey like radiation, intersection etc.

X. *Portal Line*: On completion of the survey work and plotting on the traverse sheet, the Recorder should inform the immediate superior to check the survey work. The superior will go to the field and will run a chain line which is called portal line. This line should run corner wise from one station to another and it will cut at least two Murrabba divisions. The length of portal line should not be more than 30 chains. Katans and offsets are taken on this line and can be checked by drawing the portal line on the map. Any error found should not exceed 5% for the map to be accepted to be correct. If it is found correct, the officer will mark as "checked and found correct" with signature and date bottom of the map.

XI. *Marking Dag Nos*: After portal line, dag numbers are to be marked. Marking of dag numbers starts from the North – West and ends at the South – East of the map.

XII. *U.T. Area:* The inside area of the traverse polygon is the universal area theorem and total area of the cadastral village is the geographical area. The area of the individual dags and also the geographical area are verified with U.T. area.

XIII. *Inking up of the map*: After proper checking and correction of the map by concerned staff and officers, the recorder should ink up the map with black ink. No need to ink up the traverse line, murrabba line, base line, sikimi line etc. which are taken only for drawing the map.

XIV. *Compilation of the Map*: After completion of map as per the rules Chitha and Jamabandi (Records of Right) are to be prepared. The map is then endorsed by the concern L.R. staff, officers and the officials on whose direction the map is prepared. Then the map is sent to the Director of

Land Records and Surveys, Assam for reproduction. After printing, the maps are sent to the Deputy Commissioner where the maps may be purchased by individuals.

Procedure of Record Preparation

Preparation of Chitha

REVISED CHITHA FORM

Village/town..............mauza..............circle....................District.............

Dag No.	Classification of land	Area	Type of patta and No.	Revenue		Name, Father's name and address of Pattadars	Name, Father's name and address of actual occupant (Dakhalkar) whose name has not been mutated	Name, Father's name and address of Tenant/Adhar	Type of tenancy/Khatian No. and rate of rent etc.	Name, Father's name and address of sub-tenants.
				Land Revenue	Local Rate					
1	2	3	4	5	6	7	8	9	10	11

REVISED CHITHA FORM

Village/town..............mauza circle..............District..............

1st year						2nd year						3rd year							
Uncropped Area			Cropped Area			Uncropped Area			Cropped Area			Uncropped Area			Cropped Area				
Nature of land use	Area	Source of irrigation	Name of the crop	Area	Area sown more than once	Nature of land use	Area	Source of irrigation	Name of the crop	Area	Area sown more than once	Nature of land use	Area	Source of irrigation	Name of the crop	Area	Area sown more than once	Name and number of fruit trees	Remarks
12	13	14	15	16	17	18	19	20	21	22	23	24	25	26	27	28	29	30	31

REVISED AREA ABSTRACT FORM

Year.............Village................Mauza.............Circle.............District.............

	Settled land												Unsettled land							
Page No.	Forest	Barren and unculturable land	Land put to non-agricultural uses.	Permanent pasture and other grazing land	Land under miscellaneous tree, crops and groves not shown in area sown	Culturable waste	Current fallow	Other fallow	Net area sown	Area sown more than once	Total area sown	Total settled land *i.e.* Total of Columns 2 to 10	Forest	Barren and inculturable waste	Land put to non-agricultural uses	Permanent pastures and other grazing lands	Land under miscellaneous tree, crops and groves not shown in area sown	Culturable waste	Current fallow	Other fallow
1	2	3	4	5	6	7	8	9	10	11	12	13	14	15	16	17	18	19	20	21

Chitha is a bound, continuous register, each page is used for recording crop information for two or more dags for three successive years. The pages of the chitha is numbered and certified by the Sub-Deputy Collector. During the three years for which the chitha will be in use, the entries will be annually corrected and complete and accurate record of the facts of each year.

- *Land classification and record of rights* — The columns of the chitha is filled up in accordance with the procedure described below:
  (i) Columns 1 to 7 and column 31 in part will be filled up from the previous chitha before the recorder visits the fields during the spring tour. The

field or dag number will be entered in column 1, the classification of land in column 2, and the total area in column 3, columns 2 and 3 are to be filled up for all the fields which are borne on the chitha, whether annual or periodic, settled or Sarkari. In districts where these entries were not made at the time of resettlement, the class of land as recorded for each field in the original class book will be entered in the chitha and copied out each time the chitha is written. In tracts that have not been resettled, the class to be shown in column 2 will be basti, rupit, faringati or tea etc. For unsettled plots, one or other of the following words, in addition to any class to which it may have been classified, should be entered to indicate its actual state: (a) Road embankment, (b) Under water, (c) Reserve, (d) Waste.

(ii) Column 4 will be filled up in respect of settled dag only, which should be described accordingly as they are held on khiraj (periodic or annual) or Nisf-khiraj or Lakhiraj lease. If the land is held on patta for tea cultivation, the word "tea" should be noted. The patta number should also be noted on column 4 along with the type of patta.

(iii) Columns 5 and 6 relating to land revenue and local rate will be filled up from the Jamabandi Register.

- *Field Mutation*: At the time of copying out column 7, the name of each joint pattadar should be entered in a separate line and serially numbered. If there has been a change in the settlement holder, as shown in column 7, the name of the person in actual possession must be shown in column 8 with a number corresponding to that in column 7, when there are more pattadars than one, and a word be entered to indicate the cause of change (e.g., inheritance, purchase, gift, exchange etc.). If an entry has been made in column 8 of the previous chitha, but mutation not yet sanctioned, the entry should be copied in column 8 in the new chitha. The entry in column 8 will be signed and dated by the recorder. The name given in column 8 will be transferred to column 7, as soon as the mutation is sanctioned by the Sub-Deputy Collector. But in the case of annual pattas, the names of actual occupants (dakhalkars) by right of inheritance or share only should be entered in column 8 by the recorder, and such names noted in column 8 will be transferred to column 7 as soon as the mutation is sanctioned by the Sub-Deputy Collector. In case of occupation of annual patta lands by other means or manner, e.g., by transfer, sale, gift, exchange, lease or mortgage, etc., the recorder shall note down the nature of possession (dakhal) with names, father's names and address of the occupants invariably in column 31 and not in column 8, and shall submit a report to that effect with a copy of the chitha to the Sub-Deputy Collector who will take necessary action in accordance with the latest Government orders and instructions in the matter.
- *Tenant's records*: Columns 9-11 will be filled up when special orders are issued by the Government for the preparation of record of rights of

tenants, adhiars and sub-tenants. Changes will be shown by correcting the previous entries.

- *Record of land-use:* The nature of current utilization of uncropped land both settled and Sarkari and its area will be recorded in columns 12 and 13, 18 and 19 and 24, and 25 for the first, second and third year respectively.
- The class of land-use to be recorded here will be one or more of the following classes:
  - Forests[10]
  - Barren and uncultivable land[11]
  - Land put to non-agricultural uses[12]
  - Permanent pastures and other grazing land[13]
  - Miscellaneous tree crops and groves not included in the net area sawn[14]
  - Cultivable waste[15]
  - Current fallow[16]
  - Other fallows[17].

---

[10] All actually forested areas on the land classes or administered as forest under any legal enactment dealing with forest whether State owned or private will be noted as forest. If any portion of an unclassed State forest or a private forest is not actually wooded but put to some other uses, that portion should be included under the appropriate heading of cultivated or uncultivated land and excluded from area under forest, but this will not apply to reserved forest, the total area of which should be recorded as forest.

[11] All lands that are barren and absolutely unfit for cultivation, i.e, lands under barren hills, hillocks, rock, swamps (dalani), silted lands and sandy lands will be noted as barren and uncultivable lands.

[12] All lands under house-site (basti or bari with its sub classes), trade site (beparon thai with its sub-classes) road (bat), railway, burial and cremation grounds schools, temples, mosques. Playground, land under water (panital) e.g., river, pond and fishery pond land under embankment, bunds, land reserved for other public purposes etc., will be recorded as land put to non-agricultural uses.

[13] All lands reserved as Public Grazing Reserve and Village Grazing Reserve and other grazing lands will be included under permanent pastures and other grazing land.

[14] All lands under scrub jungle, bamboo clump (whether in the home — stead or outside), thatch (kher), etc., will be noted as area under miscellaneous tree crops and groves not shown in area sown. The area covered by clumps of bamboos in the homestead should be excluded from the total area of homestead land and recorded as area under miscellaneous tree crops and groves not shown in area sown. The area of clumps of bamboos outside the homestead should also be noted as area under miscellaneous tree crops etc.

[15] All lands that are cultivable but have not been cultivated so far or once cultivated but lying fallow for more than five years will be recorded as cultivable waste.

[16] All fields lying fallow during the current agricultural year will be noted as current fallow.

[17] Fields lying fallow for more than a year and upto five years are to be noted as other fallow.

- *Record of irrigated area*: In columns 14, 20 and 26 will be recorded the source of irrigation from which an area, if any, under a crop has been irrigated. The sources should be mentioned according to the following standard classification:

Source of Irrigation	*Description*
Canal	1. Government canal 2. Private canal.
Tank	1. Government tank: a. with ayacut of less than 100 acres. b. with ayacut of 100 acres and more. 2. Private tank: a. with ayacut of less than 100 acres. b. with ayacut of 100 acres and more.
Tubewell	1. Run by electric pump. 2. Run by oil engine.
Well	1. Government: a. Masonry b. Non-masonry. 2. Private: a. Masonry b. Non-masonry.
Other Sources	
Dong Stream	

- *Crop Recording*:
  a) The name of the crop sown and its area will be recorded in columns 15 and 16, 21 and 22 and 27 and 28 for the first, second and third year respectively. The irrigated area of a crop will be noted separately from its unirrigated area and the former will be encircled to distinguish it from the latter. If, for example, dag number 55 has 10 bighas under paddy of which 6 bighas are irrigated, then the crop paddy will be entered in columns 15, 21 or 27 as the case may be, and against it, both 6 bighas and 4 bighas will be noted one below the other in columns 16, 22 or 28 as the case may be, and 6 bighas will be encircled to indicate that it is irrigated
  b) If a crop is grown on unsettled land, its name and area should be recorded in columns 15 and 16, 21 and 22, 27 and 28 for the first, second and third year respectively. The fact that it is unauthorized cultivation should be noted in column 31.
  c) When the same field or the same part of a field has borne more than one crop within the year, both will be entered in columns 15, 21 and 27 and the areas of both in columns 16, 22 and 28 for the first, second and third year respectively. Double cropping is generally effected by broadcasting rice before the crop which the recorder finds on the ground. The recorder must ascertain by careful enquiry and by inspecting the land whether there has been a preceding crop or not.

d) The area which has borne more than one crop within the year will be repeated in columns 17, 23 and 29 for the first, second and third year respectively.

e) In column 30 will be recorded the name, and number of scattered trees in areas other than the compact orchard. In case of compact orchards, their areas will be recorded in crop columns. In recording the area of compact orchards in crop columns of the chitha, the recorder will take care to see that in the case of mixed orchards the names of all the component fruits and the gross area of the mixed orchards are entered. He will then allocate the gross area to the component fruits by eye estimation.

- *Treatment of relinquished dags*: When entire dags are excluded from settlement as relinquished, the recorder shall substitute the word 'sarkari' in column 7 in place of the name of the pattadar. Should the boundaries and numbering of the relinquished field have been erased or cancelled, the chitha entry will be scored out, the area of the field being added to that of the adjacent sarkari dag, but fields of different classification should not be amalgamated with one another. If in any case, fields are amalgamated and consequent alteration in the dag numbers is involved, the fact should be noted in the remarks column of the Class Book. If the field is again taken up whole or in part, it will be dealt with in the same manner as any other sarkari dag.
- *Exclusion of faut, ferar and jotrahin fields*: A similar procedure will be followed in the case of dags that have been brought by the recorder on to his faut, ferar and jotrahin list and land excluded from settlement by order (e.g. land acquired or annulled), the name of the holder being scored out and the word 'sarkari' being substituted.
- *Recording of land under bunds*: The area under permanent bunds should be shown separately in the chitha. The area of a field bund or strip which is given a separate dag number will be recorded under the land-use to which it is put, e.g., under rupit if sown with crops; under land put to non-agricultural use if used as passage only, under miscellaneous tree-crop if used to grow trees, under grass land if used to grow grass for cattle.
- *When copying the chitha*: The recorder will reserve at least 10 pages at the beginning for the following purposes:
  (1) Remarks made and orders passed by Sub-Deputy Collector or Supervisor Kanungo when inspecting the village.
  (2) List of dags newly settled at Dariabadi or regular settlement and resettled relinquished dags.
  (3) List of dags excluded owing to relinquishment, of dags faut, ferar and jotrahin and of dags excluded under special orders.
  (4) List of dags reserved from settlement with notes of areas and purpose of reservation.

(5) List of reserved dags encroached upon with space for area of encroachment, name and address of encroachers, date of report, note of subsequent orders received and result of action taken.

(6) A list of sarkari dags of the village with areas. The original area of such dags recorded in last resettlement should be noted against each dag.

- *Old field chithas*: When a field chitha has been rewritten, the old copy will be deposited in the circle office and remain there until the field chitha has again been rewritten. It will then be destroyed with order from the Deputy Commissioner.

Jamabandi

Separate Jamabandis are prepared for: (a) periodic pattas, (b) annual pattas recorded at regular settlement, (c) annual pattas recorded at supplementary settlement. In addition, there are separate jamabandis for special tenures such as nisf-khiraj.

- *The Jamabandi Register*: The principal record of periodic and special pattas, that is to say, of land holding tenures, is the jamabandi register. This is the jamabandi prepared at the last preceding resettlement of the district. Land Revenue and local rate payable by pattadars are incorporated in the jamabandi register which is a permanent record and continues upto the terminal year during the currency of resettlement. It is maintained by the Registrar Kanungo, and kept up-to-date by making necessary corrections. Fields will be struck off as relinquished or excluded for faut, ferar or jotrahin or under special orders, or added as newly settled on the basis of the recorder's chitha. No mutation of names can be effected without the order of the Sub-Deputy Collector or an officer duly empowered.
- *The local periodic jamabandi*: A duplicate copy of the jamabandi register (called the local periodic jamabandi) is kept by the recorder for reference. It will be made available to mauzadar or tahsildar when required for the preparation of the annual collection register (wasil, tahsil or touzi). Any alteration made in the jamabandi register must be made in this copy also.
  A list of all dags which have been effected by orders of field partition together with the dates of the orders concerned must be kept permanently on a page of the local periodic jamabandi and must always be referred to when a new map is brought into use by the recorder and particularly when the map is collected for reprinting.
- Fresh jamabandis will annually be prepared by the recorder for annual pattas as recorded at regular settlement and at supplementary settlement. The jamabandis will be duly verified and checked by the Supervisor Kanungo. They need not be copied. The originals will be kept by the recorder but will be made available to Mauzadars or Tahsildars for preparation of the annual collection register (wasil, tahsil or tauzi).

- *Entry of land classing in the jamabandi*: In the annual jamabandi, columns 6 and 7 will be filled up from the relevant columns of the chitha in accordance with the nature of lands-use, and the same procedure will be followed in case of periodic jamabandi as well while making entries in the case of new holdings that have changed by gaining or losing fields and the revenue of which is to be recalculated.
- Recorder's copies of jambandis, periodic or annual, will remain with the recorder during the current settlement. The annual jamabandis of the previous years will be deposited in the circle office for three years, after which these will be destroyed with orders from the Deputy Commissioner.

Maintenance of Field Map

i. *New map when required*: In villages in which cultivation changes but little, the recorder may carry on a single map for three years, a new map being brought into use when a new chitha is rewritten. In villages in which changes are numerous, and in the case of all fluctuating villages, he will work upon a fresh map each year. The year or years for which the map is used should be clearly written on the face of the map and duly attested by the Supervisor Kanungo.

ii. *Care of map*: The recorder must keep his map clean and protected from damp.

iii. *Chain testing*: The recorder must maintain close to his house, on a level piece of ground, a measuring standard 66 feet long, whereby to test his chain and off set pole. The total distance must be marked off on the ground by large permanently fixed pegs of wood (not bamboo), must be divided into ten equal divisions of ten links each by smaller pegs. All recorders must often test their chains and rectify any errors that may be found. Every recorder must know how to correct the length of his chain viz., by opening or closing the joints of the rings.

iv. *Instruments*: All recorders should be provided with a talc or cellulose square showing Katha squares on a scale of 16 inches to a mile, a pair of compasses, a cardboard scale and a 20 link pole and an offset lip. The recorders of tracts in which cultivation fluctuates, or is spreading will also be supplied with a Gunter's chain, a plane-table, a cross-staff or optical square, a led Pencil and a piece of rubber and other materials that are required for survey work.

v. *Verification of relinquishment*: The recorder will verify on the ground all fields shown in the map in pencil, correcting the boundaries where necessary. After verifying a relinquishment, he will cross out the boundary, if it is in pencil, but if it is printed or in ink, he will leave it unchanged and deal with the field under Rule 62. The pencil boundaries crossed out as above will be rubbed out in the winter recess. The same procedure will also apply to fields excluded from settlement by order. Owing to the increase of population and the consequent demand for land, the practice of resignation even of annual lands has been much reduced and over large area is now practically unknown.

During field tours the recorder will:

(1) survey and bring on to the map all areas that have been settled upon application,
(2) survey all new cultivation and extensions of cultivation, carefully exploring the unsettled lands and sarkari dags of his villages to ensure that no new cultivation or extension of cultivation escapes notice,
(3) go round the periodically settled fields of his villages and make any corrections on the map which are needed in order to give effect to orders passed by the Sub-Deputy Collector or other officer duly empowered in mutation proceedings, and
(4) inspect all the areas reserved within his lot for public purposes (e.g., road-side lands, grazing or camping grounds etc.) and report encroachments, if any. The encroached areas in respect of Sarkari lands or lands reserved for public purposes within his lot will be plotted on the map in pencil and taken over to the encroachment register and Tauzi-Bahir jamabandi to be maintained under rule 19.

Extensions of cultivation in lakhiraj estates and fee-simple grants held for ordinary cultivation are to be surveyed and numbered in separate dags according to blocks of cultivation for the assessment of local rates.

vi. *Alteration of periodic fields*:
   (1) The recorder shall not, without the previous sanction of the Sub-Deputy Collector, alter the boundaries of a periodic field. The Sub-Deputy Collector shall give such sanction only in the case of an admitted error in mapping the boundary of contiguous fields. When the Sub-Deputy Collector gives such sanction, he shall himself revise the recorded areas and the recorded revenue of the fields concerned. Admission of such an error by the parties shall be noted in the remarks column of the chitha with thumb impression or signature of the parties concerned duly attested by the Sub-Deputy Collector.
   (2) Bad mistakes in survey should be reported to the Sub-Deputy Collector for orders.
   (3) When a portion of a dag has been transferred and when the parties so desire it, the recorder shall survey the transferred portion and shall show its boundaries in pencil in his map, but he shall not assign to it a separate dag number nor ink it and shall not make a separate entry in the chitha, without the previous sanction of the Sub-Deputy Collector.

vii. *Safeguard against assessing highland rice-fields twice* — Land which the recorder finds during his winter tour to have been taken up for cropping with highland rice during the summer following will not be surveyed or assessed by him till he commences his tour for the regular settlement.

viii. *Numbering new fields* — The following procedure will be observed in numbering new fields:

- The natural numbering of fields is from the north-west to the south-east corner of the village. The original maps were prepared on this system.
- When a new field is inserted in a map already prepared, the new field will receive a number immediately consecutive to the last number in the chitha. If the natural sequence of number is thereby broken on the map, then in the chitha and jamabandi, though not in the map, the new field will receive a fractional number which will indicate where it lies. Thus, if the last number in the chitha be 250 and a new field be surveyed in the neighborhood of field No. 79, the new field will appear in the map as 251 and in the record as 79/251.
- If a village is large and there is much sarkari and fluctuating land in it, the village should be divided into convenient blocks and certain number should be set apart for each block. Thus first block 1-75, second block 76-100, and third block 101-160 and fourth block 161-200. The blocks should be bounded where possible by natural features; otherwise by straight lines drawn between the Theodolite stations or Kanungo's dhips. The numbers should be so assigned to each block that there is no likelihood of the numbers running short. Thus, if it appears that a block will require 50 numbers, 75 may be allotted, and so on. For the purpose of numbering the fields each block will then be treated as a separate village and the system explained in clause (2) will be followed block by block. Separate pages of the chitha will be kept for each block. When a field falls in two blocks, it will be numbered according to the block in which the larger portion falls. The system of block 'numbering' will be adopted in all large newly surveyed villages which have much Sarkari and fluctuating land and also in all villages of this nature for which a new edition of the map is brought out.

ix. *Method of survey* — In surveying, the following instructions must be observed:

- All measurements must be made by means of the chain except in the case of short offsets not exceeding a chain in length, which may be measured with the 20 link tar.
- Chain lines should ordinarily run from one survey mark to another. But when the marks are far apart, or high grass or jungle intervene, triangulation may be resorted to. Triangulation may be freely used for plotting of blocks of fluctuating cultivation, or of cultivation isolated in jungle, which the recorder need not attempt to locate precisely on the map.

- New fields on the edge of permanent fields may be measured by 'tar', care being taken that the measurement is started from the boundary of a field about the correct position of which there is no doubt.

x. The boundaries of new fields and changed boundaries of old fields are to be plotted in pencil continuous lines. The recorder will show the new roads, ponds and other changes in the physical features on the map.

xi. The boundaries of periodically settled and annually settled fields (including the crossing out of obsolete boundaries) will be inked up in office. Provided that in the immature and fluctuating villages where temporary cultivation is practised and when the boundaries of holdings are subject to changes due to either floods or non-maintenance of permanent boundaries the annual dags may be kept in pencil.

xii. *Preparation of map for new field work* — When a fresh map is taken, the recorder will bring it up-to-date before leaving office for his spring tour by transferring to it all changes which are shown upon the map used by him during the tours last preceding.

When annual dags are traced on a new map, the traces must be immediately checked by lines in the field.

xiii. If the changes since the map was printed would necessitate much plotting over printed lines in a part of the map, it will suffice to make a trace of that part only which should be neatly pasted over that portion of the map of which it is a trace. On it should be shown in ink the boundaries of the village and any permanent survey marks and roads, etc. and the boundaries of the periodic fields not resigned or abandoned. If, however, the changes affect the whole map an up-to-date trace must be made for Vandyking a new set of maps as detailed in the following rule.

xiv. *Vandyking*: When a new map is to be printed under the above rule or when the stock of any map has been exhausted, it is no longer necessary or desirable to have a trace made, but two blueprints of the original map should be called for from the Assam Survey, Guwahati.

The following instructions should be observed in using them:

1(a) One copy should be taken out in the field and each dag on the map should be compared with corresponding features on the ground.

(b) Where no changes have occurred, the blue lines on the map on the boundaries of such dags should be left as they are until the map is brought to office, when they will be inked up.

(c) Where changes have occurred, the blue lines showing the original boundary (which has changed) should be crossed out in pencil, the changes e.g., change in the existing boundaries, sub-division of dags, new cultivation or changes in the course of any stream or road should be accurately surveyed, plotted in pencil and when taken to office, inked up. In case of amalgamation of two dags and to prevent any doubt on the matter when the plots are being renumbered, the link symbol "S" for connecting two plots should be drawn in pencil across the blue line that is not to be inked up.

2(a) When the revised blue print has been completed in every respect, and the dags, where necessary, have been renumbered in ink, the second copy should be very neatly and carefully inked up in accordance with the field copy of the revised blue print. The second copy should be kept flat in office and should not be rolled up, as creases or cracks will reproduce black lines in the print.

(b) The ink used should be freshly ground up Indian ink of sufficient consistency, so that all lines and letters made with it, will when dry, be perfectly black and opaque, when examined by holding the map upto the light.

(c) The lines and figures should not be drawn too fine, but should be clear, firm and not ragged. The figures should not be made too small, e.g. vernacular 3, when made, shall looks like O in the printed maps.

(d) Nothing should be pasted to either the front or back of the map, and erasers should, as far as possible, be avoided.

3. The class division of dags, whether made at the resettlement or afterwards, should be shown in dotted lines in ink in both copies of the blueprint.

4. There should be an endorsement on the fair copy of the blueprint map to the following effect under the signature of the Deputy Commissioner "This map was made under the authority of Government in (year) and has been corrected upto (year)".

5. The fair copy of the map as thus revised will be sent in original carefully rolled round a ruler to the Assam Survey, Guwahati for reproduction.

6. The Assam Survey, Guwahati can supply blue prints only when the original maps are stored there. Maps made before the Vandyke process was invented i.e. about 1907 are usually not fit for immediate reproduction. But black prints in stock in the district, if sent to the Assam Survey, Guwahati, can nearly be always reproduced in blue. Consequently, when blue prints are required, a clear copy of the existing black print, with absolutely nothing written on it, should be sent to the Assam Survey, Assam from the district stock.

If there are no changes in the existing black print, it is unnecessary to ask for a blue print for correction and in such cases black prints should be indented.

xv. In the case of all villages to be surveyed or resurveyed, the margins of the maps (and sheets) should be carefully compared and a certificate to the effect that "the margins of the +Sheet/(village map) have been compared with those of the adjoining +Sheet"/ (village map) should be signed by the Supervisor Kanungo and the Sub-Deputy Collector concerned on the copy of the map sent to the Assam Survey, Guwahati for reproduction.

xvi. *Filing of maps* — When the recorder takes out a new map, he will retain the map in previous use till the end of the following winter tour and will then file it with Registrar Kanungo who will deposit it in the record room for reference at the next resettlement, after noting clearly upon it the year or years to which it relates.

xvii. *Record of map testing by superior officers* — The recorder will maintain a notebook for all check lines run across his map by any inspecting officers, recording the name of the village, date, the number of the fields from which and to which the check line was run, and results of the check. Entries in this notebook will be made by Inspecting Officers only. The check line should also be plotted on the map by the Inspecting Officer by a dot-and-dash line. But this line need not be transferred to a new map.

Block Survey and Extension Survey

Block Survey

In non-cadastral and non-surveyed area, the survey which is carried out block wise by using chain and other instruments of chain survey for the purpose of revenue assessment in Government khas land is called block survey. Block survey is nothing but chain survey. This survey is not related with true north.

Instruments required for block survey are: Chain (1 No.), Chain Pin10 numbers to (3-4 Nos.), Pole or Nal1 number., Flags (1 No.), Optical Square (1 No.), Field book (1 No.), Plumb-bob (1 No.), Pencil, rubber and thread (1 No. each), Spade 1 No., Dao.

Block survey is generally done in char area or other non-cadastral, non-surveyed area for the purpose of revenue assessment.

Procedure of Block Survey

Block survey is generally carried out in jungle area, government *khas* land, which is newly occupied by people, mainly for the purpose of cultivation by clearing of the jungles and for the realization of revenue from the people of that area. Following steps may be taken for Block Survey.

Firstly, ascertain the area of the block to be surveyed. Secondly, stations are to be marked on the ground at convenient place and named A, B, C and D.

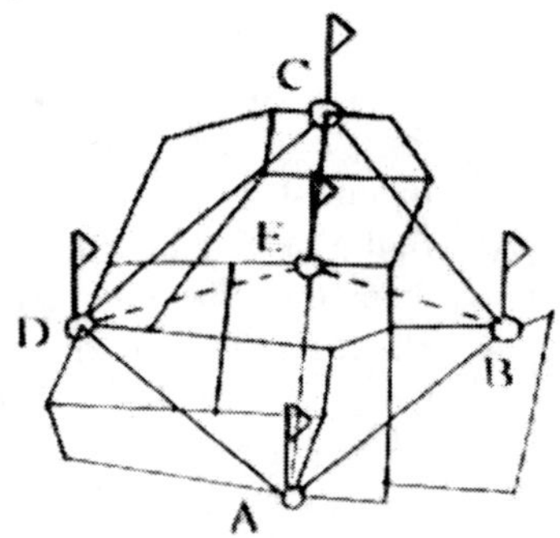

Secondly, one station should be on one side of the block, but not in the corner of the block. Then place flags on each station.

Thirdly, draw the sketch map of the block in the field book after giving a walking view surrounding the block and join AC, CD, DA, AB, and BC in straight line.

Fourthly, to survey the base line AC, by taking the katans and the nearest offsets and record it, in the field book. In the middle point of AC line, one katan is taken as substation or chanda as named "E" and join ED by dotted line in the sketch map. After completion of survey of AC line we have to start the survey of CD line by taking the katans and the nearest offsets. Same way, survey has been conducted for DA line and after completion of survey of ACD triangle, ED check line or tie line is used and note the distances of katans and leftout offsets of the ED line. Similarly, chain survey is carried out in AB, BC line by taking the katans and the nearest offsets of respective line and EB tie line as before.

Fifthly, after completion of field work, we should draw the AC base line as per distance of the field on the drawing paper. Then take the distance CD and draw an arc to the left side of AC line by taking C as the centre with the help of a divider. Again, take the distance of AD and draw an arc taking A as the centre, so that it cuts the previous arc at the point D. Now join CD and AD and find ACD. Put the point E on AC line. Like this way, draw the ABC and join the Tie line ED and EB by dotted line. After it plotting is started in the conventional manner starting from AC and later Cl) and Al) and various offsets and katans are plotted and complete the plotting of ACB. Similarly, complete the plotting of the triangle ABC also. Now join the plots as per directions given in the plotting following the field book. Then check the plotting of the triangles ACD and ACB with the help of Tie line ED & EB by taking the katans and offsets from field book. In this way block survey is done.

Extension Survey

In a non-cadastral area if an individual/individuals occupy some additional/extra land adjacent to the block already surveyed, then to survey the newly occupied area or land, chain triangulation survey is done for the newly occupied area. In such a case, new block need not be framed, only survey work is extended to the unsurveyed area by framing a triangle with the help of one line of the earlier block as base line. Such a survey is called extension survey. This extension survey is also done for the assessment of revenue only.

Procedure of Extension Survey

Suppose land is occupied to the right side of BC line. Now a station F is to be fixed. Then sketch of the extended area is to be drawn and join BF and FC line. Sub-station G is to be placed on BC line at katan G. Then Survey is done in BF line and FC line as like as block line by taking the katan and offsets. After it we have to check the BCF with the help of Tie line GF taking Katans and offsets. For plotting, draw an arc with the distance BF taking centre B of BC line of the block to the right side with the help of

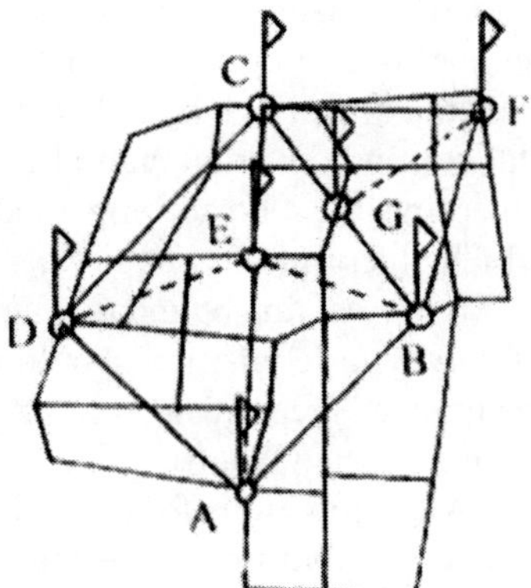

of divider. Again, draw another arc by taking the distance CF and as the centre C so that it intersects at point F. So, we find the extended triangle BCF. After drawing it plotting is started in the conventional manner on BF & FC line and various katans and offsets are plotted and complete the plotting of BCF. Joining of the plots are to be completed as per directions given in the plotting following the field book. Then check the plotting of the BCF by Tie line GF following the katans and offsets as in the recorded field book and complete the plotting.

Resettlement Operation_

Resettlement operation carried out for the modification of the rate of land revenue at which already settled lands have been assessed. Under rule 8(a) of the settlement rules, settlement of a local area or class of estates means a specific operation carried out U/S 17 to 42 of the ALRR for the formal revision of the land revenue demand. The Resettlement process is briefed below.

Preliminary arrangements for the initiation of the resettlement operations will be made by the circle Sub-Deputy Collectors under the control of the Deputy Commissioner and the guidance of the Director of Land Records. The help of the Assistant to the Director of Land Records may also be requisitioned whenever needed.

The preliminary arrangements will include the following:

(i) The instructions of the Inspecting Officers bearing on this point recorded from time to time, and also the notes of the Sub-Deputy Collectors and Supervisor Kanungos, in the recorders' notebook (Rule 55 of the Land Records Manual), shall be consulted and the current maps examined (and a classified list according to Recorders' lots prepared, vide instruction 3.iv) in the light of the instructions to find out if any entire village or any part of it requires resurvey. If only a portion (e.g., an annual block) of a village requires resurvey, the portion should be marked on the current map. If no resurvey is needed or if the resurvey of a part only of a village be needed, blueprints of the current maps of such villages shall be indented from the Assam Survey Office. If the current map of a village is for any reason whatsoever found to be substantially inaccurate but a sufficient number of survey marks exist for the purpose of resurveying the whole village, skeleton blueprints in duplicate showing only the village boundary with traverse stations and the main natural features will be requisitioned. All requisitions for blueprints must be accompanied by a clean copy of each of the current maps of which blueprints are required.

If the existing boundary marks of any villages are insufficient for the purpose of survey, a requisition should be sent for re-traversing such village. A list of unsurveyed areas of suitable size which are fit for traverse should also be sent for traversing the villages.

All requisitions for blueprints as well as for the re-traverse or new traverse should be submitted to the Joint Director, Assam Surveys, through the Director of Land Records and Surveys to the former at least six months before and to the latter at least a year before the resettlement operations start so that the blueprints and re-traverse or traverse sheets may become available before the commencement of the field work in connection with the resettlement operations.

(ii) When the blueprints are received from the Assam Survey Office, the post-resettlement dags (except the dags falling within the portions marked for resurvey, if any) will be traced from the current maps in the recorder's hand onto one copy. Nothing is to be traced on the skeleton blueprints.

(iii) A draft resettlement chitha showing the old dag numbers, area, pattadars, names, class of tenure, the present field classification (and where necessary, its area), shall be prepared by copying respectively from the first four columns and columns 12 and 13 of the current chitha in the recorder's hand except in villages which are intended to be completely resurveyed. The crops recorded in the recorder's chitha in the previous spring tour may also be copied in pencil in the proper column.

(iv) A complete classified list shall be prepared of villages for—

(1) Map correction.
(2) Map correction with partial resurvey.
(3) Complete resurvey:
- on skeleton blueprints,
- on re-traversed blueprints,
- on newly traversed polygons and the list shall show as accurately as possible the number of dags in each village.

Resettlement Processes

The resettlement of land shall consist of the following processes:

(a) Map revision (survey and demarcation).
(b) Preliminary record-writing and field classification.
(c) Record attestation.
(d) Submission of Assessment Report.
(e) Revenue attestation.
(f) Offer of settlement.

i. *Preparation of tenant's records of right:* During resettlement operations involving re-assessment of revenue, the preparation of tenant's record-of-rights if ordered under Sections 17 and 18 of the Regulation will be framed under the provisions of the Regulation and not under Chapter IX of the Assam Temporarily settled Districts Tenancy Act, 1935. The order under Section 18 of the Regulation will ordinarily specify the classes of tenants in respect of whom the record-of-right is to be framed and will state if the record is at all to extend to tenants — other than privileged raiyats and occupancy raiyats — holding land on leases the term of which is not longer than one year.

Settlement Rules 78-82F govern the procedure for the preparation of the record under the Regulation. It will be noticed that the operation consists of the following stages, namely:

(1) Preliminary survey and record-writing.
(2) Record attestation.
(3) Preliminary publication and disposal of objections.
(4) Preparation of Final Record.
(5) Publication of Final Record.
(6) Distribution of Final Record.

Of these, the first stage should be taken up and finished simultaneously with stage (a) in Settlement Rule 55. It should not ordinarily be difficult to take up and finish the second stage along with stage (6) in Settlement Rule 55. The third and subsequent stages should be taken up when the Assistant Settlement Officer is free to take them up after supplying the Settlement Officer with the material necessary for the Rate Report under Settlement Rule 58.

Should any of the stages after the stage of record attestation of the tenant's record of rights necessitate any change in the dag-boundaries inked up in black Indian ink, the Settlement Officer's order should be taken. It may be that taking the village map as a whole the corrections are so few in number that no separate map under Settlement Rule 82D showing tenancies need be printed and that the changes may be affected in red ink as badar correction.

ii. *Simultaneous disposal of settlement work*: The conduct of resettlement operations is complicated by the necessity for preparing the ordinary regular and supplementary Settlement abstracts or dauls for which, the Settlement Officer will be responsible. Enquiries into faut, ferar and jotrahin cases and relinquishment petitions have to be done as usual. Excepting in the year of map revision, the survey for regular and supplementary settlements has to be carried on each year. More specially, in chapori areas where cultivation may still be of a "fluctuating" type. But the other branches of the ordinary Land Records work, e.g. recording of mutations in the existing records or corrections of jamabandis for the field mutations sanctioned in the course of the re-settlement operations, the compilation of the crop statistics and the demarcation of estates according to the current maps are suspended.

iii. *Preparation of the ordinary settlement abstracts or Dauls*: The measurements and enquiries made by the recorders during the season of map correction and preliminary record-writing will be utilized for the preparation of the supplementary settlement abstract of the current year in the month of March as well as of the regular settlement abstract of the coming year in following August. The recorders will keep lists of the new fields measured and recorded in the course of map correction. From these lists, Dariabadi (or Halabadi), Jamabandis will be prepared in the field and without coming into office. In villages in which map correction and record-writing are not completed by the 1st February, supplementary settlement may be neglected. In established villages the supplementary settlement is generally of small account, but arrangements should be made to take up earliest in the season those villages whether in established or in fluctuating areas in which supplementary settlement is of any importance. For the regular settlement of the coming year the recorders should similarly prepare lists of new fields and of fields liable to be altered or to additional assessment, together with lists of fields to be excluded as faut, ferar or jotrahin, and should also verify relinquishments; (vide rules 19 to 23A of the Assam Land Records Manual). For this purpose it will be necessary that they should make a rapid tour of their villages during April to measure areas taken up for cultivation or going out of cultivation on account of pattadars being faut, ferar and jotrahin since the completion of map correction and to verify relinquishments. In the light of the results of these operations the periodic Jamabandis will be corrected and new Jamabandis will be written for the fields to be annually settled after the recorders have come into office. The permanent Supervisor Kanungos will at all times be responsible for the consolidation and timely submission of the settlement abstracts.

In the subsequent years of the resettlement operations, the Settlement Officer will have to make special arrangements for the annual revision of the land revenue rolls necessitated by the opening up of new lands and exclusions for faut, ferar, jotrahin cases and relinquishments.

iv. *Map Revision:* Before beginning his field work each recorder will be given a copy of the blue prints or the re-traverse or traverse sheets pertaining to the villages in his lot the other copy remains with the Registrar Kanungo in case the first copy is spoilt in any way. In the case of areas which are not marked out for fresh survey (as distinct from map correction) all post-resettlement dags if not already in print should be traced on the blue prints in pencil from the current working map of the permanent recorder. In the case of areas marked out for resurvey or fresh survey no such tracing should be done in the blue prints or re-traverse or traverse sheets, as the case may be.

Each of these prints or sheets will, before commencing field work thereon, be mounted on a strawboard by pasting a narrow piece of fine Malmal cloth along the borders and covering the edges of the sheet and the strawboard, and the sheet will remain so mounted till the resettlement work thereon is finished, the map is inked up in Indian ink and finally passed for despatch to the Survey Office for vandyking. Every care must be taken to keep these (original) maps neat and clean and free from any mark of coloured ink other than the lines, figures, etc., in Indian ink meant to be reproduced in the process of vandyking. It may be noted that neither the blue ink lines — printed or drawn — nor any pencil marks on the blue prints will come out in vandyking. It must be clearly understood that nothing is to be drawn by pen on these maps in the field except with the drawing pencil only.

Besides the prints or sheets indicated above, the recorder should have the current working map and the classification map of each village also for reference.

v. *Map Slip:* To each map, a slip for Inspecting Officers' remarks will be attached at a corner of the strawboard. Before the field work begins, the Assistant Settlement Officer will examine each map, and if he finds that in any village it is necessary to direct special attention to any particular branch of map revision (e.g., the examination of sarkari fields where concealed cultivation is suspected, the survey of a changed river, the resurvey of a block of annual or kabula lands, etc.), he shall make a note to this effect on the slip for the guidance of the recorder.

During the inspection of field work, the Inspecting Officer should record on the slip attached to the map a very brief note showing exactly what testing he has done and in what part of the village and containing his opinion of the quality and speed of the recorder's work,

vi. *Scope of map correction:* Map correction includes the careful examination of the boundaries of all fields, the correction of all boundaries which are not correct according to present possession, the inclusion of any occupied land which has escaped unassessed, the amalgamation of similar adjacent fields in the same ownership and the division of partitioned fields.

The re-numbering of dags in the map and the re-calculation of areas will ordinarily be done in office after the fieldwork is over.

vii. *Unit of interior survey:* The unit of plotting is the dag, that is to say, a parcel of land Unit of forming (i) if settled, the whole or part of a single estate or holding and constituting a compact block, generally similar in character of its soil or cropping (e.g., basti, rupit, faringati, bao, chara, patit, etc.) or (ii) if unsettled, a block of fairly uniform character (e.g., hills, rivers, railways, roads, paths, culturable lands, etc.). Dags which can be amalgamated in accordance with the above description may be amalgamated. The holdings of tenants must be plotted separately except when they are found to be inoccupation on leases the term of which is not longer than one year.

It will be found that, whether from mistakes in the survey or changes since the survey, cases occur in which the dag boundaries of the map supplied do not indicate correctly the limits of the pattadar's actual present possession. The recorder should begin his fieldwork by running at least two cross check lines across each village between theodolite stations and make a chanda and put in a peg at every five chains: he will make corrections of the field boundaries separately within each block so formed by the pegs and the village boundaries. If the map is found on the whole to be fairly accurate, the recorder must walk along the boundaries of each field, with the map, comparing by visual inspection the field and map boundaries, frequently verifying measurements with a 20 link ter (pole) and making necessary corrections in the boundaries of dags in pencil according to possession; rice fields adjoining sarkari lands or occupied high land must be specially tested, as it is in such cases that encroachments are most common. Errors not exceeding the length of a far (20 links) need not be taken into account unless the land be very valuable, e.g., in towns,

If due to distortion of map, the cross-check lines reveal a discrepancy of more than 14 per cent between the ground and the map measurements, the matter shall at once be reported through the proper channel for the orders of the Settlement Officer. Such a village may have to be re-traversed and resurveyed.

If on running the cross check lines it appears that the changes in the internal survey are very numerous indeed, the existing map may be discarded and a fresh survey may be made, but no such resurvey of a whole village shall be commenced without the sanction of the Settlement Officer. If there be any serious error extending over a whole block of printed dags re-survey of the same may be undertaken with the previous sanction of the Assistant Settlement Officer.

In Nisf-khiraj and Lakhiraj estates the interior survey must be overhauled according to the present possession of tenants and, if feels necessary, a resurvey is to be made. Each tenant's holding must appear on the map. As in such estates numerous changes may have taken place since the last resettlement, special attention should be directed to their survey.

viii. *Map correction post resettlement fields*: Every field added to the map since the last resettlement must be very carefully examined as to the accuracy in its survey. If such dags were printed in blue they should be specially marked on the blue print. Blocks of 50 bighas or under of such land must be paralleled by the recorder by running one check line and larger blocks by two or more lines. Such lines should be run, if possible, between theodolite stations, but if this be found very difficult, short lines may be run, between Kanungo's dhips or the chandas marked in the cross check lines of the village, provided the points selected are first carefully verified. Triangulation from any two fixed points may be freely resorted to. Fields adjoining cadastral fields may be verified by tar measurements in the method described in instruction 24 but the position of new fields inside sarkari blocks must be verified by check-lines or by two measurements from the nearest block of cadastral fields.

If in any block, an error of a chain is discovered, the whole block must be resurveyed. Errors of 20 links and under may be neglected.

ix. *Disputes*: Should any dispute occur during map revision or chitha-writing, the recorder will survey according to possession marking out the disputed area on the map if necessary with a suitable letter and a note the existence of the dispute by entering the word "bibad" in the remarks column of the chitha. In the case of petty disputes, the Kanungo should endeavour to bring the parties to agreement and, if successful, should take their signatures in the chitha.

x. *Fresh survey*: Fresh survey may be undertaken either on a blue print, a skeleton blue print, a re-traverse sheet of an old village or a new traverse sheet of an extension survey village. In either of these cases the survey must be done on the correct principles of cadastral survey, detailed instructions about which will be found in Schedule-A. A fresh chitha will have to be written for the village in each of these cases.

No change will be made in the numbering of the existing dags on the map until the completion of map revision. In the case of amalgation the dividing line between the two dags the map, will be crossed out in pencil and the amalgamated dag encircled on the map and the chitha entries pertaining to the dags scored through. When a cadastral dag is split up into two or more parts one part will retain the number of the parent dag and the rest will be allotted numbers consecutive to the last number in the chitha; the latter will also be entered on the spare pages at the end of the chitha with cross reference against the original dag.

All pencil boundaries of dags will be inked up in blue (cobalt) at the recess office. In map correction, villager dags will then be serially renumbered in vernacular figures in blue (cobalt), the renumbering starting from the north-west corner ending at the south-east corner. The changed numbers will also be entered in red ink against the old ones in the chitha. In the case of fresh surveys, if the dag numbers used in the field have run serially from the north-west to the south-east corner of the maps, the same shall be retained and inked up in blue (cobalt).

xii. *Map certificate*: On the completion of map revision in a village the Kanungo or the Assistant Settlement Officer, after finally checking the work, will write on the face of the map the following certificate in pencil: "Certified that the recorder has finished map revision, and that, after examining his work, I am satisfied that it is correct."

Problems/Issues faced at the field level while conducting Traditional Survey Operations

- The maintenance and regular updating of old records is cumbersome and time consuming.
- The records in some rare case do not portray the correct picture on ground regarding the ownership and boundaries.
- Some Current maps are flawed due to the difference in the area of Jamabandi (Annual Register) and maps due to the wrong Tarmeem (division). In cases of land allocation, division and decree, numbers are inserted in the Jamabandi without any Tarmeem (division) modification in the maps.
- Traditional survey system is highly delaying, expensive and flawed and due to this, the area of the Jamabandi (Annual Register) and the map is different.
- There is difficulty in updating the map according to the present situation and the Jamabandi (Annual Register).
- Hence, when the existing record is converted into digital format, the digitized version reflects the same errors and as a result it may vary from the ground reality.
- With the development in Urban areas, the traditional methods of survey is getting difficult. Inter-visibility is one of the major issues.

Necessity for Resurvey

1) Creation of an updated Cadastral Map and Title database
2) Creating an integrated view of textual and graphical information of land records on GIS platform
3) Replace manual records with digital records, update the records and ensure consistency of information across the departments
4) Portraying the correct picture on ground regarding the ownership and boundaries
5) Enabling a seamless integration of different departments and create accurate and updated land records — which are a pre-requisite for rapid economic development.

Modern Land Survey Initiatives Taken

With the advent of modern survey instruments/technologies like Electronic Total Station (ETS), Differential Global Positioning System (DGPS) etc. Survey department also uses these instruments for survey of villages. Presently for providing control framework and in preparation of Traverse Polygon, ETS and DGPS instruments are used instead of Theodolite and Chain. Further detail surveys of the villages are carried out by the conventional methods as discuss earlier.

Presently, the Government has undertaken the large scale mapping of the rural abadi areas with no records of rights on 1:500 scale using Professional Survey Grade UAV/Drone. The survey has been initiated under the central government scheme SVAMITVA.

With the help of Survey of India (SOI), Government of Assam is going to generate up-to-date digital topographical maps (GIS data) of rural abadi areas where no records of rights are there. Under this programme, geodetic infrastructure comprising Continuous Operating Reference System (CORS) Network and Geoid model will also be established.

GIS data comprising rural abadi property boundaries, topographical features, and other relevant attributes collected from ground. The non-spatial attribute data provides by State government preferably in digital format.

Scope of Work

- Establishment of Continuous Operating Reference System (CORS) Network by SoI in the state of Assam. Following work stages will be followed:
    1. Completion of the tendering process for outsourcing
    2. Site selection and reconnaissance for CORS stations
    3. Civil construction work by outsourced agency
    4. Installation and commissioning of CORS stations by outsourced agency
    5. Establishment of Control Centre and DR in SoI premises
    6. Operation and Maintenance of CORS Network for five years from the date of commencing

7. Development of Geoid model for entire state
8. Notification for Drone Survey in the target areas by Government of Assam
9. Marking of property boundaries with Chuna lines before the drone flying in the area
10. Acquisition of Aerial images using Professional survey grade drone/ Unmanned Aerial Vehicle (UAVs) by SoI. Following work stages are followed:
    - ➢ Drone Flying of rural unmapped abadi/habitat/areas with no records of rights of villages.
    - ➢ Drone data acquisition at better than five centimeter Ground Sample Distance (GSD).
    - ➢ Drone data Processing involving Block Adjustment & AT (Aerial Triangulation), Ortho Rectified Image (ORI) generation, DEM (Digital Elevation Model)/DTM (Digital Terrain Model) generation.
    - ➢ Extraction of 2D features and generation of digital spatial data as per SVAMITVA scheme guidelines by SOI.
    - ➢ Attribute linkage of all attribute data provided in digital form by Government of Assam as per jointly finalised schema by Government of Assam and SoI.
    - ➢ Numbering of properties will be entered as per numbering system provided by Government of Assam.
    - ➢ Ownership data collection and Ground validation of property ownership boundaries will be done by Government of Assam
    - ➢ Ground-truthing and validation of topographical features shall be carried out by SoI.
    - ➢ Generation of final GIS data, Village maps, Land Parcel Maps will be prepared.

Methodology

- Horizontal and Vertical Ground Control Points: Identification, Establishment, Densification and Utilisation of Ground Control Points (GCPs) using SoI GCP library points. In areas covered with CORS Network GCPs shall be carried out using CORS Network rovers.
    - I. CORS Network shall be established by SoI in the State under SVAMITVA scheme.
    - II. Area/site for CORS stations installation to be selected. These stations should have electricity supply and physical security to be ensured by the State Government.
    - III. The SoI shall be responsible for operation and maintenance of CORS network stations and to provide CORS network services to State Government for next five years.

- Existing Geodetic BMs (Benchmark) of SoI shall be utilized for vertical ground control point extension and geoid model development.
- Property boundaries marked with Chuna lines or any suitable alternative before the drone flying in the area. Government of Assam will organise the Gram Sabha or such appropriate village level forum to intimate the schedule of the survey and to sensitize the villagers about the project work and its intended benefits.
- Extent of the rural abadi area with no cadastral records for drone based mapping will be provided in digital form or with co-ordinates or as kml file for mission planning for drone flying.
- Acquisition of Aerial images using drone shall be carried out by the SoI for the extent of area given in Sl 3.4.
- Drone data Processing will be carried out by SoI involving Block Adjustment and AT (Aerial Triangulation), ORI, generation, DEM/DTM generation.
- 2D Feature Extraction (FE): The ORI shall be used as base image layer to extract the topographical features as per jointly finalised schema by State Government and SoI.
- Attribute Data Collection: Attributes data shall be provided by Government of Assam as per feature/wish list. A standardized data collection format shall be provided as an effort to simplify and speed up the process. The correctness of attribute data shall be the responsibility of Government of Assam. The attributes collected/provided (as in point 3.8.1) shall then be linked with their respective features, thereby creating a digital spatial library of all the features and their respective information.
- Boundaries of properties and numbering of properties/structures within village abadi area will be as per numbering the existing system.
- Generation of updated Land Parcel Maps (LPM) in suitable soft copy formats and in printing formats. GIS data prepared shall comprise base map overlaid with layers of topographical features, land parcel information, district/tehsil/village boundaries information, etc. with attributes.
- Ownership data collection and Ground validation of property ownership boundaries will be done by Government of Assam.
    - Ground validation of topographical features as derived from ORI shall be carried out by SoI.
    - Inquiry process for finalising the objections shall be carried out by respective Government of Assam.

Additional Notes

Guidelines, Manuals, Acts responsible for Survey and Settlement in Assam

1) The Assam Land and Revenue Regulation, 1886
2) The Assam Land Revenue Re-assessment Act, 1936
3) Assam Land Revenue Manual

4) Assam Land Records Manual
5) Assam Resettlement Manual, 1948
6) Handbook of Government Circulars

Assamese Land Measurement

Assamese Land Measurement (Area) Unit	*Old Measurement Unit of Barak Valley, Assam*
1 Lessa = 144 Sq Feet	16 Chattak =1 Kotha
1 Kotha = 20 Lessa	20 Kotha = 1 Bigha
1Bigha = 5 Kotha = 100 Lessa = 14400 sq. Feet	1 Bigha = 14400 sq Feet

Glossary of important vernacular words

Batwara Partition.

Batta When numbering the plots in a map serially, if one is left out, the last or the available number is subsequently put and for the sake of convenience in locating the plot on the map, a reference to the plot near which it is situated is given in the chitha and also part of the map e.g. 20/206. This will show that plot No. 206 is nearer the regularly numbered plot No. 20

Bigha Unit of land measurement 1 *Bigha*=14400 square feet.

Chanda A mark left on the ground at the time of survey for future reference.

Chitha Field catalogue.

Deriabadi Supplementary settlement.

Daul Settlement abstract.

Dhip Survey mark,

Ejmali Joint.

Faut Dead without any heir.

Faringati A land classification of usually high land.

Frar Absconded.

Halabadi New cultivation.

Hal dag Present or existing dag.

Istafa Relinquishment.

Jotrahin Insolvent.

Jamabandi Register where 'Jama' or revenue is entered which is also the record-of-rights.

Khiraj Full revenue paying.

Kabula Application for settlement of wasteland.

Lahi Transplanted paddy grown on moderatively low land.

Nisfi- Khiraj Half revenue paying.

Patta Lease.

Safa A full page of chitha or Jamadandi.

Tauzi-Bahir OutsideTouzi—not included in Daul.

2.3

Bihar

Manoj Kumar Jha and Chandan Kumar

Background and Introduction

In modern Bihar, the first land survey was begun in 1873 under the Survey Department of the Government of India. The present Land Records and Survey Directorate came into existence in the year 1956, which functions as a directorate under the Revenue and Land Reforms Department of the Government of Bihar. Under this directorate, there are district settlement offices, under which land survey and settlement work is being done in the districts.

Land survey and settlement work started in the year 1873 in various districts of Bihar state; the chain survey eventually ended in the year 1925 to 1926. In this way, the existing cadastral *Khatian* was created and the cadastral map was prepared by this survey (cadastral survey) in all districts of the state of Bihar. Originally, this survey was carried out with the basic aim of collecting revenue and resolving disputes among different *Zamindars*.

After the abolition of zamindari in Bihar, in the year 1952, the revisional survey of land started under Chapter-10 (Section 101 to 115) of the Bihar Tenancy Act for updating the land records and correct identification of tenants. But the revisional survey work could not be completed in all the districts till the year 2009-10, as the survey work was based on traditional method and took huge time and was too time consuming.

After the cadastral and revisional survey, there has been extensive change in the geographical structure. The identification of the reference point *Mustakil* and Tri-junction that was established during the earlier survey operation is almost unrecognized or ruined. With the increase of population, the size of parcel has become small and irregular and settlement or habitation area have increased in all revenue villages, due to which the verification and ownership determination of land area was problematic and taking too much time in preparing the map using the traditional method.

For the implementation of the scheme of Computerization of Land Records sponsored by the Government of India in which updation and computerization of the land records necessarily required updated information before entries are made in the computer. In addition, for the fulfilment of modern and technical requirements, it has been found necessary to carry out land survey work by using modern technology, which is compatible with computer and field operation.

In this light, the Bihar Special Survey and Settlement Act, 2011 and Bihar Special Survey and Settlement Rules, 2012, were enacted, and it was decided to carry out special survey and settlement work by using modern techniques.

Under the Bihar Special Survey and Settlement, 2011 Act, Government of Bihar adopted hybrid survey method to prepare maps with the help of aerial photography out of aerial photography/satellite imagery. Along with this, there is a provision for on-site ground truthing of the map and thereafter Record of Rights (*Khatian*) to be prepared by field functionaries. The Department has analysed both the methods of satellite imagery and aerial photography and found that from the resolution of aerial photography, a structure/object up to 10 cm can be seen, while in advanced satellite imagery a structure/object smaller than 60cm cannot be seen. Based on that, the option of aerial photography was selected and after that for onsite ground truthing ETS/ DGPS was to be used for surveying of land parcels, as the size of the fields are small and irregular in shape due to the high density of population. Under the new act, using the modern technology all the survey activities will be computerised and the process of map creation can also be done quickly through modern software. Thematic map and base map creation facility will also be readily available in this process.

Survey and settlement work in 45899 revenue *maujas* (villages) in all 38 districts of Bihar state excluding urban area is being done by the Directorate of Land Records and Survey using hybrid technology of aerial photography and ground-truthing by ETS/DGPS equipment. Even traditional method is also being used whenever required. The main objective of special survey and settlement is the maintenance, preservation and updating of digitized Records of Right and maps with the help of modern technology so that in future all the Land Records can be updated real time.

Establishment of Bihar Project Management Unit

With the objective of providing necessary support in implementation and monitoring of various components under the central sector scheme NRLMP/ DILRMP of Government of India in 2011 provided guidance to establish Project Management Unit as a society. In the light of the guidance provided by the Government of India, after the approval of the Hon'ble Chief Minister, Bihar, "Bihar Project Management Unit" was constituted in the year 2012 as a registered society for providing necessary support in the monitoring of various activities of State Government. Two committees have been formed to run this society office:

(A) Executive Committee;
(B) Governing body.

The Executive Committee is authorized for the implementation of the scheme. The governing body is authorized to take policy decisions. Apart from this, posts are sanctioned for technical experts and personnel in the society office, in which GIS consultant, Land Information System consultant, programmer, accountant, assistant, data entry operator and office attendant have been appointed. The executive committee and the governing body organize meeting time to time.

Process of Special Land Survey

Under the Bihar Special Survey and Settlement Act, 2011 and Rules, 2012, procedure for the phase wise preparation of map and land-records/documents is as follows:

- *Aerial Photography*: Aerial photography is being used in the special survey for preparation of map of revenue villages on the basis of which the map and authorized record/document will be finalized after field verification, the work of aerial photography and revenue village map preparation has been outsourced to aerial agencies.
- *Notification and Proclamation*: The district in which revenue villages are to be surveyed is notified by the State Government, and then the proclamation of revenue village to be surveyed is done by the Settlement Officer of the said district.
- *Formation of Survey Camp*: A survey camp is established for the 20 villages ideally. The camp consists of one Assistant Settlement Officer, two Kanungo, two clerks and one executive assistant per camp and one Amin per village.
- *Kistawar*: Generally, *Kistawar* means to construct a map according to ground reality of latest geographical location. Earlier this work was done manually, in which the geometry of each plot/Khesra/Revenue village or in other words 'Chouhaddi' was outlined on a plane table. It was a laborious task and quite time consuming. Now through aerial photography and computer software, it is possible to do this work in relatively very short time.

Under *Kistawar*, there is an obligation to complete four works as per the new Act: Base Mapping, Village Boundary Demarcation, Parcel Demarcation and Ground Truthing. Under the Act, *Kistawar* is a time bound process. It is edited in a gradual and phased manner, as follows:

- Establishing Ground control point
- Identification of Tri-junction (Tri-simana) and their observation
- Ortho-photograph verification
- Verification of village border and matching of margin line
- Polygon rough numbering and Area Statement.
- *Khanapuri*: Khanapuri generally means to associate the name of its owner/ entitled with the plot or polygons in the map. This work is being done on the basis of old records available and during the field verification based on the documents provided by the tenant. During the course of Khanapuri, the process of the creation of the genealogy of the tenant as per the revised numbering of the plots, the maintenance of the Yaddasht register and the physical specifications of the land in the plot register format. The

construction of plot register is virtually the backbone of the creation of the Records of Rights.

- *Amendment of Special Survey Map by the Aerial Survey Agency*: In the process of Kishtwar and Khanapuri, the revised map is made available for further action after incorporation of field updates in the special survey by the Aerial Survey Agency.
- *Distribution of LPM on the basis of Khasra Register and Adjudication of Claims*: After the distribution of form-7 under rules, a software generated Land Parcel Map (LPM) also on the basis of khesra plot register is distributed among the same ryots, objections are invited from ryots. The objections are adjudicated under the prescribed procedure.
- *Draft Publication of Records of Rights (Khatiyan) and Map*: Objection received on LPM and Form-7 is adjudicated and finally published in Form-12. Again claim/objection is to be invited from the tenants.
- *Adjudication of Claim-objection against Draft Publication and Recess*: The records of rights prepared after compiling the adjudicated claims-objections received after draft publication as per the rules, the compliance of all the passed orders during the period of recess to be ensured and action to be taken to validate the prepared maps and land records accordingly. The map is then published after the final correction
- *Preparation of Rent Roll and Final Publication and Settlement*: After the verification under the recess, the final publication of rent roll and record of right is to be prepared through the software.
- *Hearing of Claim/Objection after Final Publication of Record of Rights*: There can also be a claim/objection on the record of rights published finally under the rules. For hearing of these claims/objections, and passing the order, settlement officers are the competent authority.

Initial Phase of Special Survey and Settlement Programme

In the light of Bihar Special Survey and Settlement Act, 2011, firstly for preparation of updated revenue map and survey work of Bhagalpur, Saran, Munger, Nalanda and Sheikhpura districts through aerial photography, an agreement was signed with third-party solutions. But after agreement in 2011, till the year 2013, special survey map of all revenue villages of the said districts was not made available. Also, ETS and ETS operators etc. were not made available at the field level and technical problems were also found in the maps provided.

Phase II of the Special Survey and Settlement Programme

In view of the shortcomings found during the initial stage and to conduct the special survey on the basis of modern technology, an agreement was signed, in the year 2013 with Aerial Survey Agencies through open tendering.

After aerial photography, ortho-photographs and digitized special survey revenue maps were prepared by these aerial survey agencies. Aerial photographs were sent to the Ministry of Defence and Survey of India for security vetting and permission was obtained for further action. After the security vetting up to the year 2017, permission to prepare a special survey map was obtained for all the districts.

In the year 2015, special land survey was started in 13 districts of Bihar i.e. Begusarai, Lakhisarai, Khagaria, Nalanda, Sheikhpura, Munger, Saharsa, Madhepura, Supaul, Katihar, Araria, Kishanganj and Purnia. In these districts, a map of 9217 *maujas* out of a total of 10180 *maujas* were provided by the concerned aerial agencies at the time of survey. The survey was conducted from the year 2015 to 2017 in which village boundary verification of 1225 *maujas* were done, *Khasra* register of 688 revenue villages and records of rights of 266 villages were published.

Regarding the ongoing survey work in the said districts, it was found in a review meeting chaired by the Development Commissioner on 08.02.2017 and chaired by Principal Secretary, Revenue and Land Reforms Department, Bihar, Patna on 20.06.2017 that the Pre and Post Monumentation, to be done by the aerial survey agencies for the correctness of village boundary, has not been done properly. Also, it was reported by the Settlement Offices that the village-boundary demarcated by the agency is not verified on the ground. In the course of reviewing the special survey work, the need for amendment in Bihar Special Survey and Settlement Act and Rules and requirement of a updated new technical guideline was felt and many technical and practical errors were also revealed. It was also found that due to lack of sufficient number of technical personnel, special survey work is getting hampered.

Phase-III of the Special Land Survey and Settlement Programme in 20 Districts of Bihar

Based on the experiences deficiencies found during the Land-survey of 13 districts and after addressing the deficiencies, the decision was taken to undertake fresh survey and settlement work in 20 districts of Bihar State i.e. Begusarai Khagaria, Lakhisarai, Jehanabad, Arwal, Shivhar, Kishanganj, Araria, Katihar, Purnia, Sitamarhi, Supaul, Saharsa, Madhepura, West Champaran, Banka, Jamui, Sheikhpura, Munger and Nalanda

Under the policy decision, it was felt necessary that as a pilot project, land survey and settlement work should be started after removing the previous technical difficulties and deficiencies and more importantly during the survey, the Directorate of Land Records and Survey and the Settlement Officer of the district should keep close watch on actions at every level to identify the future problems of land survey. In this light, according to the procedures provided in the technical guideline a pilot project, keeping the legal compatibility of the work done in the past, based on the available workforce, three Anchals of Bihar state,

Ghatkusumbha (Sheikhpura district), Pipra (Supaul district) and Sadar Anchal (Begusarai District) work was started.

Various dimensions of the ongoing Bihar Special Survey and Settlement Programme

Under the Bihar Special Survey and Settlement Act, 2011 and Rules, 2012, the following action has been taken in connection with the selection of districts and establishment of technical facilities for the special survey.

- *Notification:* All the 38 districts of Bihar state have been notified under special survey and settlement programme.
- *Selection of 20 districts for the first phase*: In view of the availability of resources and personnel, for the survey and settlement programme, 20 districts of Bihar state viz. Begusarai, Khagaria, Lakhisarai, Jehanabad, Arwal, Shivhar, Kishanganj, Araria, Katihar, Purnia, Sitamarhi, Supaul, Saharsa, Madhepura, West Champaran, Banka, Jamui, Sheikhpura, Munger and Nalanda have been selected.
- *208 Special Survey Camps:* Out of a total of 220 anchals of 20 districts in the first phase, a total of 208 special survey camps have been set up in 89 anchals.
- *Posting of personnel in Special Survey Camps*: The total vacancies of Special Survey Assistant Settlement Officer, Special Survey Kanungo, Special Survey Amin, Contract Amin, Special Survey Clerk and Executive Assistant are 275, 550, 4950, 550, 550 and 275 respectively out of which 220 Special Survey Assistant Settlement Officers, 340 Special Survey Kanungo, 3450 Special Survey Amin and 362 Special Survey Clerks, have been posted in districts and camps. The policy decision to appoint a data entry operator in place of 275 executive assistants is currently under process.
- *To provide technical material to the personnel of the Special Survey Camp*: The equipments such as laptop, Android mobile, plank tripod, etc. have been made available to the Special Survey Assistant Settlement Officer, Kanungo and Special Survey Amins.
- *Providing equipment and basic facilities in the camps*: Equipment and basic facilities have been provided in each camp.
- *Deputation of Nodal Officers*: Nodal officers have been deputed to supervise the work of special survey going on in the districts from the level of Revenue and Land Reforms Department and Directorate of Land Records and Survey.
- *Establishment of IT Cell under the Directorate*: A separate IT cell has been set up in the Directorate of Land Records and Survey for carrying out various tasks related to modern technology and making software as per the requirement, in which seven computer operators under the supervision of MIS analyst is employed. A call center with 15 computers has also been

established under IT cell. This call center will work to address the problems raised related to the special survey.

- *Establishment of a separate website for the Directorate of Land Records and Survey, Patna*: A website (dlrs.bihar.gov.in) has been created by the Directorate separately from the Department of Revenue and Land Reforms, on which all information, letters, related videos, etc. related to the Directorate of Land Records and Survey, are available.
- *Bhu-Survekshan software*: Directorate of Land Records has in-house developed a software for capturing field data from Form-1 to 22, as provided by Bihar Special Survey and Settlement Rules, 2012 as amended, 2019, for the work being done by the Directorate under the special survey process. With the help of this software, it will be possible to integrate the Textual and Spatial Data after completion of the special survey process. In this context, Bhu-Naksha software is also being developed by NIC, Bihar, through which the work will be done to update the maps in future.
- *Bhu-Naksha software*: After the completion of the special survey, to keep the integrated "Village Revenue Map" and "Records of Rights" constantly updated with the transfer of each land as well as to modify both the records and the map, it will be required. This "Bhu-Naksha software" will be used to modify the map. After the division or consolidation of the plots/parcels with each mutation, the changes in the shape and size of the plots will be edited with the help of this software so that computerized land records management can always be Real Time. Thus, in future no more survey will be required for the preparation of land records.
- *GCN Software*: With the modern technology, the number of control points[18] has a central importance in maintaining accuracy in the process of map creation. Control points have a sequence of hierarchy. All types of control points also act as a reference points over a period of time, which greatly facilitates the measurement of local land. All such control points are maintained in the computerized database with the help of this ground control network software. In this, the following control points will be fixed and can be projected on ortho-photograph on any scale.
- *R2R Personnel Management Software*: The software named Online Survey Personnel Management System has been developed by the Directorate for the management of personnel. Through this, joining, posting, maintenance of service books, etc. of special survey workers will be done in large numbers at present. Through this software, online application and planning, dispatch of appointment letters, joining of selected candidates, posting and transfer, issuance of all types of orders, etc. are being done. In the

[18] Primary Control Points, Secondary Control Points, Tertiary Control Points, Touching Points of three boundaries of Revenue Village, Auxiliary Control Points.

coming year, new features like maintenance of service history, e-leave and payroll management will be added to this software.

- *MIS Software*: Special survey and settlement programme has to be implemented in mission mode. This software is being used to prepare reports related to computerized monitoring and supervision of all the officials and employees involved in the survey. Amin, Kanungo and Assistant Settlement Officers will maintain their daily work in the software. Through this software, comparative reports of daily achievement of Amin can be obtained, as well as weekly and monthly achievement comparative reports can also be obtained of special survey camps, Anchals and districts. All weekly and monthly reports of individual, camps. Anchals on district can be obtained on daily, weekly and monthly basis. This software is also related to the email system and the analysis and performance of the finished work is sent to all the concerned officials through the software itself.
- *Operation of various digital platforms for the citizens*: To overcome the problems of common citizens, the Directorate has set up a call centre in the Directorate, as well as various option of interaction available for citizens on various digital platforms viz. Twitter, YouTube, Facebook, Instagram etc. are also being utilized.

Pilot Project of Special Survey and Settlement Programme

In these pilot project Anchals Ghatkumbha (Sheikhpura district), Pipra (Supaul district) and Sadar Anchal (Begusarai district), the technical team of the directorate, representatives of the aerial survey agency and local personnel after starting the survey work of village boundary demarcation & validation along with the last cadastral survey map the special survey maps were provided by the Aerial Survey Agency. The procedural and directive measures were adopted to remove the gap-overlap.

During the previous operation the difficulty in determining the boundaries of two revenue villages was identified because revenue village's boundary was validated in isolation, due to which the problem of gap-overlap persisted. Therefore, in order to overcome this obstacle in the pilot project technically, the work of verifying the village boundary was done in the clusters simultaneously. By taking the clusters of the villages which were adjacent, it was found that the problem of gap-overlap is verifiable and rectifiable. It is noteworthy that if the difference of area between the cadastral/ revision survey map and the special survey map is less than 5 percent of the total area of the revenue village, then it is considered to be accepted for further survey processing.

In view of the difficulties arising in the process of uploading the prepared map on Bhu-Naksha software and entries done in Bhu-Survekshan software for the data received from survey work an operating manual was prepared and accordingly the software was also customized.

During the survey of land in these pilot projects, the survey officials from departmental and directorate level visited the villages to supervise the survey work on the spot and also directly interacted with the local landholders. Based on the experiences gained from the field visit the work of providing necessary resources to the camp offices was done to enable the camp offices to undertake land surveying.

Through all these digital platforms, information about the latest activities and important information is shared by the Directorate with the citizens and necessary action is being taken on the basis of their views and feedback.

Shortcomings diagnosed and solution at various stages of Special Survey and Settlement Programme

After review of the problems arising during the special survey, the following deficiencies were diagnosed and necessary actions were taken for their solution:

- *Provision related deficiencies*: Lack of necessary provisions in the Bihar Special Survey and Settlement Act 2011 and Rules, 2012 as per the work.
  Action taken: In the Bihar Special Survey and Settlement Act, 2011, necessary amendments were made in the year 2017, and again in accordance with this other detail necessary provisions were made in the amendment in the Bihar Special Survey and Settlement Rules 2012 in the year 2019.
- *Lack of Technical Guideline*: Preparation of Technical Guideline in compliance with Rule 21 of Bihar Special Survey and Settlement Rules.
  Action taken: The Technical Guideline was published in the year 2019 by the Directorate of Land Records and Survey, which was notified by the Revenue and Land Reforms Department on 15.03.2019.
- *Technical problem in village boundary verification*: Given the extensive changes in the map and geographical reality before the Bihar survey work, the technical problem faced in the determination and verification of the village boundary in the map construction.
  Action taken: The technical guideline contained the solution of technical problems faced in the determination and verification of village boundary as well as Tri-junction.
- *Shortage of technically competent personnel*: Problems arose due to lack of technically competent and necessary workforce.
  Action taken: Bihar Special Survey Honorarium based Contract Recruitment Rules, 2019 was formulated in the month of February, 2019 with the aim of availing the service of technically skilled personnel, in which the technical qualification based process of recruitment and appointment such as civil engineering degree and diploma holder competent personnel was initiated.

  In the process of recruitment of skilled personnel against the created posts, action has been taken to post these personnel in first phase of survey districts.
- *Infrastructure for training*: Lack of basic infrastructure facilities for training of personnel engaged in special survey.
  Action taken: In view of the lack of basic infrastructure for training related to revenue and survey in the state, training institutes have been established in Patna and Bodh Gaya.

- *Shortage of training material*: Lack of training material for training of special survey personnel.
  Action taken: For the purpose of providing training material to the personnel engaged in special survey and settlement work, classes related to revenue and survey were organized by subject experts.
- *Lack of training programmes*: The lack of regular training sessions required for special survey and settlement programme.
  Action taken: At the directorate level, training of Amin, Kanungo, Assistant Settlement Officers, and other officials were given to make them master trainer.
- *Lack of public awareness*: Lack of awareness in the general public towards special survey and settlement work.
  Action taken: "Public awareness series" through newspapers were published by the directorate for ensuring public participation and public awareness in the special survey and settlement programme of Bihar.
- *Pre-survey maps not being accessible*: To ensure availability of maps in a universal manner to the general public for special survey work.
  Action taken: All the old maps like cadastral/revisional/municipal/consolidation have been made available on the website through bhuabhilekh.bihar.gov.in software so that the general public can view any map related to any revenue villages from anywhere. One can also see his *Khasra* in these maps. Due to this facility, the obligation to purchase all the map-sheets of any big revenue village is removed. The public can identify the map-sheets related to their *Khasra* on the website. The government has arranged the digitized maps for the door step delivery to the applicant's home along with the prescribed fee based on the requisition.
- *Help from the best practices and procedure of other states in special survey work*: During special survey and settlement work, it was found that the difficulty faced by the survey in preparing the map of revenue villages and preparing the records of rights. Help is being taken by the use of modern methods being carried out in other states for the process of updating the records of rights in future.
  Action taken: International, national and state level seminars and workshops were organized to understand the process adopted for the preservation and updating of special surveys maps and revenue records in other states and countries. Experts from government and non-government institutions of various states including Karnataka, Uttar Pradesh and Andhra Pradesh and country Bhutan were contacted and technical expertise was obtained from them. Apart from them, technical information has also been obtained from the experts of the top technical institute like IIT, Kanpur.
- *Non-availability of map and records of last survey*: Cadastral survey has been done in all districts of Bihar state about 120 years ago and the revised

survey was done about 60 years ago. Due to this, the RoR (Records of Right) and maps of the surveyed revenue villages in many districts have either been destroyed or are not available due to certain reasons. In this situation, there are difficulties in carrying out the special survey.
Action taken: In case of non-availability of RoR (Records of Right)/records, the search is going on and if the records of rights are not available, a policy decision is required as to how special survey work should be based on other revenue records like Jamabandi Register, *Khasra* Register in this regard

- *Lack of software for entry of data and facts collected during the survey*: During the survey operation in 13 districts, in various ways under the manual operation, a lack of meaningful software was felt for the digitization and creation of the database for the collected data. From future point of view also it was an imperative for the use of digital data.
Action taken: For the digitization of the data and map obtained during survey, various software's "Bhu-survekshan" software, "Bhu-Naksha" software, "GCN" (Ground Control Network) software, etc. have been made.
- *Lack of independent settlement officer*: From the very beginning, the work of the settlement officer was being done by the district collector. The district collector was finding it difficult to give adequate time to supervise survey due to various reasons.
Action taken: At present, the independent Settlement Officers have been appointed for the 20 districts of the state of Bihar where special survey work is going on.
- *No independent Charge Officer (Officer-in-Charge) is working for the Settlement*: At present, the Additional Collector of the districts has been notified as the Charge-Officer (Officer-in-Charge) for the special survey and settlement work. Apart from revenue related and land reform works, other works of the district are associated with them, due to which there is a lack of supervision and control at their level in special survey and settlement work.
Action taken: The matter is still under process with regard to the policy decision to notify and post the charge officer (incharge officer) independently for the ongoing special survey and settlement work in the districts.
- *Lack of GIS Lab*: Due to non-establishment of GIS (Geographical Information System) Lab under GIS Advisor. Bihar Project Management Unit, there is difficulty in analysing data obtained from agency and pointing out lapses or loopholes in it.
Action taken: Correspondence has been made with the Government of India for the establishment of GIS Lab. Immediate action has been taken to get the GIS lab working by deputing the personnel employed for the Bihar Special Survey.

- *To make provision for survey of unsurveyed land*: During the cadastral survey and the revisional survey in the past, the riverine belt was not surveyed. Settlements are presently inhabited in these areas. Also, some other areas which were disputed during the last surveys could not be surveyed. The revenue records and verifiable maps are not available for the survey of these unsurveyed areas/revenue villages, hence the provision for special survey of these regions, consent from competent levels is required.
  Action taken: Policy decision is under process for undertaking special survey of unsurveyed revenue villages/areas, especially in the riverine belt.
- *Third party verification of data*: Proposal for verification of submitted data by aerial survey agencies by an external agency (third party).
  Action taken: A sufficient amount of geospatial (Raster and vector) data is being produced by aerial agencies. Accuracy of data, generation of map and its need in future is a sensitive matter. Therefore, physical and logical validation of all soft data (DTDB-Digital Topographic Data base) is required to be done by external agency. In this light, consultations with various technical institutions are under progress.

2.4

Gujarat

Ashok Nada and Jani Jyotinkumar Prahladbhai

Introduction

Land is not commodity which can be obtained as and when man desires. Land is becoming scare and inevitable need of the time, therefore, updating of records and introduction of modern technology are the need of the hour to register land records on real time basis with utmost accuracy and better management of land related matters. In Gujarat, the vision is to undertake detailed survey and create updated land records including textual and spatial information, to enabling of such a system which will help in the regular maintenance of land records and provide ready and smooth access to all stakeholders – including citizens and Government.

Before moving into the subject, the history of land records in Gujarat is necessary to refer as every present or future activity is based on the past practices. In Gujarat, the original survey was carried out in 1886-1920, with the traditional chain and cross staff method and area measurements for each field (Known as "*Tippan*").

Land revenue and land records system in Gujarat are still governed by the following Acts, Rules and Manuals:

- Gujarat Land Revenue Code-1879
- Gujarat Land Revenue Rules-1972
- Bombay Survey and Settlement Volume Part-1 (Historical) by R.G. Gordon, ICS
- Bombay Survey and Settlement Volume Part-2 (Technical and appendices) by R.G. Gordon, ICS
- Land Survey Manual by R.G. Gordon, ICS
- Revenue Accounts Manuals for village, Talukas, and District by F.G.H Anderson, ICS.
- City Survey Manual by F.G.H. Anderson, ICS.

Resurvey manual in English as well as in Gujarati is published by the Revenue Department in 2012 for official use only. The resurvey has been carried out as laid down in resurvey manual. No amendments are enacted in prevailing laws and rules.

Gujarat has a rich and legally documented survey and revenue records of almost all land parcels. All these manually written records after the span of time get deteriorated and brittle. For the future benefits of citizen, government introduced the latest perspectives to incorporate it in making the records up-to-date and on real time mode by using various technologies. Under the SRA and ULR scheme Government of Gujarat has initiated modernization of land records and introduces modern technology for updating land records.

The project of resurvey was initiated in Jamnagar District as a pilot-project under SRA and ULR scheme in 2008-2009. Thereafter, in phase wise whole state of Gujarat is covered under NLRMP Scheme (now known as DILRMP) and updates rural land records. The entire work has been carried out by private agencies with the control, guidance and superintendence of Government Officials of various committees from village level to state level under the direct supervision of Settlement Commissioner and Director of Land Records, Revenue Department.

It may be noted that in the Land Revenue Code-1879, amendment has been made to introduce a new chapter 9-A (of Transitional Area Land) to issues Records of Rights to urban properties by paying compounding fee.

The history of Land Revenue Administration in Gujarat (1407A.D. to 2021 A.D.) may be divided in various parts, such as; Medieval period, period during Princely State of Baroda, British era, Post-British era and current Land Revenue Administration (1960-2021).

By the Bombay Reorganization Act, 1960, the state of Bombay was bifurcated into two new State namely, Gujarat and Maharashtra with effect from 01 May 1960. The present Gujarat state inherited the survey, classification settlement and revision settlements, categories of Non-Agricultural lands, tenures and terms of settlement is mainly governed by Gujarat Land Revenue Code 1879 and Gujarat Land Revenue Rules 1972.

The City Survey of Gujarat was introduced in five cities namely: Balsar (Valsad), Rander, Bharuch, Surat and Ahmedabad in 18th Century. The city survey was conducted based on the City Survey Manual by following methods of Plane Table Survey and Minor Triangle was compiled by F.G.H. Anderson, ICS (Retired).

History of Land Records Department

The early Survey Classification operations resulted into the organization of the Survey Department in its openings stages. At the commencement, the new survey was an isolated experiment of a local character in the Poona District. At the outset, therefore it was under the direct control of superintendents Goldsmith and Wingate without any intervening authority. As the operations, however extended to Kokan and Gujarat it became impossible for these superintendents to supervise these operations single handed. Hence, Assistant Superintendent usually Military Officers were appointed and the Survey and Settlement Department came into existence and when revision survey operations were nearing completion, this Survey and Settlement Departments was brought to a close and the regular Land Records Department was created in 1884 A.D. The Director of Land Records was the Head of the Department who was also the Director of Agriculture and Registration. The Department was then entrusted with the work of maintenance of Land Records.

The separate post of Survey Commissioner was abolished from 01 April 1901 and the powers of the Commissioner of Survey were conferred on the Director of Land Records and Agricultural (R.5370 of 31 July 1901).

In December 1905, a new post of Joint Directors of Land Records was created (R.9189 of 10 November 1905) to supervise and control the work of maintaining the Land Records. Subsequently the two Departments of (1) Land Records, and (2) Agricultural came to be separated from each other, and controlled by different heads (i) Director of Land Records and Registration and (ii) Director of Agricultural (R.6634 of 11 July 1906). In 1907, the Director of Land Records, being mainly responsible for Settlement work (the survey operation having been closed) was given the status of "Settlement Commissioner" (R-6337 of 26 February 1907).

Functions of Land Records Department

The functions of the Land Records Departments are to collect and provide statistics, necessary for the sound administration of all matters connected with land, to help reduce, simplify and cheapen litigation in Revenue and Civil Courts by providing reliable survey and other records, and to supervise the preparation and maintenance of the Record of Rights, for the protection of those who hold any title to, or interest in land. The department is also responsible for conducting all the periodical Revenue Settlements Operations in the State, and for training the Revenue Officers in Survey and Settlement Matters.

The work done by the department provides essential data, and forms the basis of the land revenue administration of the whole state. The Department is required to maintain the voluminous Survey and Classification records up-to-date, by keeping very careful note of all changes, by regular, day-to-day fieldwork. It also organizes and carries out village and City Survey for private individuals and for public bodies (such as survey of Inam Villages, Surveys in connection with Railways, Municipal and Local Bodies) and survey (and measurement work) for the defence and other Government Departments, and for the Centrally governed States (viz. Dadra-Nagar-Haveli and Daman). It is also responsible for the up-to-date maintenance of all village maps and their re-printing and sale and service distribution to various departments for administrative purpose. It also supplies permissible extracts from the Survey Records to the public on payment and free extracts to other departments for administrative purposes. In brief, it supplies the basic data to various departments (particularly to the Revenue Department) for sound administration and for undertaking any agrarian reform. Thus, the

Department is closely connected with the Revenue Department and in the past it was a part and parcel of the Revenue Department. The department is headed by Settlement Commissioner Director of Land Records who is also the Ex-Officio, Secretary to Revenue Department. A manual of Rules and Standing Orders relating to the Duties and Supervision of Land Records Establishments in the Gujarat State defines duties and responsibility of the various officers and staff of Land Records Departments.

Revenue Survey History and the Present Position

1. Surveying is the art of ascertaining by measurement and of representing the form of earth's surface and the relative positions of objects upon it.
2. The originator of the system of surveys which is the feature of Moghal period is said by Abu-Fazal to have been Sherkhan, the conqueror of Humayun. It was the genius of Akbar, however, aided by his famous minister Todarmal who began this system to its fullest development. He first fixed the size of the unit of measurement, the '*Bigha*' and then standardized the instruments of land measurement the '*Gaz*' or 'Rod' and the *tenab* or chain.
3. In 1827 Mr. Pringle, the Assistant Collector at Poona was placed on special duty to devise a system of Survey and Settlement for the Poona and surrounding Districts. The systems comprised two main operations:
   (i) Survey of all the cultivable lands field by field, and
   (ii) An assessment of every field was done by chain (of 16 *annas*=33 feet) and Cross-staff and the standard of area was the English Acre with its sub-division the *Guntha*. No Attempts was made to produce maps, the areas of fields was only being ascertained and a descriptive record of their boundaries prepared.
4. In 1839, at the suggestion of Lt. Davidson sketch map was substituted by a scale map by plotting the individual fields to scale separately from the measurement and then transferring these plotted sketches to one sheet by tracing paper thus forming a village map.
5. Until 1864, however no attempt was made to construct an accurate taluka or district map; but in that year a system of traverse survey of village boundaries by the Theodolite was introduced which enabled a highly accurate Taluka map to be constructed by fitting together the traverses of individual villages.
6. The second operation is that of detailed measurement. These comprises of the division of the village into survey numbers with their sub-divisions, *pot* or *phalni*[19] numbers and then measurement by Chain and Cross staff, Plain, Table or Theodolite as the case might be.

[19] Sub-division of a survey number which the area and the assessment are separately entered in the land records under an indicative number subordinate to that of the survey number of which it is a portion.

7. Various types of Land Records:
   A) Theodolite Records
      1) Theodolite Field Book
      2) Traverse *patrak* (shows the computation of Traverse of the village boundaries)
      3) Contour Map (shows the boundaries of the village and other important topographical features as originally fixed by the theodolite surveyor).
   B) Measurement Records
      1) Rough Field Book (*Kachi* Book)[20]
      2) Fair Field Book (*Paki* Book)[21]
      3) Area Book (*Vaslevar* Book or *Gunakar* Book)[22]
      4) Rough Village map (*Kacho Naksho*)[23]
      5) Fair Village Map (*Pako Naksho*)[24]
   C) Classification Records
      1) Classification Book (*Prati* Book)[25]
   D) Settlement Records
      1) *Pahani Sud*[26]
      2) *Darvari*[27]

Challenges and Problems Faced by following present survey system and during preparing of records

- In Gujarat, Survey and Settlement work was carried out from 1886 to 1920, the system of measurement was mainly based on manual of Land Surveying. The Use of old technology for survey with chain and cross staff consisted of general principle of measurement upon to simple propositions:

---

[20] a. Contains sketches of survey numbers drawn roughly but not to scale. b. All detailed measurement for divisions of cultivation, such as dry-crop, rice and garden

[21] This book contains the sketches of survey numbers drawn to scale and also the details of area calculation.

[22] This record contains detailed calculation of the area of survey numbers.

[23] Is drawn to scale concurrently with the measuring work in the field season and differs from the fair field map in having two sets of numbering to the survey numbers.

[24] It is according to scale and it gives (1) the numbering of the fields according to the final series, and shews (2) all details of survey boundary marks, roads and nalas within and on the boundaries of survey numbers.

[25] a. contains sketches of survey numbers divided for purposes of classification with the details of soil and water classification and b. the culturable and kharab area of each description of cultivation and the total culturable area of the numbers as finally fixed

[26] This paper shows the details of area for every field together with the old (maji) and new numbers attach to each and also the names of the occupants.

[27] The survey numbers of the village were arranged in groups.

right-angle triangle, trapezium with measurement units in *pratianna* (a measurement units), *annas*, chains, *gunthas* and acres. The principle of measurement was based from part to whole method with inclusion of tolerance limit where the real area of the field cannot be precise by cross-staff method, these lacked of accuracy in field measurement resulting non-acceptance of that records now a days. The cross-staff method recorded every individual land parcel (*Tippan*).

- Some of the *tippans* and the area did not match with actual field area with a tolerance limit up by 5% which was permissible on actual ground measurement area. Adding the totals of right-angled triangle and trapezium, final area over 8 (eight) *annas* count as 1 (one) *guntha* and 8 *annas* or under, are discarded. (In Local Language called "Dharchhod"). This cross and staff methodology has its own limitations regarding accuracy in comparison with latest modern measurement instruments.
- The measurements for each field were written and drawn on a paper and the area has been calculated manually by using a ready reckoner. The chain and cross staff measurement system may bore tolerance limit in land parcel map (Tippan), lacking of accuracy with regard to measurements and old technology which had its own limitations. The old records by the span of time torn, deteriorated and became brittle, sometime missing and destroyed by way of fire, water, climate, termite or human mishandling to find out original old records that make the present survey very challenging and time consuming as the new technology does not adopt the old records as it is.
- On the passing of time, during British period the measurement of land by theodolite machine and by the plane table surveys and minor triangulation system was introduced (Described in Chapter-12 of city survey manual-1918). The plane table survey is much faster, accurate and easy survey method in comparison to cross and staff method. Nowadays cross and staff method is discontinued in the State of Gujarat. The measurement instruments such as DGPS/GPS/ETS machines are used and the data is processed in AUTOCAD software which is compatible on GIS environment.
- In The Land Revenue Code-1879, prescribed to carry out Revisional Settlement operations at the interval of 30 years. But, the measurement of sub-occupancies, survey corrections such as KJP [kami-jasti-patrak] or survey correction, sub divisions of fields, amalgation of fields etc. were not carried out timely as a result, disparities are found in Records of Rights and Survey Records. The tremendous changes on ground reality in survey records did not match the occupancy records or the records of rights. To correct those, it requires tremendous efforts from the Revenue Administration and Survey Settlement Department and also need participation of the public as well.

- The splitting of large survey numbers, changing of land-use classification, introduction of new systems of measurement etc. resulted the mismatch between textual data and spatial.
- Shortage of expertise and experienced officials and staffs, lack of establishment, less capacity building and training of modern instruments and non-participation of private agencies in survey operations etc. resulted delay to carried out revisional surveys.
- Apart from these, there are so many other field-level challenges faced by the official during survey or preparation of records.
- There was no ground control network grid to show the exact latitude and longitude of the every land parcel [*Tippan*].
- The maps and areas of river were not separately shown in survey records.
- The landholders some time resists to change their fields boundaries as per survey records.
- The number of cases of encroachment on Government land as well as on private lands noticed during the land survey operations.
- The landholder does not agree to resolve the problem by mutual consent.
- The non-voluntarily disclosure of possession, boundary marks and change of boundaries as per Government survey records and revenue records lead to dispute among the landholders and burden on revenue and civil courts.
- Khatedars [Landholders] are not serious enough during the survey to remain present and showing their boundaries, or sub divisions of lands which leads to disputes.

Learnings from Past, overcome the challenges and initiate Pilot Project on Modern Survey

In 1974, scheme called Re and Revision survey was carried out in tribal areas of the State, and it was incorporated with Resurvey as it did not has ground control network and digital survey data. The scheme was very much prior to resurvey manual and it was monitored by SCDLR office and executed by the own revenue officials. But the scheme obtained limited results. Now the whole Re and revision Survey has been merged under DILRMP scheme. Before introducing full-fledged resurvey for the entire state, a pilot project was conducted in Jamnagar District and in Mansa taluka in Gandhinagar District by SCDLR in year 2008-2009. During the pilot survey modern instruments like DGPS/GPS/ETS etc. were used followed by ground truthing to prepare digital records.

During Re and Revision survey in tribal areas, there was no ground network (specific ground control network grid to carry out work) system adopted, but numbers of learning were found such as:

- For survey, primary procedure to be adopted at village to get involved the villagers and co-operation of people for the measurement by theodolite survey machine and connectivity to GTS stations.

- Every field was measured by plane table method. Fixing of survey numbers and allotting them a separate numbers, super imposing with original survey records and finding out an encroachment on Government wasteland, roads, finding out amalgamation of different land tenure lands which is a breach of rule-11 of Gujarat Land Revenue Rules, 1972.[28]
- Finding out *pot-kharab,*[29] unlawful mutations of block numbers under Prevention of Fragmentation of Agricultural lands and Consolidation Act-1947, non-procurement of land acquisition awards of roads, canals etc., fixing the boundaries of village and there after fixing the boundaries of the fields.
- Deciding final area by finding out any clerical or arithmetical mistakes in old survey records, (in-local language it is called *senkda-bar*[30]), preparing new village map, *khetarvar patrak* (fields wise register), *akarbandh* (showing area and assessment according to survey), and *Kayam khardo* (showing area tenure, type of land, cultivated land and assessment value of agriculture land) correction in new record.

Pilot project of Resurvey

Improved methodologies and steps were involved to conduct the Jamnagar District Resurvey Pilot Project. These are as follows:

- Creation of ground control network (GCN) in whole district, establishment of iconic point or area of interest point, checking of primary, secondary and tertiary stones. Permanent monuments of ground control network.
- Involved Gramsabha during the planning of resurvey and creation of Gram Samiti and declaration of resolution with Talati Mantri, (Talati-cum-secretary of local panchayat body), Surveyor and Survey Agency.
- Utilization of RoR data for resurveys work and data entry.
- Detailed measurement of land.
- Preparation of final records and its checking.
- Record promulgation process.

Present Methodology of Survey and preparation of Survey Records

Based on the level of accuracy in the pilot project, the same methodology of survey has been rolled out for the entire state. The resurvey has been carried out under the Resurvey Manual, Land Revenue Code and Land Revenue Rules.

---

[28] (see rule11: any survey number or sub-division of a survey numbers may be amalgamated with any other coterminous survey number with the sanction of the Collector and upon the application of the holder, whenever all the parcels of land proposed for amalgamation are held by the same holder upon the same tenure).

[29] Uncultivable land of the survey number

[30] Change in area of survey number due to arithmetical or clerical mistakes found during survey.

The procedure that is followed is laid down as below:

Under section 95, 106 and 135-G of Gujarat Land Revenue Code (1879), a legal sanction is obtained and tender process is done. Under the direct supervision of land survey agency resurvey work carried out. More over a special NLRMP cell (now known as DILRMP cell) at state level is created for technical supervision, checking of data and training.

Prior to resurvey, presurvey activity through the offices of the Revenue Department were carried out and kept the records ready, both the textual records and spatial records for the surveying agency and digitized village map was given to the agencies.

State has opted for ground truthing survey methodology with the help of DGPS/GPS and ETS. After establishment of Ground Control Network,[31] a detailed measurement of every field is carried out with the help of DGPS/ETS machine. Creation of ground control network in whole District was established by taking measurement through Differential Global Positioning machine for particular district to ensure perfect fitting of maps in prescribed frame before starting detailed resurvey measurement activity. Main control point of particular district is connected with network to master control point of the state along with main point of adjoining districts by observing through DGPS. Grid designing, iconic point or area of interest point, ground control network, checking of primary, secondary and tertiary stones, permanent documentation of ground control network, regional, primary, secondary and tertiary stones through DGPS machine are also been created.

For active participation of people, a calendar of Gramsabha (Village community meeting) is published, presence of maximum citizen is ascertained and information of detailed measurement in Gramsabha is declared. The formation of Gram Samiti is created and resolution of resurvey in Gramsabha is passed. In Gramsabha, 4-layer committee has been formed for smooth operation of resurvey activity.

The data entry is done in local language, all the data entered in form "A" is checked with village form No. 7×12. The detailed measurement by ground truthing method (with the help of DGPS/ETS) is carried out in the presence of landholder and taking signature for it. In form "B", the survey or fills all the details as per ground measurement position (current status). The modern instruments like, DGPS/GPS/ETS provides an accuracy of ±15 centimeter, earlier in the old Cross & staff method, the tolerance limits was 5% permissible land area. In the new method, the tolerance limit is removed and as per the actual area, possession, boundary marks and taking into consideration of the all nearest

[31] Creation of GCN: Regional Station (if required) is between 40-50 km, primary control point at 16×16 km. secondary control point at 4×4 km, tertiary control point at 1×1 km. and auxiliary control points at 150 to 200 meter or sufficient distance for surveying through electronic total station machine.

boundary survey number holders during the survey and preparation of new records. The new measured area is finalized and the register called *vadh-ghat* (the difference in area of an old area and the new area) is maintained and the new area is to be accepted in reality. If any mismatch found between the old data with the newly generated data as per possession or boundary marks are also been noted. After the completion of measurement, the Government surveyor checks the measurement details and there after the Government surveyor signs a LPM (Land Parcel Map) notice to landholder to raise any objection (if any he/she has within 10 days from the date of receipt of notice). At village level an objection register is maintained and whosoever has objections, that is been noted down at village level.

The biggest challenge in the resurvey project is the acceptance of new survey record by the landholder of land. Therefore, all concerned offices checked all the records. The newly prepared resurvey record is compulsorily carried out promulgation of the records. Survey Settlement official/Revenue Officials checked the following records prepared by the survey agency:

- Main register
- Area difference register
- Annexure 4 (1), 4 (2), 4 (3)
- Aakarbandh
- Kayam khardo
- Khetarwar patrak
- Survey charges register
- Land register of old and new survey number
- Village map
- New village Form No.7 with map shown with Latitude/Longitude

The revenue officer through online process promulgates the records. Prior to promulgation a notice of 30 days is widely published at village levels and on the date of promulgation the objection recorded are remanded for further actions to concerned officer. Once the promulgation is affected the new resurvey records become effective and legal. Even after promulgation a landholder may raise an objection if there is a dispute among landholders for area, size, shape, and boundary marks, possessions etc. by submitting simple application to SLR/DD (Superintendent Land Record/Deputy Director) without engaging an advocate or filing an appeal. For verification of the objection raised by the landholder, surveyor disposes the objection by revisiting field and it corrections by passing special order through SLR/DD and DILR is empowered to make necessary changes in RoR also.

If there are any extraordinary changes in area and possession is found, it is reconciled with old records and if there does not seem any encroachment on Government land or public land, the holders are required to accept new area obtained by modern instruments.

How Survey has been taking place

1. Prior to full-fledged implementation of DILRMP, in old times Cross and Staff method survey with chain of 33 feet having 16 links was used and tippan of every LPM was prepared as described on land survey manual.
2. There after the use of the theodolite machine and plane table set system were introduced. Plane table system give map in scale, and prior to measurement a notice to remain present on site is given to landholder. The possession, bounding marks, and limit of dimensions on site are measured in presence of landholder and shown as per his knowledge and beliefs.
3. The survey super imposes the measurement sheet prepared by plane table system and matches it with old tippans. If anything found irrelevant of tippan, surveyor shows the encroachment in measurement sheet. In short, tippan is a final and primary evidence to show the actual boundaries of LPM. A Panchnama is drawn on the site and the surveyor shows the boundary marks on the field and fixes the boundary of the field according to tippan only. Any type of measurement including sub-division, partially sale of land, amalgamation, acquisition is co-related with tippans only.
4. After introduction of resurvey, every LPM is measured by DGPS/GPS/ETS machines only with established GCN, the measurement instruments are replaced by DGPS/ETS. The old survey records particularly "TIPPAN" is referred to resolve any of the disparity of possession, boundary marks and encroachments.
5. No survey is authenticated without verification of survey records and revenue records as well.

City Survey in Gujarat

The necessity for the survey of towns and cities as an adjunct to municipal administration is sufficiently obvious and the matter of fact in such survey were undertaken during British rule. Under this regime, during the revenue survey two towns were also been surveyed one was Surat (surveyed in 1821) and another one was Ahmadabad (surveyed in 1824).

The objectives of City survey are mainly threefold; (As per chapter-12 of Survey and Settlement Manual by R.G. Gordon, ICS and the City Survey manuals by FGH Anderson):

- Survey of all lands within the site of the area to which the survey has been extended including all occupied land and unoccupied areas, roads, tanks etc. with a view to provide a map for administrate purpose.
- The fiscal object is to ascertain the revenue due from land.
- The legal object is to clear all titles to existing holding to support and better define those which are good and to eliminate those which are lend to prevent vexatious litigation between owners and to remove doubts and private claimants and local bodies or Governments.

The general course of the operations is as follows:

- Government directive to survey of the lands other than those ordinarily used for the purpose of agriculture within the site of the particular village, town or city.
- Survey by mean Traverse, minor traverses, details measurement of land.
- Inquiry:
  - The actual work of inquiring into title.
  - The determination of survey fees.
  - Issue of Sanand

Maintenance of the City Survey records

Now some of the methodology narrated in city survey manual, the present Government has added a para no. 129 (A) and enabling private agencies to be outsourced for city survey work for certain purpose only. City Survey traditional old method was long and time consuming. The Government made various resolution and methodology to introduce City Survey. Recently Government has introduced out sourced agencies in Municipal corporation area and 1450 villages.

1. On attaining the non-agriculture status through NIC portal property cards are prepared based on RoR, KJP, and non-agriculture order since 2014.
2. On finalization of town planning scheme, based on its records, property cards are prepared.
3. In village site area and in municipal areas by publishing tender, out source agencies are awarded the work of survey, data entry, record preparation etc. The data provided by agencies is approved by Government official and prepare property cards.
4. As per Gujarat flat ownership act, every individual unit flat holder in multi-storied building is entitled to separate property card. Separate property card of land and constructed building unit is given separate city survey numbers. This system is operational in Gujarat.
5. On introduction of a new Chapter 9 (a) in land revenue code, claimants are given property cards by recovery of compounding fees.

Modernized Survey and preparation of accurate records: Overall Development, innovative actions and implementations of various policies

1. All agricultural or non-agricultural land in the state surveyed only by using ETS/DGPS/GPS.
2. Developing the LPM (Land Parcel Map) using GIS technology with latitude and longitude for precise location of each parcels.
3. The state has 18,046 villages out of which 18,033 villages are measured, 11,988 villages are promulgated, a total survey number approximately 1.20 crore are measured. A total 4,58,925 objections are received after promulgation. After completion of resurvey and records promulgation,

state is able to provide a single updated revenue records (RoR) with map. All data is kept in single-point source in SDC (State Data Centre).

4. Special care has been taken on establishment related issues at different level. Modern compactors are provided to revenue as well as survey offices to preserve the physical records in the states.
5. In case of any survey corrections, DILR (District Inspector of Land Records) is authorized to make appropriate changes in survey as well as in revenue records in e-Dhara
6. As a Revenue Reform, Revenue Department has developed IORA (Integrated Online Revenue Administration) to provide all revenue related services under one umbrella, that creates simplicity and transparency to citizen.
7. For Citizens, Mojani portal has been launched. Applicants may apply for parcel measurement, sub division and land hold area verification. In this portal, randomly allotment of applications to surveyors and time bound services are provided, measurement sheets are provided to the applicants by email.
8. The urban land record (city survey) is introduced in the state under Chapter 9 (a) of Land Revenue code-1879 and Chapter 10 of Land Revenue code-1879. The state has carried out amendment in para-129(A) of City Survey Manual, permitting private agencies to carry out survey and prepare city survey records but finalisation can be attributed by Government officials only.
9. Town planning lands converted in city survey and every urban property whether it may be village site survey, city survey or non-agricultural land, every individual unit of a multi-storied building is entitled to have a separate property card.
10. All Urban/Rural (village site area) properties revenue records are being converted into property cards for non-agricultural area in CSIS (City Survey Information System). Fifty four lakh property cards are operational. It is important to note that Government of Gujarat has taken initiatives to issue an individual property card to every unit of multi-storied buildings.
11. The Government has empowered the survey officer to promulgate the resurvey records, city survey records. In Gujarat Land Revenue Rules-108, Government has empowered the District level survey officer to dispose the disputed mutations of city survey.

Policy Recommendations

1. A programme of maintenance, repairing and establishment of boundary marks as per survey records and revenue records should be preconditioned prior to introduction of survey.
2. All Presurvey activities to be completed including Revenue Records and survey records to be updated and matched with ground reality.
3. The dependency on private agencies being minimized and Government appointed surveyors should perform the survey. Only mechanical type of work should be assigned to agencies.

4. Where survey records are in good shape and available in accurate form, Re and Revision survey should be taken in a limited phase and it must be compatible with old records for the verification of possession and LPM boundaries.
5. Survey methodology and its accuracy must be spread over to public to accept it by IEC.
6. After record promulgation and considering curtain principle, public is required to accept the new digital records both in survey and revenue records so the verification checking and monitoring system by renowned Government agencies other than the survey department be deputed.
7. Fresh application of measurements must be disposed in context to digital map, land co-ordinates and variation in new survey records within the limit of tolerance limit looking to the mirror principle.
8. Further new technology including CORS (Continues Operating Reference Station) may be adopted.

Guidelines on Survey and Settlement

Settlement is defined in Section 117(C) (1) of Gujarat Land Revenue Code. “Settlement” means the result of the operations conducted in a zone in order to determine the land revenue assessment. Chapter VIII A talks about assessment and settlement of land revenue of agriculture land. The rates of land revenue assessment of agriculture lands in the erstwhile Bombay state villages are fixed and levied as per settlement made and approved by Government under the provisions of the Bombay Land Revenue Code 1879. The details regarding the year of original and revision settlements carried out in force at present till the revision settlement are introduced as per the provision contained in section 117-R of the Land Revenue Code. The rates of land revenue assessment were lastly fixed in 1959-60 are in force from 1959-60; till regular settlement under Chapter VIII-A of the Bombay Land Revenue code is made or next revised whichever is earlier. Thus, the land revenue assessment rates are fixed for all the areas of the state.

1. Revenue survey may be introduced by state government into any part of India to which the act extends.
2. Government may direct a fresh survey and revision of assessment without classification of land with a view to revision of land of such area. Under section 106 of BLRC 1879, Government has introduced a fresh survey without revision of settlement rates.
3. A settlement shall remain in force for the field of 30 years but in Gujarat, no fresh settlement has been carried out.
4. A detailed Settlement procedure is narrated in Chapter-VIII of The Bombay Survey and Settlement manual by R.G. Gordon, ICS.
5. In resurvey project starting from Jamnagar district to covering whole state, no revision settlements are conducted but the old rates are continued and in proportionate to fresh measured area is calculated.

6. In present era no need of old system of classification of land is required as the scientific ways are available to decide land fertility and the land faults to decide classification of land namely dry crop, rice or garden land.
7. The classification value of the land was recorded by surveyor having regard to its soil, water and other advantages. The proportion of whole revenue income from the land amounts to some of 25 per cent and was of course enormously larger in pre British days. From 01/08/1997, the Government has suspended the recovery of revenue in Gujarat, so, in present system the revenue income is not of paramount importance.
8. No fresh settlements are required as new scientific methods are available to classify the land and law permits Governments to carry out survey without settlements procedure, and methodology has become a history.
9. Village boundaries are precisely demarcated and then after every land (plot) it may be private or Government, river, water bodies, reservoir, tanks. And the vacant Government land is measured and given a separate survey number showing boundaries and adjuring survey numbers.
10. No use of cross and staff method and plane table method is allowed for any of the survey whether it may be survey/resurvey/city survey.
11. Every survey is carried out in presence of a landholder and its neighbour survey number holders.
12. Survey is carried out looking actual possession of land/mirror principle/ mirror image as per ground reality with reference to co-ordinates of the boundary marks and possession of the land with DGPS/ETS/GPS machineries.
13. If Government land is adjacent to a private land, the original *Tippans* are enlarged to scale and the measurement done on site is superimposed with original *tippan* and the final boundary as per *tippan* is fitted and the remaining area is treated as enlargement on same land and such enlargement is entered in enlargement register and such enlargements are evicted by the Revenue Officer.
14. Wherever original Tippan is not available, other related records are checked and the boundary is fixed as per DSO (District Survey Officer) records only and not as per possession.
15. The land boundary marks erected earlier may be washed or uprooted due to land delusion/elusion, the naturally erected new boundary marks among the coparceners or heirs on inheritance or on family partition, sale or transfer of land or partially sale of land resulting in altering land boundaries marks are found and measured as per ground situations. With passing of the time and non-compliance on part of the landholders to maintain their boundary marks, it is always possible that there may be some change in boundary marks which do not result in survey number or major portion of land do not move in adjoining survey number and within permissible limit of 5 per cent of area tolerance with new measurement by ETS/GPS Machine.

16. With the consent of adjacent landholders only which is not supported by RoR or DSO records, only actual possession of the land is not considered for resurvey records.
17. The provision of Section-119 of Land Revenue Code-1879 which defines how to fix the boundary of survey number is taken care of.
18. In absence of landholder or in absence of neighbour landholders if any landholder shows his unlawful possession which does not cancel with onsite tippan and onsite boundary marks and claims for more possession on site, he cannot make lease after resurvey.
19. Unlawful possession which is not compactable with RoR and DSO records cannot be claimed to be true.
20. In sub-division or part sale or partition, family partition, court degree partition, the landholders whose names are in RoR have to put their consent before surveyor and are duty bound to show their sub-divisions.
21. Where there is a dispute among sub-division holders of the land, partially sold landholder and they do not agree to it survey will measure the land. Sub-divisions as per their say and the matter may be decided by Revenue officer and per the revenue officers order, the boundary as sub-divided plot holder is fixed by surveyor.
22. Every type of survey such as Town Planning, Land Acquition, Railways, National Highways, SEZ, Forest Land, Sanctuary, Government Land, Land allotment the DILR office is responsible to carry out survey or to certify the survey from survey agencies deputed by any of the institution.
23. After survey, the measurement is reconciled with old survey records for extra ordinary changes of land area, shape, dimension, encroachments, etc. The survey prepared digitized survey map, process it in AUTOCAD software, prepares a signed measurements sheets and draws *panchnama* in presence of landholder and submitted to DILR office.
24. Headquarter Assistant, a superior of survey and who is responsible for District Survey Office Records, a scrutiny survey checks the measurements sheet with DSO records and Headquarter Assistant finally approves it, thereafter, a certified copy is given to applicant and further survey corrections are carried out in DSO/RoR records.
25. No manual method of computation of area, measurement of land preparing new village map is allowed only digital map is prepared and correction on all the allied records including RoR are synchronized as real time by.
26. As per guideline, every LPM must bear latitude/longitude and it is based reiterate measurement of Land in digital form, digital map in village Form No. 7.
27. Earlier 7/12 was a collectively forms but after resurvey, Form No.7 is a separate RoR and Form No. 12 is a separate form showing cultivation of land type of cultivation etc.

28. The Government regulation is circulated to collector to inspect and maintain government boundary marks and GCN stones to be declared as Government boundary marks. Survey & Revenue officials are directed to inspect all GCNs and no one should damage the stones must be ascertain.
29. Orientation training to probationer IAS, Deputy Collector, Mamlatdars, Surveyors is held particularly on DGPS/ETS/GPS/AUTOCAD/Record Management/Reconciliation of Village Marks/Tippan, Computerisation/GIS Data Processing, etc.
30. SOP is circulated to address the objection of landholders after record promulgation.
31. Where in it is compulsory for Government surveyor to measure the land in presence of landholder and adjustment neighbouring landholders in reference to GCN. The redressal is complete after an order of DD/SLR and he sends an order to DILR to implement it in survey records and revenue records.
32. All guidelines published by department of land resources, GOI are implemented and the various guidelines described in resurvey manual-2012 are observed.
33. DILRMP CELL and a unit of GIS LAB checks the village maps, super impose it with old maps, change in use of land, latitude and longitude of LPMS. Government Land Acquisition Correction soft and hard data processed by agencies are checked from the level of surveyor to promulgation officers and periodically the committees form in four layers resolve the problems, if any.

2.5

Haryana

Mohinder Kumar, IAS (Retd.)

Introduction

In the early period, the sovereign earned the major share from land revenue. From the very time of the Sultanates, extended for more than 300 years, *Jagirdar*, King, *Inamdar*, *Nawab*, *Subedar*, *Mirja*, *Zamindar* etc. were made intermediaries who passed on the revenue to the sovereign. Indian land records originated during the Mughal period. Dewan Todar Mal attempted to reform the system for the first time during Sher Shah Suri's reign. Under the reign of Mughal Emperor Akbar, Raja Todar Mal, the then Finance Minister transformed the land revenue collection and assessment into a systematic practice by appointing a clerk in every Village. This system of maintenance by patwari is still used in the Indian sub-continent which was improved by the British and the Government of India.

Status of Land Records in Haryana

Haryana's land records system is as old as that of the Mughal and the British period. The last land settlement was held in 1909-10 in United Punjab during British period. At the time of separation from Punjab in 1966, Haryana had seven districts and having a land area of 44212 square kilometers. Now there are 22 districts and 7085 villages. After independence, land consolidation was done from 1952 to 1964 in United Punjab. Land was divided into uniform grids of acres. Each acre is called a *killa* (unit of area), having dimension of 40 *karam* (unit of length) x 36 *karam* and each *karam* is equal to 5.5 feet. Lowest land unit is *Karam*. Killa grid of 25 acre is called *Murrba.*[32] One *Mussavi* (mapping sheet) contains 16 *Murrbas* i.e., 400 acres of land. *Mussavi* is the basic map of identification and location of ownership of land and prepared as per village area. Whole village area was shown in *shajra* map called cadastral map. Land ownership transfer details in book and Field Books were prepared.

Mutation is a legal proof of change in any rights in the holdings occurred after preparation of last *Jamabandi* (supporting documents of land ownership).

---

[32] Unit of Area, each musavi comprises of 16 murrba and each murrba comprises of 25 killas.

Mussavis remained un-updated for 50-60 years. Owners have changed but the land records continued to be in joint names and only share of land is registered as land ownership, which created disputes.

Guidelines regarding Land Survey in Haryana

Survey Numbers

Definition of a survey number – the following definitions of survey number is given for guidance in making new surveys or corrections there of:

(i) In all survey work each parcel of land lying in one spot, in the occupation of one person, or of several persons holding jointly, and held under one title, should ordinarily be measured as a separate survey number, but large areas may be broken up into convenient fields.

(ii) A survey number may have part of its area cultivated and part uncultivated or part of one soil and part of another. Survey numbers should not be multiplied merely on grounds of this kind unless it is convenient to measure wasteland separately and not to include irrigated with unirrigated cultivation, as this leads to errors in totalling the village area.

(iii) Care also should be taken not to multiply survey numbers merely on account of cultivation ridges or other purely temporary divisions. In normal state of cultivation, there is usually no necessity to treat each ridge made for convenience of cultivation, as separate field boundary.

(iv) But in the case of valuable lands cultivated by tenants who are frequently changed, special care should be taken that the measurements are made to show the boundaries of parcels in which the land is usually held for cultivation or irrigation. In such lands, the survey numbers will necessarily be smaller than elsewhere.

(v) In places where land is of little value, if an occupancy tenant has extended his field by ploughing out, and there is no boundary between the new and old land, nor other evidence, such as payment of a different rent by which the new land can be separated from the old land, the *patwari* shall survey the whole in one number. In such a case, it is not his duty to distinguish between old and new land.

(vi) Field names, if locally used, should be written under the survey numbers.

(vii) In short, every care should be taken to make the survey simple, but not to omit details convenient for the annual *girdawari* (harvest inspection) and *jamabandi.*

(viii) Where the boundaries of a survey number is known, but is not marked on the ground owing to rich cultivation or sandy soil, the boundary should be delineated on the map by broken lines.

(ix) Where there is a large area of undivided waste it may be cut up into survey numbers corresponding with the limits of the survey squares.

(x) In all cases in which a new map of any estate is prepared and regarding canal requirements, and so far as may be possible the limits of canal irrigation, as ordinarily practised, must be shown in separate numbers.

Maintenance of Survey Marks

The land surveying practices in Haryana are based upon the survey marks placed by Survey of India (SoI) and by the State Revenue Department, therefore, maintenance of survey marks is necessary.

i. *Marks Placed by the survey of India (Great Trigonometrical Stations)*
    - Base line stones placed in the course of riverain surveys.
    - Traverse stations supplied in estates not surveyed on the square system.
    - Other traverse data such as corner stone's indicating blocks in the regulation carried out by the survey department.

    Note: Traverse data supplied by the Survey Department are not intended to be a guide to patwaris in the execution of their survey except where the ground is so hilly or broken that accurate squares cannot be laid down, where for special reasons, e.g. in riverain tracts a scientific traverse has been made as the foundation for the patwaris field surveys.

ii. Marks Placed by the Revenue Department
    - Tri-junction pillars or platform or *sihaddas,* erected at every point where the boundaries of more than two estates meet.
    - *Burjis* (mud pillars stone slabs), set up at every angle on the boundary line between two *sihaddas.*
    - Masonry or stone pillars at the corners of survey squares or rectangles.

iii. *Tri-junction pillars*: The completion and maintenance of tri-junction pillars in every village is a matter of great importance, because under the existing system of village survey, these points are the connecting link between the patwari survey and the survey of India, furnishing a basis (1) on which the results of the patwari maps can be checked against the data of the survey of India and (2) by the aid of which the topography of the patwari maps can be incorporated into the sheets of that survey section.

iv. *Maintenance of Great Trigonometrical Survey stations and international boundary pillars*
    - The deputy commissioners will maintain in their offices a list of the Great Trigonometrical Survey stations in their districts and shall see that the instructions given below are carried out.
    - In his field inspection the Patwari, in whose circle such pillar is situated, should note whether the mark is in good repair in the manner prescribed for *pakka* survey marks in the instructions given in chapter on Harvest Inspection.
    - On the completion of the kharif harvest inspection each *patwari* shall send a report to the tehsildar for submission to the Deputy Commissioner.

v. Should any pillar not be situated within the boundaries of any one revenue village, the tehsildar shall make special arrangements for the inspection of such pillar and for the preparation of the prescribed report by a patwari or kanungo (Supervisor of patwaris) as soon as possible after the kharif harvest inspection.

vi. *Maintenance of base line stones placed in the course of riverain surveys*: Index maps have been supplied by the survey department indicating the base line stones fixed by them in the Course of riverain surveys. These stones are of essential importance, in connection with the maps of riverine tracts with boundaries after emergence from the river. Now those almost all riverine boundaries are fixed. Deputy Commissioner will prepare a list of base line stones from Index maps, but the report to be submitted by the patwari. They will send an annual return in the following form to the Director of Land Records with the annual report on the Land Records of the districts

vii. *Maintenance of traverse stations supplied in estates not surveyed on the square system*: The orders will also apply to traverse stations supplied by the Survey of India in hilly areas.

viii. *Maintenance of other traverse data fixed by the survey of India*: The orders in clause will also apply to other traverse data fixed by the Survey of India.

ix. *General orders relating to maintenance of all Survey marks*: All classes of survey marks set up by the Survey Department and tri-junction pillars and pillars at the corners of survey squares and rectangles will be given a red ink entry without number, after the field number, in which they are situated, and the patwari will at each harvest inspection note in his diary if they are in good repair.

x. *Proper preservation and inspection of survey marks*: The proper preservation of survey marks of the above kinds is of such importance that the special attention should be paid by Deputy Commissioners and Settlement Officers in the matter. When inspecting girdawari work all Revenue Officers should satisfy themselves that the patwari has noted whether these survey marks are in good repair. When a tehsildar or Naib tehsildar or field kanungo visit a village containing such marks he should invariably inspect them and should, as far as possible, put them in good order if he finds them out of repair. If the repairs require expenditure, he should report the matter to the Deputy Commissioner. He should always make an entry in his diary nothing the state in which he has found the marks.

xi. *Mention about the condition of surveys mark in the annual reports*: In the annual report on the Department of Land Records, Deputy Commissioners and Settlement Officers should specially note whether the condition of all marks has been examined during the year and whether they have been put in proper order where necessary.

Surveys during Settlement: Instructions regarding re-measurement and map correction

Survey implements and mapping paper: Instructions as to survey implements and mapping paper will be found in Chapter No.3 (Patwaris). In hilly and broken land where squares cannot be used, application for plotted traverse sheets should be made to the Director of Land Records, and that officer, in communication with the Survey Department, will supply suitable sheets for the patwari's use.

Responsibility given to Patwari for measurements: The main portion of the measurement and record work should be done by the circle patwaris, the settlement patwaris being looked on primarily as an aid to them in their work. A patwari must in no case be excused from doing both measurement and record work.

Riverain measurement Rules hitherto observed by the Survey Department: The rules are made under which riverain measurements have been carried out throughout the Haryana in conjunction with the Survey Department.

Such points as the Settlement Officer may require should be traversed and where necessary marked on the ground by the Officer-in-charge of Riverain Survey. These should include –

(a) All existing tri-junction pillars
(b) Recognizable physical features of a permanent nature
(c) The survey part's traverse points. These should not be more than 340 meters apart and should invariably be close to the district or tehsil boundary
(d) A number of points in the kacha area to facilitate internal measurements by the patwaris.

The kanungos who were employed with the traversers may now be appointed by the Settlement Officer to supervise the detailed measurements. It is advisable to have a special naib-tehsildar in charge of the whole cadastral survey of riverain areas.

It is in connection with remeasurement of the kacha area that boundary disputes arise and discrepancies have to be reconciled, and this requires careful treatment. The naib-tehsildar will first of all mark the external boundaries of the village as shown in the settlement Shajra. The Patwari will then easily be able to fix the field boundaries which he should show to the owner concerned. In the case of settlement, shajras are in such a dilapidated state that they do not clearly show the village boundaries or in case the boundaries of two villages overlap or an area has been omitted from measurement in both maps, the naib-tehsildar should prepare a statement of the cases illustrated by tracing from the mussavis, and submit it to the Settlement Officer for his decision which will be marked on both sets of mussavis. His report should include the statements of lambardars and owners interested in the matter. To enable him to deal properly with disputes, the naib-tehsildar will require –

- the settlement shajras of village on both sides of the river.
- all record of previous disputes and decisions. If any of the villages involved are situated in another district, it is necessary to obtain the cooperation of those authorities.
- The most convenient course is to obtain jurisdiction for the Settlement Officer over the whole of the riverain area of the adjoining district.
- Lambardars should be made responsible that the pegs and survey marks are not removed or destroyed. A list should be maintained by the village patwari in the following form:
  a. No. of Chanda (point of demarcation)
  b. Field No. in which the chanda is situated.
  c. Owner's name
  d. Name of the tenant.
  e. Signature or thumb impression of lambardar (village headman).
  f. The position of the pegs and chandas should be marked by the kanungo on one of the patwari's maps, it will then be easy to fix responsibility.

Procedure for Correction of Field Maps in the Interval between Two Settlements

The following instructions are issued for the purpose of collecting material from year to year for incorporating in the field map changes, which occur in fields in the interval between two settlement.

i. *Changes due to transactions*: The Changes in fields, which ought to lead to the correction of a field map in the interval between two settlements, and the methods by which the map should be corrected, are stated in the following instructions:
Firstly, changes which are due to transactions on account of which a mutations order has been, or should be, passed. The chief examples are –
(a) Partitions.
(b) Sales.
(c) Mortgage with possession.
(d) Redemption when part of an old field has been mortgaged and in consequence a new number has been made, the result of redemption being the restoration of the original number.
(e) Exchange.
(f) Gifts.

ii. *Changes due to nautor and hissadari kasht*. Secondly, other changes of a sufficiently permanent character. Examples are:
(a) Nautor (Bringing uncultivable land under cultivation).
(b) Conversion of part of a barani field into irrigated land when the change is of a permanent nature. Such changes will especially occur when a new well has been sunk or some other new means of irrigation has been provided.

(c) Separate cultivation of share-holders in fields jointly owned (hissadari kasht) when arrangements for separate possession has lasted for not less than four years. Such arrangements when once made usually continue until a partition is carried out under the orders of a Revenue Officer.

Method of Preparation of Tatimma Shajras

i. *Based on Permanent changes*: In the case of new numbers due to transactions on account of mutation order the Revenue Officer must not sanction the mutation in the absence of a proper map of the new field numbers attested by the kanungo and checked by himself. When the patwari enters up the mutation he will draw to scale on the back of the mutation sheet and its counterfoil the numbers effected and will enter under them the details prescribed for the field book referred to in paragraph 4.26. The new field will be temporarily numbered, e.g. 155/1 155/2 etc., permanent numbers not being adopted lest the mutation be rejected or the new fields be affected by subsequent mutation. The kanungo will check on the spot the dimensions and areas of the new numbers and will sign his name at the foot of the map with a note "attested on the spot". In the case of mutations due to sales, etc., the kanungo is responsible for seeing that the measurements correspond with the area actually transferred. In the case of partitions it will not always be possible to show the new numbers and field book details on the back of the mutation order. If so, they will be shown on separate mapping sheets. The tatimma shajra in the case of a partition will be a copy of that prepared as soon as the partition is completed. The kanungo who attests the tatimma shajra in the case of a partition will be held strictly responsible that the map really shows the land allotted to each share-holder and pointed out to him. In case of a transaction based on a registered deed the revenue officer should immediately on receipt of the registration memorandum from the Registration Officer, direct the kanungo and the patwari to proceed to the spot and prepare a tatimma shajra, if one is necessary, on the basis of the material given in the registration memorandum and that alone. On the completion of the tatimma shajra it shall be submitted by the kanungo to the revenue officer.

ii. *Based on hissadari kasht etc.*: In the year in which the quinquennial jamabandi of an estate is to be prepared the kharif girdawari must be made with great care, and the field kanungo is responsible that no number which has changed permanently escapes detection. After the girdawari is finished he will prepare the tattima shajras on mapping sheets of the same size as the sheets used for jamabandis. Field book details will be entered on the back of these maps. In the case of villages measured on the square system these mapping sheets will have two squares marked on them. The field kanungo will check the tatimma shajras on the spot during the cold weather before the end of January.

iii. *Boundaries and dimension of new field numbers to be shown in red ink*: In the maps prescribed by the two last paragraphs all new boundaries and other amendments will be shown in red ink. It is unnecessary to re-chain such of the boundaries as have undergone no alteration, and if a side of a new field includes the whole of a side of an adjoining field which is not being amended only the remaining part of the side of the new field need be re-measured. When an old field number is divided into two or more new numbers the patwari will re-calculate the areas of each of the new numbers. To facilitate identification one adjoining number which has not altered will be shown in the tatimma shajra.

iv. *Preparation of field book of new field numbers*: In the case of any further changes brought to light at the rabi girdawri and when it is completed the patwari will enter all the new field for which tatimma shajras have been prepared

v. *Tatimma shajras to be bound with the jamabandis*: The original tatimma shajras prepared will be bound up with the Government copy of the jamabandi, and copies checked and signed by the field kanungo will be bound with the patwari's copy of the jamabandi.

vi. *Check of tatimma shajras and keeping up-to-date of maps*: The tehsildar and naib-tehsildar shall check on the spot at least 25 per cent of the tatimma shajras prepared in each village in the period intervening between two jamabandis and they are responsible for the general accuracy of the measurement. The patwari's copy of the settlement map and the fair copy kept in the tehsil should include all changes from time to time brought to light and all recently settled districts, maps should be kept completely up-to-date.

vii. *Renewal of patwaris copies of shajra kishtwar*: The patwari shall in future have in his custody only one copy of the settlement map for use at girdawari and for all other purposes. The karukan (sides-measurement) will be shown in the copy. The patwaris copy will be on *latha* cloth (shajra parcha). The fair copy of the settlement map formerly in the custody of the patwari will hereafter be permanently kept in the tehsil. The patwaris copy of the map of every village must be renewed at the time of filing of every other jamabandi of that village. For special reasons, however, a fresh copy may be prepared after the lapse of a shorter period under the orders of the collector.

viii. *Incorporation of amendments in the parat*[33] *tehsil maps and in the shajras kishtwar kept by patwaris*: The new lines of amended fields should in the first instance be shown in pencil by the patwari and then inked by the kanungo after comparison with the tatimmas concerned. The kanungo must carefully compare the changes made in the maps with those shown in the tatimma shajras, and must state in his note of the result of checking the jamabandi that he has done so. The tehsildar and naib-tehsildar shall also examine the incorporation of 25 per cent, of the tatimma shajras in the parat tehsil mussavi.

Preparation of Tehsil and District Maps based on Patwari Surveys

Preparation of the grouped (mujmil) map – Where fairly recent survey or other maps on a sufficiently large scale showing village boundaries does not exist the

---

[33] new settlement record

Settlement Officer should prepare for each tehsil a grouped (mujmil) map on a scale of two centimeters to a kilometer. The grouped map is made on tracing cloth and is an exact reproduction of the index maps. In the case of large tehsils with big estates and much wasteland it may be convenient to reduce the index maps to the scale of one centimeter to a kilometer.

It should for two reasons be started as soon as the index maps are available, and should not be deferred to the very end of the settlement, for

(i) in piecing together the index maps errors in the boundaries are often brought to light, which are real errors of further inspection of the ground, and
(ii) there are differences in practice as regards the showing of roads, canal cuts, etc. indifferent patwaris or kanungos circles, and uniformity should be secured.

A copy of the mujmili map, should obtain materials for showing new roads, canals, dak bungalows, power stations, bridges, railway lines, communication towers/mobile towers etc., in revised editions of their maps.

Preparation of district map – If no convenient survey maps of the district exist, the Settlement Officer should reduce the grouped tehsil map by pentagraph to a smaller scale (1 centimeter to 2.5 kilometers) and prepare a district map.

Dispute Resolution

It often happens that a landowner trespasses on the land of the adjoining owner; under such circumstances the aggrieved person need to apply through an application to the revenue officer, revenue officer forward it to concerned tehsildar/naib tehsildar/kanungo for pointing out the boundary in dispute. The kanungo does the work on the spot. The tehsildar should ensure that the work is not done in a perfunctory manner.
If a boundary is in dispute:

a) the Field Kanungo should re-lay it from the village map prepared at the last settlement. If there is a map which has been made on the square/rectangles system; he/she should reconstruct the square/rectangles in which the disputed land lies. He/she should mark on the ground on the lines of the squares/rectangles on the places where the map shows that the disputed boundary interacted those lines, and then to find the position of points which do not fall on the lines of the squares/rectangles, he/she should identify through the map and set out all the points and boundaries which are shown in the map.
b) but if there is no map on the square/rectangles system available, he should then find three points on different sides of the place in dispute are or near (not more than 200 kadams) which are shown in the map and which the parties admit to have been undisturbed. Then the official start surveying with chain from one to another points and compare the result with the

map. If the distances when thus compared are matched with then lines can be drawn on maps by pencil and draw perpendiculars with the scale from these lines to each of the points which it is required to lay out on the ground. Then checking with cross-staff whether the distance from one of his marks to another is the same as in the map or not.

If a question is raised on disputed boundary according to the field map of the settlement records with the current settlement, that also should be demarcated on the ground and also shown in the copy of the current field map. The areas of the fields abutting the boundary in dispute as recorded at the time of last settlement and those arrived at as a result of the measurement on the spot, should be mentioned in the Field *Kanungos* report with an explanation of the cause of increase or decrease if any discovered.

Recent Practices on Resurvey

Survey under Digital India Land Records Modernization Programme (earlier NLRMP)

Haryana Space Application Centre (HARSAC) which is the nodal agency for the state for geospatial application was assigned the task of National Land record modernization programme by the State Government. In 2007, prior to launching of NLRMP, HARSAC took up resurvey for one village as a pilot project. With successful completion of the pilot project, the exercise was extended for whole of Sirsa district. Central Government appreciated the pioneer work of HARSAC.

i. *Objective*: The Government of India launched the NLRMP in 2008 to modernize land records which would reduce land disputes and enhance transparency in land records maintenance system. Land records having long historical link have errors coupled with missing documents created difficulty to update data by Revenue Departments. The resurvey component under NLRMP aims to develop planetary data of land record with geo referenced cadastral maps of record data. As per the project, every state has to modernize the land record data accurately.
ii. *Methodology*: HARSAC's land digitization model is based upon accurate geo referencing of planetary data, this reduces field visits and survey.
The entire work has been executed through three broad-parts:
Firstly, scanning and digitization of mussavi and cadastral map generation.
Secondly, correcting maps using high resolution satellite data using primary control points as a monumentation for accurate photogrammetric process.
Thirdly, development of documents management system.
iii. *Scope of work:*
    - *Patwaris* and other revenue officials were trained.
    - NLRMP's business processing unit is established inside the premise of *Patwari* Training Center where workstations were connected to main server manned by the HARSAC.

- On field, every vendor must have district coordinator with the revenue officers.
- Margin of acceptable error was set less than 1%.

iv. *Process followed*

a) Geo-referencing of land surface: For accurate geo-referencing of cadastral maps, monumentation easily identified in satellite images, of entire state was done as shown in the figure.

Initially, 35 Primary control points by the Survey of India were used to build reference map. Another 121 primary control points at a distance of 20 km followed by 589 secondary control points at distance of 8 km distance and finally 18000 tertiary control points were added to the network by HARSAC as shown in the figure.

b) Photogrammetric process: High resolution satellite data was acquired for photogrammetric process. Triangulation and digital terrain models were created for ortho rectification afterwards to establish ground control points as shown in figures.

c) Digitization of Mussavis for cadastral map and vector generation: Digitized mussavis were printed and sent to respective Patwaris for matching with record of rights and updating it. Corrections were made, thus a corrected and updated Mussavi was prepared.

All *mussavis* of a village were made to cadastral map and verified by *Patwari* and *Tehsildar,* subsequently vetted by villagers. After the consent, cadastral map was super-imposed upon geo- referenced image.

d) Document Scanning: All documents of land ownership like *Jamabandi, Misal Haqiyat (Record of Rights),* Field Book, Mutation, *Shajra Nashb, Girdwari (harvest inspection)* and registry deeds were scanned. Scanned documents were uploaded onto 'Document Management Retrieval System' software. This data in DMRS was verified again

v. *Output:*

- Geo referenced cadastral map was linked with DMRS and Record of Rights data. Whole digitized data is shown to villagers in "Jalsa-e-Aam" (Gramsabha) for their approval and also social auditing by end users.
- 100% success rate in respect to land titles till date is observed.
- In this way, all documents are available online to everybody.
- All districts are preparing their data.
- Change can be swiftly and easily updated.
- Simultaneously hard copy of updated digitized cadastral map is given to *Patwari, Tehsildar* and DRO as a proof of land record.
- After concealing whole digitized data of a particular village in a PDS device with a GPS chip, the same will be given to *Patwari. Patwari* can measure village land area correctly with PDS device using the GPS.

vi. *Benefits*

- Decrease land disputes.
- Updated land record data available online.
- Facilitate government development, infrastructural project by simplifying land acquisition process.
- Increase government revenue and the efficiency of government machinery.
- Time saving.
- With this model any state can modernize their land record efficiently.
- To resolve the following:
    - Millions of land disputes lying pending in courts.
    - Farmers going countless rounds of courts and administrative officers for searching proper records of their land.
- Government, Panchayat and common land is being encroached upon and trespassed.
- Compensation of land acquisition and natural calamities are not settled.
- Land administration and management is becoming difficult due to fragmentations of land parcels.
- Nobody can cheat in land selling.
- Crop loss due to natural calamities will be calculated through modernized land records.
- Land registrations are easily checked.

Abadi area survey under SVAMITVA scheme

The Svamitva scheme was first implemented in Sirsa, Haryana in order to have better land records, provide property rights to the residents of the village and have improved land revenue. The scheme became a success in the pilot phase and therefore, it was decided by Government of India to implement the scheme at a national level, so that every individual living in the most remote areas could get their land rights.

Laal Dora was first introduced in our country in 1908 by the Britishers. It was introduced in order to categorize that portion of land which is a part of village 'abadi' (habitation). These lands were to be used non-agricultural purposes only and were exempted from building by laws.

The government of Haryana has launched the campaign to make the villages of State free from 'Lal Dora'. The Lal Dora is a land in every village and city of the state which is used for residential purposes without any revenue record. Haryana is one of the six states selected by the Centre to run the pilot project. At least 2231 villages of 22 districts of the state are covered under the scheme till date.

Problems/issues faced at field level by practising the current survey and land recording systems

The digitization of the revenue maps of the villages have been carried out as per the revenue record and have been observed that in some of the adjoining villages there are either overlapping or a gap between the common village boundaries. In some of the villages, where the Killa lines of the adjoining villages are not same, the angles on the turns are also not matching and at a common point both the angles are different within the common boundaries between two adjoining villages.

The total area of a village as per the village revenue record and as per the digital output under NLRMP is also coming different. Though it is almost very near to the figure of the revenue department and may be due to the methodological implementation of the traditional tools at that time. On the basis of the modern tools and technologies those have been used under NLRMP, the issues of overlapping and gap areas as well as variations in total areas can be overcome with a positive intervention of government officials and the respective villagers in a judicious way.

The measurement for Murrbabandi and Kilabandi (rectangular measurement) must follow jareeb system only and in residential area, ETS and DGPS machine should be used.

Acts and Manuals for Survey and Settlement in Haryana

- Settlement Manual 1965
- Haryana Administration Manual 2013
- Haryana Land Records Manual 2013
- Punjab Land Revenue Act 1887

Additional Notes

---

1. Equipment with patwari for measurement:

i. Chain/Jareeb: A metalled chain of 10 Karam in length
ii. Cross: A wooden platform for drawing perpendiculars
iii. Flags: Flags are used for the monitoring of progress of demarcation in straight lines.

Survey equipments: The following survey equipments will be supplied to each Patwari, the cost thereof being met from the Patwari contingencies:

1 Chain with 10 iron pins
1 Cross staff
12 or 15 Bamboo flag staves
1 Plotting Scale
1 Board 75 X 60 centimeters

Note: In hill circles plane table and sighting and will be supplied in place of the board.

2. Units of Land Measurement

Length: (Instructions for converting local measure into hectares) Prior to the Agricultural year 1971-72, the land measure used in all revenue work varied in different parts of the State. From the Agricultural year 1976-77, the metric measure has been used along with the local measure of total *(mijan)* of the *hudbast* (village wise serial number in tehsil) at the end of the *jamabandi.*

The units of length and area in different parts of the State and their equivalent are as under:

I) Throughout the State from the agricultural year 1976-77 the following metric measures have been in use.

1 Meter	39.3701 inches.
1 Centare (Square meter)	1.19599 Square yards.
Are (100 Centares)	119.599 Square yards.
1 Hectare (100 Ares) ...	11959.9 Square yards

II) In all the areas consolidated on the basis of the Standard measure of a karam of 66 inches:

1 Karam (66 inches) ...	1.6764 meters
1 Sarsahi (Square karam) ...	2.81031696 Square meters
1 Marla (9 Sarsahis) ...	25.29285264 Square meters
1 Kanal (20 Marlas) ...	505.8570528 Square meters
1 Ghumao (Acre of ... 4840 Square yards-8 kanals)	4046.8564224 Square meters

III) In the area consolidated on the basis of the local measure and the non-consolidated area of Gurgaon, Rohtak, Faridabad and Panipat.

1 Karam of Gatha (57.157 inches)	1.4517878 meters
1 Biswansi (Sq. Karam or Sq. Gatha)	2.1076878 Square meters
1 Biswa (20 Biswansis)	42.153756 Square meters
1 Bigha (20 Biswas – 1008.33 Sq. yard)	843.07512 Square meters

***Area*:** Where the consolidation operation has been completed and record has been handed over to revenue department, scale adopted is 66 (inches) to a karam and killa

I) To get area from given lengths.

36x40 karam = 1440 sarsahi
9 sarsahi = 1 marla
1440/9= 160 marla
20 marla = 1 kanal
160/20= 8 kanal
8 kanal= 1 killa or acre or ghumao

II) To get a side when area and other side is given

8 kanal x 20= 160 marla
160 marla x 9= 1440 sarsahi
1440 sarsahi/36 = 40 karam

(Conversion of area of a killa into bigha and biswa [where the killa is 36x40 karam in the scale of 99 (inches) and bigha is in the scale of 66 (inches)].
1killa= 4840 sq. yards
1bigha= 3025 sq.yards
1sarsahi= 1sq karam or 1sq. gatha

4840 sq.yards x 5/8 = 3025 sq. yards
1440 sarsahi x 5/8 = 900 sarsahi/9 = 100 marla/20 =5 kanal =3025 sq. yard
160 marlax 5/8 = 5 kanal = 1 bigha = 325 sq. yard
8 kanal x 5/8 = 5 kanal =1 bigha = 3025 sq. yard
5 kana lx20 = 100 marla x 9 = 900 sarsahi = 3025 sq. yards or 1 bigha
8 kanal = 1 bigha 12 biswa in the scale of 99 inches
4840 sq. yard = 3025 sq. yard + 151.25x12 = 4840 sq.yards because 1 biswa = 151.25 sq. yards in the scale of 99 (inches)

Conversion of area from killa to bigha and biswa when killa is in the scale of 36x40 karam in the scale of 66 (inches) and bigha is in the scale of 57.157(inches)

1 bigha= 1008.33 sq.yards
4840 sq.yards x 5/24= 1008.33 sq. yards
8 kanal= 4 bigha 16 biswa= 1 acre
4840 sq. yards= 1008.33 sq. yards x 4+50.42 sq. yards x 16 = 4033.3 sq. yards + 806.7 sq. yards = 4840 sq. yards = 1 acre or 1 killa or 1 ghumao.

3. Useful terms for Land Survey and Settlement in Haryana

Metric Rod: The Patwari's metric rod should not be of wood, but of bar iron (about eight millimeter square). Two rods should be supplied to each Patwari. The field Kanungo is responsible for their agreement with his own rods. These should be kept safe in hollow bamboos.

Addas: At every village where a Patwari resides, there should be marked out on a level piece of uncultivated land a standard length (adda) exactly corresponding with the Patwari's 20 metres chain. The extreme ends should be marked by two pegs driven deep (60 centimeters, if possible) into the ground. The measurement of the adda should be reckoned from the outside edge of the peg to the inside edge of the other; that is to say, when the handle of one end of the chain is placed over one peg, the other end should touch the inside of the other peg. If the adda itself needs correction, it can be shortened by cutting from the outside of the pegs, or lengthened by cutting from the inside.

Importance is attached to the correct maintenance of these addas, and revenue officers in their visits to patwaris offices should see that the orders for their maintenance are duly observed and that the length of the adda is strictly accurate. Field Kanungo should be held responsible for any inaccuracies in the addas and for any neglect of the orders relating to them. Full instructions for preparation of these addas will be found in the Mensuration Manual.

Patwari's chain: The Patwari's chain should be made of soft iron and constructed exactly as directed in the Mensuration Manual. Variations of patterns are forbidden. Chains should be made up locally not at other distant workshops. In testing the length of a chain, see that it is well shaken out and stretched only to the tension at which it is used. Test either on the adda or by rods as may be convenient. In the latter case use two rods, placing them on the ground alternately and see that they touch truly.

Patwari's cross-staves: The Patwari's cross-staff – A pattern will be supplied to each district by the Director of Land Records. It should be made up locally, strictly in accordance with this pattern. Elaborations and additions to the pattern are forbidden.

Measuring flags for Patwari's: Bamboo flag-staves – A Patwari cannot survey on the square system with less than 12 or 15 flags. Of these 4 or 5 should be 450 centimeters high, and the rest three hundred centimeters. Each should have a pointed iron ferrule at foot, and completed in this way.

Plane-tables sometimes required: Plane-tables are necessary only for hill surveying. When necessary for this purpose, a pattern should be obtained from the Director of Land Records and they should be made up locally according to the pattern so supplied. Patwaris of plain villages require only a board, in size 75x60 centimeters strengthened on the underside with battens. Care should be taken to employ brass, not iron, in repairing the sockets, etc., of plane-tables.

Sighting Rods: Sighting rods are not required except in hill tracts, where it is necessary to use plane-table. In such case, a pattern should be obtained from the Director of Land Records and the sighting rods should be made up locally according to the pattern.

Mussavi: Original map, prepared for every revenue village at the time of settlement, showing position and boundaries of all fields.

Shajra Kistwar (*Field Map*): A field map for every revenue village is prepared at the time of the Settlement. The original map is called 'mussavi'. Its updated version is called 'shajra kistwar' and these are kept in safe custody in the Record Room. A wax copy called 'momi' is available in the Tehsil. All changes in field boundaries occurring due to partition, sale etc. attested in Mutation are entered from the Parat Sarkar Mutation onto the momi. A copy on cloth called 'latha' is kept and updated by the Patwari.

Shajra Nasb: Prepared in every estate at the time of settlement, it forms a part of record of rights. Shajra Nasb is a pedigree table showing succession to ownership rights occurring from time to time in an estate. It is revised after every five years along with Jamabandi and in the interval; changes occurring from time to time are reflected in the Patwari's copy through suitable references. The Shajra Nasb also serves as an index for locating an owner's accounts (Khata Numbers) in the Jamabandi. In the new Jamabandi owner's accounts are arranged as per arrangement in the Shajra Nasb. The name of owner in the Shajra Nasb is arranged according to caste and sub-caste.

Settlement: Settlement is a comprehensive term that covers all aspects of land survey and measurement, preparation of revenue records and assessment of land revenue.

Jamabandi (*Mutation Register*): All changes in title or interest are incorporated into the Jamabandi through attestation of mutation. The Patwari enters the mutations on the basis of a document/verbal information presented by the concerned parties for the change in title/interest on land. This information is first entered into the Patwari's Diary (Roznamcha Wakyati) giving serial number, date and then into the mutation register referencing the Roznamcha number. However, the final changes in the Jamabandi are made only after the Revenue officer has attested the mutation. The mutation form has 15 columns and every entry is given a Serial Number, which is called Mutation Number. This Mutation Number runs continuously from one settlement to another for each estate. The Mutation register is maintained by the Patwari and all entries are made in duplicate. The Patwari's copy (parat patwar) contains the brief substance of the Revenue Officer's order, while the other copy (parat sarkar) contains the detailed order and is kept in the Tehsil in separate estate-wise bundles. Whenever a mutation is entered, the Patwari makes a note in the remark column of the Jamabandi in pencil giving the Mutation No. and type of mutation. When the mutation is attested, he makes the entry in Red ink, giving Mutation No., type and date of attestation. When the new Jamabandi is written, all the mutations accepted are attached to the new Jamabandi for cross-reference and an index sheet linking the mutations to the Khatas is placed in the Jamabandi.

Jamabandi Register: It is prepared quinquennial in duplicate for every estate on the basis of entries existing and changes recorded on the Mutation Register, Khasra Girdawari Register and Fard Badr over a period of five years. It is the document to which a presumption of truth is attached. The form of the Jamabandi has 12 columns and gives Khewat/Khatoni number-wise information of total holding of each owner of land in a particular revenue estate. It also indicates cultivation, rent and revenue and other cesses payable on land and constitutes an up to date record of various rights in land. The new Jamabandi is prepared by the Patwari and is attested by the Revenue Office in a public meeting of local villages. Two copies of the revised Jamabandi are prepared, one copy is filed to the District Record Room and other copy remains with the Patwari. All changes in title/interests of the revenue estate coming into the notice of Revenue Authorities are duly reflected in the Jamabandi according to set procedures.

Khasra Girdawari: It is a register of harvest inspections unlike the Jamabandi, which is Khewat-wise, the Girdawari, is Khasra-wise. The Patwari conducts field to field harvest inspections every six months in the month of October and April. He records the plot-wise details regarding crop grown, land description and status of the cultivator This register is considered important as it acts as master file for the preparation of many returns and reports. This document is retained in the custody of Patwari for the period of 12 years after which it is retrieved from him and destroyed. No presumption of truth is attached to this record though entries in it are often used as evidence in courts. Changes in the tenancy however are made through mutations in view of Section 10-A on the Tenancy Act.

Lal Kitab (Village Note Book): Popularly known as "Lal Kitab" these are prepared at the time of settlement. The kitab has valuable information regarding crops grown in the estate, soil classification, area under different crops, land use, transfers in land, wells and other means of irrigation in the village and abstract of the livestock and cattle census in the village. The data is updated regularly through harvest inspections and revisions of other records, which are the main source of the data to this kitab. These Lal Kitabs are prepared at village, tehsil and district level and maintained in the Patwari Office, Kanungo and Sadar Kanungo respectively.

Shajra Kishtwar: Original copy of the field map prepared at the time of settlement of consolidation is kept in Tehsil Record Room. The patwari has another copy of the map with him, which is prepared on cloth for working purposes. The changes in the fields usually occur in two sets of circumstances viz. the transfer by way of mortgage with possession, sale, gift or exchange etc. for which mutation entry is made and disposed of the competent authority and secondly through separate cultivation of shareholders in joint holdings or a permanent changes in classification of land. The former set of changes in the field map are reflected on the back of the relevant mutation sheet through Tatima Shajra or supplementary maps. The latter set of changes usually comes to notice through periodic harvest inspections.

Instructions contained in para 4.24 of the Punjab Land Records Manual stipulate that in the year when a new Jamabandi is to be prepared the patwari while doing the Kharif and Rabi Girdawari of the concerned estate will carefully observe and take note of the latter type of changes and the fields which have undergone change of a subsisting nature will be X marked by him in the Girdwari in column number 10,15 and 20 of the Register as the case may be. At the end of the Girdawari, a list of fields number so marked, is prepared and passed on to the Patwaris for measurements and preparation of new maps on mapping sheets of the size of the Jamabandi. The dimensions and the area of the new fields are made out on the back of the mapping field.

The new field numbers are given a survey number according to a set of procedure. For example, a survey number is represented by the rectangle number and killa number. A rectangle covers 25 killas of one acre each. The rectangle number is indicated in red ink and the killa number is indicated in blank ink. Thus field number is written as 2//4 means killa number 4 lies in rectangle number 2. If due to some transfer, the killa number 4 is splits in two fields, the new fields number will be 2//4/1 and 2//4/2. If field no 2//4/1 is further undergoes a change and splits in two new fields, it will be numbered as 2//4/1/1 and 2//4/1/2. The patwari incorporates these changes simultaneously in his copy of map. The tatima plotted on the mapping sheets are bound with new Jamabandi and consigned. At the time of consignment of Jamabandi, the patwari brings his own copy of map, amends the original copy of the map lying in the Tehsil. However, temporary changes relating to mortgage, redemption and cultivation arrangements are not transplanted to the original copy. Thus at a particular point of time, the original copy lying in tehsil record will reflect the position as on the date of the consignment of the last Jamabandi while patwari's copy will normally reflect the present position.

Latha (Field Book): Popularly named as Shajra. Patwari keeps a copy of the Shajra on Cloth called 'Latha'. It gives survey numbers and dimension of a field, now-a-days usually prepared on the scale 40 Karam to one Inch. It is prepared at the time of settlement or consolidation. Original copy is retained in Tehsil record room and is updated every five years. Patwari's copy is kept up-to-date through field inspection and incorporation of all transfers attested from time to time.

Shajra Nasab: Prepared in every estate at the time of settlement and forming a part of record-of-right. Sharja Nasab is pedigree table showing succession to ownership rights occurring from time to time in the estate. It is revised and brought up-to-date every five years and in the interval changes occurring from time to time are reflected in patwari's copy through suitable references.

The Sharja Nasab, prepared at the time of settlement, is a source of information regarding the previous proprietary, history of estate and the devolution of proprietary rights from time to time. One copy of it along with Jamabandi prepared at the settlement is consigned to district record. The Second copy remains with Patwari and is retrieved from him after coming in force of the new settlement, when it is kept permanently in Tehsil or District Record Room.

2.6

Karnataka

Dr. Ashok Sanganal

History of Land Survey in Karnataka

Every year 10th April is celebrated as National Land Survey Day in India to commemorate the beginning of scientific land survey by British Col. William Lambton on 10-04-1802. This survey had commenced from Marina beach in Madras and is known as the great trigonometrical survey of India. Although earth is round and undulated, it is the responsibility of surveyors to ensure 100 per cent accuracy in the measurements and mapping of land by creating an overall survey framework in which topographical and revenue survey details are incorporated. The state of Karnataka from pre-British period till date had undergone huge transformation in the land survey practices from the simple methods of measurements using chain to the latest survey technologies such as, ETS, GIS, GPS, Drone/UAV. It is worthy to note that the state government launched series of programmes to bring all land property records that were earlier surveyed by different methods such as chain survey, plane table survey, cross-staff survey, compass survey that were preserved in paper format for a long time, have now been completely digitized and are easily accessible to the Landowners at almost no cost and time without errors.

The old preserved land survey records were subject to frequent wear and tear due to their day to day repeated usage leading to deterioration. But they have still remained the basic land records for today's revenue administration. For instance, cadastral surveys conducted in those days were to serve the limited purpose of revenue taxation on agricultural lands. Also different surveying practices were adopted to the convenience of administration.

The collection of land revenue and the existence of the institutions of the state have been coterminous. A historical analysis of ancient policy suggests that tax on land played a pivotal part in the evolution and maintenance of the systems of governance. In ancient times, land revenue was possibly the only source from which the entire income of the State was derived. Further, its incidence was on a large section of the population as a major proportion of the people relied on land for their livelihood and existence. Thus, tax on land proved to be the primary source of the State's wealth and the Revenue Department was established to regularise it. The Revenue Department is the oldest department and considered as the mother of all departments with its history from pre-British period.

The Kings derived their revenue only from the lands. More cultivable land means more land revenue. To secure regular income from all arable lands year after year, the kings needed land settlement and administration. The British gave importance to reform land administration. In India, the systematic surveys were started during British period. They have created and maintained a wonderful system of land management which is very relevant even today, even after 150 years. The department has continued the British legacy both in measurement system and in management of records.

The historical background of the survey and land records system in India shows a bewildering variety from state to state. Even within a state, also there are many variety of surveys and land records systems.

The department aims at preserving and safeguarding various forms of rural and urban land records through computerisation and modern technology in order to facilitate easy and speedy delivery of services related to land records to the farmers and urban residents.

The department is thus responsible for the preparation of records relating to agricultural land, and identifying and preserving the property rights and boundaries of villages, towns and cities in excess of the population according to the Land Revenue Act. As a result of this, urban governance work has been implemented in almost all the cities and towns in the state, including the Belgaum divisional villages and towns.

Pre-British Era

For the first time 1831 soon after assuming the administration of Kingdom of Mysore by the British, it was decided to collect the land revenue based on measurement and survey of land in place of *Ryotwari* and *Bhatayi* systems which were considered to be unscientific and arbitrary.

An hereditary right of occupation was attached to all *kandayam* lands[34], and as long as the occupant paid the Government dues, he had an absolute tenant right, so that when the Government required any occupied land for a public purpose, they had to pay compensation fixed either by mutual consent or under the Land Acquisition Regulation.

Complaints regarding indiscriminate land revenue in Malnad regions in Karnataka namely for areca nut and other crops was reviewed by the survey superintendents in more than 14,000 gardens and plantations. As a result of which the land survey work in the entire Mysore state was completed in 1899.

---

[34] The *kandayam* lands were held on annual leases or pattas but the assessment was seldom altered and hardly ever raised. Under the batayi system, the land was held direct from Government but the share of Government was paid in grain. A hereditary right of occupation was attached to all *Kandayam* lands, and as long as the occupant paid the Government dues he had an absolute tenant right, so that, when the Government required any occupied land for a public purpose, they had to pay compensation fixed either by mutual consent or under the Mysore Land Acquisition Act VII of 1894 as amended from time to time.

For purposes of assessment all cultivated land in Mysore state was classed either as kushki (dry), tari (wet), or bagayat (garden) and plantation. The first class is cultivated with dry grains which are entirely dependent on the rainfall; the second with rice, sugar-cane or such other staple productions that require artificial irrigation and the third with coconut, areca nut tree and other garden produce. The fourth with coffee and tea plantation. The land measures in Mysore at that time corresponded with the measures of capacity and depended on the area of land which could be sown with a given quantity of seed. The measures therefore varied greatly on dry and on wet or garden land. This mode of measurement, however, afforded incompetent or dishonest revenue officials, plausible excuses for laxity of practice and fraud.

After much consideration and discussion, it was decided in 1863 to introduce a regular system of survey and settlement into the State on the lines of that in force in Bombay, as this was found cheaper and more expeditious than the Madras system. In 1863, Haihara taluk in Karnataka was taken up and survey work was done by land classification, revenue settlement rules, appoint of surveyors to address the complaints. The Survey and Settlement Department started work in 1863-64 with the following objects, namely

- The regulation of the customary land tax so as to secure an adequate revenue to Government
- The progressive development of the agricultural resources
- The preservation of all proprietary and other rights connected with the soil.

Until the year 1888, however, there was no codified law regulating the land revenue administration of Mysore. The Mysore Land Revenue Code (IV of 1888) supplied this deficiency and this was the principal law relating to Revenue Officers to the assessment and recovery of land revenue and to other matters connected with the Land Revenue administration.

A register called 'The Settlement Register' showing the area and assessment of each survey number, the name of the registered occupant were prepared by the Survey Office.

During British Period

The mode of assessment and collection underwent a change when the British took over the administration. Lands were measured and village records of lands were gradually built up. Thus, closely linked to the collection of land revenue was the creation of an array of land records wherein collection of revenue could be systematized and recorded. Sir Thomas Munro, Governor of Madras (1820-1827) had said, "In India whoever regulates the assessment of land, really holds in his hand the main spring of the country." This is true till this day.

Different systems of survey and classification were followed in different regions of the state before the unification of Karnataka. But survey methods are invariable, scientific and of universal application, therefore little opportunity for basic variation in the system prevailed. In Old Mysore regions of Bombay and

Hyderabad areas, original survey has been completed by Cross-Staff and Chain. In Bellary, South Canara (Madras areas) and Coorg District the original survey has been completed by Theodolite and Chain (*khandam*[35] and diagonal offset system). The survey records thus prepared differ from region to region and were completed in the following years in respect of original survey and revision survey.

	Original Survey		*Revision Survey*	
Regions	*From*	*To*	*From*	*To*
Old Mysore	1863	1899	1900	1917
Bombay Karnataka	1840	1863	1906	1921
Madras area	1863	1904	1923	1935
Hyderabad Karnataka	1875	1888	1906	1916
Coorg	1806	1816	1906	1912

Survey Documents prepared during 1863-1899

Original survey tippan is a hand drawn sketch representing the shape of the individual lands along with measurements such that the land is divided into triangles and trapeziums. Each individual land within the village boundary is given serial numbers are *chalta* numbers (a serial number of each individual land within the village boundary) are given to each land. Names of the *Khardadars*[36] are also recorded.

Original survey pakka books: Original survey *pakka* book is a drawn sketch of the original tippan and the area is calculated by drawing the area of the triangles and trapeziums. *Chalta* numbers and names of *Khardadars* are recorded.

Original survey Prathi books: In which, Classification of the Soil is made and recorded. Survey numbers are given against the *chalta* numbers recorded in the *tippani* books (The sketch of a number not drawn to scale but showing the measurements, the book containing *tippans*) for individual properties.

Phoot Kharab means a piece or pieces of land classed as unarable and included in a Sy. No. Some agricultural land contains certain interior land which cannot be cultivated which are brought under Phoot Kharab at the time of classification. Phoot Kharab includes lands in a field covered with buildings, burial ground which may be disused and brought under plough, track and paths which are not used. Phoot Kharab details and type of fields are recorded. (i.e. dry, wet garden and plantation). (As per Rule 20 of the Karnataka Land Revenue Rules, 1966)

[35] The maximum error possible in theodolite surveys is 6feet a mile in co-ordinates under the present system, each village boundary is traversed and a number of interior traverses run, dividing each village into sub circuits, called *Khandams* of from 100 to 250 acres.

[36] the occupant or the eldest or principal of several joint occupants, whose name is entered in the government records as holding un-alienated land whether in person or by his co-occupant, tenant, agent, servant or other legal representatives.

Resurvey Documents prepared during 1900-1917

On 24-10-1900 resurvey work was taken up in the entire Mysore state by adopting new land revenue code mainly to correct the errors in the area, survey numbers and boundaries. Resurvey was although considered as unimportant since original operations were to be considered good and accurate, and pointed out that at least a reclassification of water supply to wet and garden lands was absolutely necessary in the interest of both the Ryots and of Government. Following resurvey works were carried out.

Resurvey Tippans: On the basis of traverse data, individual land is measured in the respective district with maximum and minimum extent of area being allowed. Serial numbers or *chalta* numbers are given to each land. Names of the *Khardadars* are recorded.

Resurvey Pakka books: Measurements of the each *chalta* numbers are recorded, and the area calculated. *Chalta* number and names of *Khardadars* are recorded.

Resurvey Prathi books:

(i) In which classification of the soil is made and recorded.

(ii) Survey numbers are given against the *chalta* numbers recorded in the *tippani* books for individual properties.

(iii) Phoot Kharab details and type of field are recorded (i.e., Dry, Wet Garden). (As per Rule 20 of the Karnataka Land Revenue Rules 1966).

Survey Documents prepared during 1928-1950 and onwards till date

Hissa survey Tippans: The land of each of the tenants is surveyed with details of area, name of the holder, type etc., with a survey number is called *hissa* survey.

Hissa survey Pakka books: It contains details such as survey number, *hissa* number (a piece of land which has been assigned a Survey Number is divided into multiple Sub-Divisions, each Sub-Division is assigned a "*Hissa* Number"), name of the holder, area, dimensions, *phodi* details etc.

Reclassification Prathi books prepared between 1958-1966

- *Prathi* book: Original survey *pakka* book is a drawn sketch of the original tippan and the area is calculated by drawing the area of the triangles and trapeziums
- *Bhagayat taktha*: It means agricultural land other than garden and plantation land
- *Darwari*: The ranking of the land and assigning of *bhagane* (16 anas = 1Rupee) based on soil fertility at a depth of *mola*[37] (1.53ft) and water facility. This method is called dharwari ranking.

---

[37] soil fertility and water facility of the agricultural land at a depth of 1.53 ft.

- *Classer Register*: The land is divided into six classes based on the water availability for crops. For example classification is done in the following manner
  1st class – water flow availability for crops up-to end of April
  1 ½ class - water flow availability for crops up-to April 15th
  2nd class - water flow availability for crops up-to end of March
  2 ½ class - water flow availability for crops up-to March 15th
  3rd class - water flow availability for crops up-to end of February
  3 ½ class - water flow availability for crops up-to February 15th
  4th class - water flow availability for crops up-to end of January
  4 ½ class - water flow availability for crops up-to January 15th
  5th class- water flow availability for crops up-to end of December
- Statement showing the bifurcation of soil and water assessment
- *Akarbandh*: Akarbandh is a record that describes the total area of the land comprising all survey numbers with different classes of land namely dry, wet, garden and plantation including the revenue for acre water facility, approach road, streams, etc.

Kanara system was followed in the North Kanara region of Bombay region. In the Kanara system land was classified into Rice (further classified into sweet and salt), Khushki (dry), Garden, *Pulan*[38] and Mithagar (salt-pans).

In the Southern Maratha Country System different systems were adopted in each of the Belgaum, Dharwar and Bijapur districts. The Dharwar system was introduced into the Deccan Survey by Colonel Andersen about the year 1877, after which it was universally employed for the classification of rice lands.

In Bombay-Karnataka land survey methodology carried out during Chatrapati Shivaji period was adopted. Survey was done using chain and cross-stop and area was measured in acres and guntas.

In the Madras region of Karnataka in 1863 topographical survey for village mapping was initiated. Triangles, plane table, block map, D&O method (dividing the area into triangles) and trapeziums were used to measure the land areas.

In 1853, Hyderabad-Karnataka under the king Salarjang, agriculture land and boundary measurements were carried out and bigha (3600 sq.ft.) revenue system was adopted and farmers tilling the land were encouraged to own the land on agreement for three years.

The second reclassification (1958-1966) survey work was carried out to identify land-based changes in the crop, water source and increase or decrease in the area of land under cultivation on the farm. *Hissa* survey work (1928-1945)

---

[38] *Pulan* defined as "the sandy plains situated in the immediate neighbourhood of the sea and tidal creeks; they are sometimes found quite bare, producing nothing, sometimes covered with *kaju* and *undi* trees, and are generally easily converted into rice land.

carried out (all land records of alaida tenants brought under one survey number). The main purpose of reclassification survey work during 1958-1966 was for assessment of agriculture land based on water resource and cropping pattern to identify and facilitate increase or decrease of karab land.

After Independence and Unification of Karnataka State

The Department of Survey Settlement and Land Record is one of the oldest departments in the state of Karnataka. After the unification of Karnataka in 1956, different regions of Old Mysore region, Bombay region, Madras region, Hyderabad region and Kodagu region were merged together to form the State of Karnataka (then known as the Mysore State). As most of the original survey in the state was completed before independence, only maintenance, revision survey and settlement works were taken up.

As different procedures were prevailing in the integrated area, there was an urgent need to evolve a unified procedure. A Revised Survey and Settlement Manual was prepared vide government order RD-11-SYS-60 dated 27 April 1960 with common procedure for all the integrated areas. In order to bring uniformity in survey procedures the following were adopted:

- Powers and duties of the officers and officials were defined
- The terminology of technical terms used in the survey were defined
- Decentralisation of survey record and preservation of the same at district and sub-division headquarters. Two fold benefits were achieved by this system. Firstly, the records were within the easy reach of the ryots. Secondly, it has facilitated the departmental officers to function and dispose the land related cases promptly.
- Introduction of 'A' and 'B' record system. Technical records were preserved in the survey office on the Bombay pattern. According to this system the present records of the villages were to be sorted out in two parts viz. A and B list (pherists) and preserved in two separate buildings. If any record listed in any of the lists is damaged or lost, the same could be built up on the basis of record listed in other lists
- Introduction of Plane Table Survey. According to government order No. RD 369 SST 58 dated 11 June 1959, all future surveys were adopted the plane table survey method.
- In accordance with the Standard Weights and Measures Act of 1956 final figures of area and measurements were worked out in the standard weights and measures.
- The dual control of Revenue and Land Records Department over the Taluk Surveyors were abolished. All works relating to survey, *hudbust* (fixation of boundary), *phodi*, mutation etc., were allotted by a single agency at Sub-Division level.
- The different forms which were unclear have been standardised to save the duplication of printing of forms, labour and government money.

- The different procedures followed in the matter of maintenance of survey and boundary marks under the provisions of different statutes in force in the integrated areas have since been made uniform in the entire State of Karnataka consequent on the enforcement of the Karnataka Land Revenue Act, 1964 with effect from 01 April 1964, which has repealed these erstwhile enactments such as Madras Survey and Boundaries Act 1923, the Coorg Land and Revenue Regulation 1898, the Mysore Land Revenue Code 1888, the Hyderabad Land Revenue Code 1898 and Bombay Land Revenue Code 1879.

Current Practices of Land Surveying

The administration of land in the state of Karnataka is dealt by three levels of organisations namely Survey, Settlement and Land Records Department, Department of Stamps and Registration and Tahsildar Offices at taluk level. All these three organisations are under the administrative control of the Department of Revenue, Government of Karnataka. Transactions in land require the coordinated efforts of these three organisations and involve sharing of data between the respective application systems manually or through interfaces between the same. The basic unit of reference for all transactions is the survey number. *Survey number* means a portion of land of which the area and other particulars are separately entered under an indicative number in the land records.

It is the duty of the department to index every change in the land usage and ownership periodically owing to developmental reasons and the tax is collected by the government as per the scientific assessment of revenue.

Agricultural land of the individuals will be measured and survey numbers are given based on the classification of land and revenue to be paid to the government is fixed as per the Karnataka land revenue survey manual Vol-2, Part-2 and Chapter-4.

When is the survey taken up?

When a portion of a survey number or of a sub-division of a Survey number is claimed by a tenant, a proper survey should be done indicating the portion and calculating its correct extent and mentioning the boundaries of its location. The survey should be done before the tribunal passes its order. Otherwise many defects with regard to its extent, survey number may creep in and later resulting in several problems at the time of incorporation in land records by survey department. The tribunal alone is empowered decide whether the land is tenanted or not and the applicant is entitled to be registered as occupant or not.

Survey Instruments and Methods used in the State

In Karnataka, for land revenue survey including city survey, the following survey instruments are used.

Chain and Cross-staff: The principle behind this type of survey is mainly to divide the area to be surveyed into triangles and trapeziums thereby making the irregular figure into simple geometric figure and hence the area.

Chain is used for taking linear measurement in the field. As per Standards of weights and measurement Act, 1956 metric chains are being used, the length of chain, being 20m, comprising of 100 links. Each link thus measures 20cm. Types of chains used:

Guntur chain: It is 66 feet long and divided into 100 links. Each link measures 0.66 feet or 7.92 inches.

Anna chain: It is 33 feet long and divided into 16 equal parts. Each part is used to be called as one Anna. This was used during Original Survey, Resurvey.

Links Chain: It is 33 feet long and divided into 50 links. To facilitate counting brass rings were provided for every five links and circular tally for 25 links.

Metric Chain: As per Standards of Weights and Measurement Act, 1956, metric chains are being used, the length of chain, being 20m, comprising of 100 links. Each link thus measures 20cm.

Cross Staff: It is an instrument used for setting out right angles from the baseline to offsets. A wooden square block (4"x4"x 2") is mounted over an iron rod of 4 feet to 5 feet in length, the bottom end being sharp.

Diagonal and Offset System: In this method of survey, in addition to simple triangulation concept offsets are also being taken to bend points with the help of cross staff. Even today, the same method is adopted in old madras area of Karnataka. The area is computed by using Area-square paper also termed as Tal-square paper.

Plane Table Survey: Plane tabling is a graphical method of survey. The distinctive feature is the field observations, measurements and plotting proceed simultaneously, i.e., instead of recording the angle and distance of lines in the field and plotting them afterwards, we draw their directions in field itself on the plane table sheet. When chain survey method becomes inadequate, plane tabling survey becomes necessary. Regions in Karnataka, where the Plane Tabling is mainly used:

- Coorg district and some *Malnad* areas.
- Belgaum division area for maintenance survey.
- Detail survey mapping in city survey work.

The plane table consists of:

1) Plane table with tripod
2) Alidade
3) Trough Compass
4) Plumbing Fork
5) Spirit Level
6) Drawing Paper with Rain Proof Cover.

THEODOLITE

Compass Survey: In compass surveying, the horizontal angles are measured with the help of a magnetic compass in addition to the linear measurements with a chain or a tape. As a magnetic compass is not a precise angle-measuring instrument, the compass survey is not very accurate. However, it is more accurate than a chain survey.

Theodolite Survey: A theodolite is a very precise instrument for measuring horizontal and vertical angle and topographic survey. The theodolite surveys can be broadly classified into two types: Traverse and Triangulation.

Prior to the advent of modern surveying instruments, distances were usually measured manually by taping and chaining. Taping and chaining process in the stony, thorny, hilly rough terrain were really painstaking process. Angles were also measured and recorded manually by instruments like sextant and theodolite. The measurement of distances and angles with the old conventional instruments were really hard and laborious work if the accurate results were desired. Electronic Total Station (ETS) is deployed in the state for accurate measurements and all recent survey and resurvey works both in urban and rural areas especially in the city and village survey as part UPOR (Urban Property Ownership Records) and RPOR (Rural Property Ownership Records).

Electronic Total Station Instrument: The major advancement in surveying in recent years is the development of Electronic Total Station instrument. The total station instruments have become most common and certainly also one of the most important instruments used by modern surveyors.

Total Station Survey: A total station is an electronic/optical instrument used in modern surveying. The total station is an electronic theodolite (transit) integrated with an electronic distance meter (EDM), plus internal data storage and/or external data collector. Total stations are use for:

- Control Survey (Traverse).
- Detail survey i.e., data collection.

- Height measurement (Remove elevation measurement – REM).
- Fixing of missing pillars (or) Setting out (or) Stake out.
- Resection.
- Area calculations, etc.
- Remote distance measurement (RDM) or Missing line measurement (MLM).
- Coordinate Geometry (COGO)

Advantages of Total Station Survey
Among others following are a few of the important advantages:

1. The chief advantages of total station are the speed and accuracy.
2. Quick setting of the instrument on the tripod using optical/laser plummet.
3. On-board area computation programme to compute the area of the field.
4. Greater accuracy in area computation and mapping.
5. Integration of database (exporting map to GIS package).

Disadvantages of Total Station Survey
Among others following are a few of the important disadvantages:

1. The instrument is costly.
2. For surveys using ETS, skilled personnel are required.
3. Visibility of the target reflector will always be a problem over significant distances of broken or heavily vegetated terrain.
4. For an overall check of the survey, it will be necessary to return to office and prepare the drawings using appropriate software.

Photogrammetric Survey: Photogrammetry is the science of taking measurements with the help of photographs. Photogrammetric Surveys are generally used for topographic mapping of vast areas.

EDM Survey (Electronic Distance Measurement): Trilateration is a type of triangulation in which all the three sides of each triangle are measured accurately with EDM instruments.

Modern Surveying Practices Deployed in Karnataka

Need for Modern Survey in Cities

Urban local bodies in Karnataka were maintaining land property records in the form of 'Khatha' for the purpose of tax collection, which really were not the Record of Rights (RoR) or Record of Tenancy and Crops (RTC) as issued in respect of agricultural land. Therefore, GoK extended the existing city survey system to all the major cities of the state as UPOR (Urban Property Ownership Records). The main objective is to ensure accurate survey of private and government properties like buildings, houses, roads, playgrounds, parks etc., generate a survey sketch including other property related documents and accord permanent identification numbers to each property. Five cities were selected on a pilot basis Mangaluru, Ballary, Mysuru, Hubballi-Dharwad and Shivamogga. Project is implemented through Public Private Partnership (PPP) – BOOT model for city survey work. While the Private Service Provider (PSP) is in-charge of creation of both spatial and non-spatial data under the supervision of survey settlement department, Technical Service Provider (TSP) is to provide software.

Surveying Methodology in Cities under UPOR

The spatial data involved establishment of control networks via, primary, secondary and tertiary control points and maps. The non-spatial data includes: i) Collection of data and verification of documents, ii) Measurement of properties, iii) Preparation of index mapping, iv) Master database, v) Collection of original documents, vi) Scanning of documents, vii) Preparation of property cards. The photos of the control points taken from the field are given below.

Primary Control Point, PCP

Secondary Control Point, SCP

The city survey includes: a) establishing control networks, b) conducting a detail survey of each property, c) title enquiry process and preparation of property cards, d) citizen service delivery.

Deployment of ETS instrument: ETS instrument is deployed for ensuring accuracy and exact measurement of properties. A base map on scale 1:20,000 was compiled for Mysuru city using Survey of India maps and satellite images. Survey of India established primary control points (PCP) that were plotted on the base map. The PCP and SCP (Secondary Control Points) were extended to mainline traverse (MT) and secondary line traverse (ST) by providing tertiary control points (TCP). Main line traverses commence from PCP and SCP and get converged into PCP and SCP network using ETS for securing high degree of precision and accuracy. TCPs are set up in such a way that there is at least one TCP within a range of 100 meters from the other one with a fair inter-visibility and the total station readings are taken. Since each individual property is unique in terms of coordinates, the measurement of entire city of Mysuru was divided into 11 zones, 50 sectors and 42 villages. 32 surveyors were appointed by the Department of Survey Settlement for measurement of individual properties. Government surveyors were deployed to identify property owners which are critical to determining the exact boundaries if the properties and private partner is not allowed to take decision in this regard. Values are fixed for all properties including roads, lakes and public establishments in the city for measuring individual plots/sites and houses. Boundaries are fixed using ETS to arrive at coordinates. Finally, using UPOR vectorisation software, detailed survey map for the entire city survey jurisdiction depicting houses, roads, public establishments generated. This is followed by validation of properties randomly by selecting 5000 properties in each sector. As per the coordinates drawn using ETS, variation between one per cent minimum and two per cent maximum are ignored. The entire sector is resurveyed in case the variation is 10 per cent in each sector. In the last stage, property documents were collected from Mysuru Urban Development Authority, City Corporation, Housing Board, Housing Societies, Private developers, individuals and all other owners and these were scanned by UPOR software before porting the same and master date base is generated. Property cards are generated. The UPOR certificates are delivered to the individual owners after verification of the original documents in UPOR Centres established in the respective cities. The status of implementation of this scheme in three cities (up to 2020-21) is given in the table below:

Progress of UPOR -2020-21

City	*Total number of properties measured is*	*Number of draft P.R. cards prepared*	*Total number of properties stored in the record of ownership*
Mysuru	3,23,616	1,75,937	2,19,123
Shivamogga	1,01,389	64,623	73,832
Mangaluru	1,59,000	67,213	89,641

Source: Survey Settlement and Land Record Department, GoK

Now the government has made UPOR certificates mandatory for all transactions involving urban properties. In the absence of this certificate no transactions on the property will be allowed by the government.

Resurvey Methodology using Drone/UAV Technology in Villages in Karnataka

MoU is signed between Government of Karnataka and Survey of India to implement this project using Drone. Initially pilot survey of urban properties was undertaken in Jaynagar 4th Block of Bangalore. Around 6000 properties are mapped and finalization of ownership by the SSLR department staff is under progress. Establishment of GCP (Ground Control Points) to carry out resurvey in Ramanagara and Tumkur district is completed. Drone flying was started in both the districts. Around 800sq. km is measured and surveyed under Drone by Survey of India (SoI). The data collected for 10 villages from SoI is under the process of finalization by the SSLR department.

SVAMITVA – Survey of Villages and Mapping with Improved Technology in Village Area

This scheme commenced on 24 April 2020 aims at providing an integrated property validation solution for rural India. The demarcation of inhabitant land in rural areas would be done using Drone surveying technology in collaboration with Ministry of Panchayat Raj, GoI, State Panchayat Raj and State Revenue Department.

The main objective is to create "Record of Rights" of properties within habitats and issuance of Rural Property Ownership Records to the owners. Apart from demarcation of individual rural property, other Gram Panchayat and community assets like village roads, ponds, canals, open spaces, school, Anganwadi, health sub-centers, etc. would also be surveyed and GIS maps would be created. Further, these GIS maps and spatial database would also help in preparation of accurate work estimates for various works undertaken by Gram Panchayats and other Departments of State Government. These can also be used to prepare better-quality Gram Panchayat Development Plan (GPDP). Karnataka state has been selected as one of the states in the first phase of implementation with the target of 16,600 villages during the year 2020-21. State Government has selected 16 districts covering 16,543 villages for the year 2020-21.

The following departments are the stakeholders for implementing the project under the guidance of GoI:

- Revenue Department (SSLR) – is the nodal department in implementing the project
- Panchayat Raj Department – is the major beneficiary of this project
- Survey of India (SoI) – Drone survey and mapping using GIS

SoI will establish the Continuous Operation Reference System (CORS) network and measure the habitat area using drone technology and mapping (digitization) will be done under the guidance of Survey Settlement Land Records (SSLR) department and submit the map for validation. Once SSLR validates the maps, draft property cards are generated and issued to the owners by the SSLR department. This is followed by calling of objections and if no objections are received, final RPOR (Rural Property Ownership Record) is issued to the beneficiaries as prescribed under KLR Act, 1964 and Rules, 1969.

Initiatives taken on Land Survey and its related Services to the Citizens

- *Digitisation of Village Maps:* **The work of digitising all village maps has been started in t**he state in collaboration with Karnataka State Remote Sensing Application Centre, Bengaluru in the year 2006. A total of 32,664 village maps have been digitised out of 33,891 village maps. The digitised village maps are available for general public at https://landrecords.karnataka.gov.in/revenue maps online.
- *Phodi Mukta Abhiyana*: *Phodi* means bifurcation of land by dividing a survey number into many parts, once a survey number is divided it is given a temporary number known as *phodi* number and then a *hissa* number. In the year September 2015, Karnataka started a drive to make agriculture lands free from *phodi*. This drive is taken to convert many RTCs which are having multiple ownership into single ownership.
- *Aakar Bandh Digitisation*: *Aakar Bandh* is a document containing full details, such as the survey number, its extent, revenue payable, etc. Digitisation of 28,136 village *aakar bandh* documents was already completed out of a total 30,014 documents taken up across 177 taluks in the state. The surveyors of the survey settlement department along with private partner are executing the project.
- *Sameeksha Mobile App*: This mobile app is developed to enable surveyors for speedy measurement and delivery of day-to-day works related to land records in the form of computerised maps and record. The work was started in the year 2018 and ₹400 lakh has been approved by the government to procure mobile devices for the surveyors and for other works.
- *Dishaank*: *Dishaank* is a mobile app which helps the citizen to see the survey number details of any spot by mere tapping a screen. It was started in the year 2018. Under this project around 30,662 village maps were digitised in collaboration with Karnataka State Remote Sensing Applications Centre. This application lets users know the survey number and owner details of his current location and get village maps. It also allows surveyors to give feedback on survey number details and get to know their land details like owner details and area of their land.
- *Mojini*: *Mojini* is a web based Internet application to regulate all the survey activities of the department. It gives easy access to information through the Internet and Mobile phones. It is implemented across the State in coordination with *Nadakacheri* and involves both Survey and Revenue staff. It helps in comparing both RTC and *Aakar bandh* area data. It is useful

for management Information System Reports for Deputy Commissioners, Assistant Commissioners, DDLR's and Tahsildar.

Below are the services provided in the *Mojini* application:

1. Survey department circulars
2. A web based Internet application to regulate all the survey activities of the department. (www.bhoomojini.karnataka.gov.in/sslr)
3. Easy access of any information through the Internet and Mobile phones.
4. Implemented across the State in coordination with *Nadakacheri.*
5. Involvement of both Survey and Revenue staff.
6. Piecemeal approach for matching both RTC and *Aakarbandh* area data.
7. Management Information System Reports for Deputy Commissioners, Assistant Commissioners, DDLR's and Tehsildar
8. The status of application by entering the application number.
9. The status of allotment by entering the application number.
10. To view 11E sketch, alienation and *phodi* sketch.
11. To view village map (revenue map)
12. *Mojini* reports of disputed cases
13. *Mojini* MIS report.

- *Tatkal Phodi Yojane*: Tatkal *Phodi* Yojane was started in the year 2008 to facilitate speedy disposal of *phodi* in all taluks in the state. The applications for tatkal *phodi* measurements are received at the hobli level Atal Ji Jansnehi centres through online *Mojini* application. The measurement of *phodi* land and related works are carried out and delivered to the farmers online through *Mojini.*
- *Pahani online i-RTC*: Pahani Online is simply getting the original Record of Rights, Tenancy and Crops on the Internet anywhere and anytime. A citizen can pay ₹10 online per RTC and get his/her RTC. For the first time in the country, this unique initiative was done by the Government of Karnataka.
- *E-Swathu*: E-Swathu is a Government of Karnataka scheme that helps to see ownership details of properties. This is a web application used by the department of Rural Development and Panchayath Raj for issue of property records at Gram Panchayats.

Concluding Remarks

The chain, cross-staff and plane table survey carried out earlier manually are time consuming and expensive. All the agricultural land surveyed with these methods were in paper format and hence were subject to wear and tear. Therefore, the government of Karnataka launched series of programmes to resurvey the lands using latest survey methods and digitise the survey records by creating master data base. The latest survey methods such as ETS, GIS, GPS,

RS and UAV/Drone technologies adopted in urban and rural areas in the state for resurveying of land properties have been able to store the land records in the digital form and thereby enabling the farmers and urban Landowners to seek error free land property ownership documents at their convenience without any hassle. Drone technology adopted for surveying of urban and village land and properties through UPOR and RPOR helped the administration for speedy and error free mapping along with ETS, GIS and chain survey for ensuring accurate measurement of property boundaries of each individual land property. It is seen that wherever drone technology is used for surveying, ETS and chain surveying were also deployed in order to ensure accuracy of measurements on the ground.

Plane table survey method is the most used and suitable method for surveying and preparing small scale maps. In this method, all possible human and machine errors can be eliminated as the surveying and plotting are done simultaneously in the field.

Chain surveying is the simplest method of surveying used for small areas with a fair degree of accuracy.

ETS and GIS (Geographic Information System) used in UPOR and RPOR in the state could able to map the land properties and all public establishments with details at a central location for data and analysis. It allows professional land surveyors a way to provide more accurate and less expensive surveys.

From the above discussions, we can see that Karnataka state steadily brought modifications in the surveying and land management practices from pre-British period to the current stage. The state of Karnataka implemented various revolutionary reforms in order to ensure error free speedy delivery of land survey records to the people both in urban and rural areas. The interface with various stake-holders like private partners, Landowners, NGOs, registration department, land acquiring bodies, banks etc., helped in seamless surveying and delivery of services to citizens. These innovative solutions through the process of digitisation and application of modern technology to the land survey and land management practices in Karnataka are a major step towards revolutionising the land management system.

Additional Notes on Land Records Management initiatives taken by Government of Karnataka

- *Bhoomi*

The land records in the state of Karnataka were earlier maintained by manual system. For the first time in India an innovative computerised land records management process through the flagship project named Bhoomi was launched in 2001. Under this project, all the manual Records of Rights, Tenancy & Crops (RTCs) were digitized and made available to the public.

This project was undertaken under a centrally sponsored scheme 'Computerization of land records'. Manual RTCs maintained by Village Accountants were computerized through data entry work. Verification and validation of the digital data with each manual RTC was done by Revenue department officials.

Need for Bhoomi Project

- Manual RTCs were prone to tampering and destruction
- To curb the harassment to the citizens especially farmers and enforce the procedures prescribed and to avoid Point of Contact/corruption
- Effective multi-level monitoring
- Move from localized village level manual records to taluk level database
- Flexibility to increase on-demand citizen service delivery points for issuing of computerized RTCs
- Government was facing the challenge of acquiring land for development projects in the pre-Bhoomi stage in the absence of computerised land records.

- *Electronic Integration of Bhoomi with Land Registration process*
  Kaveri Online Service is a web portal developed by the Department of Stamps & Registration, Government of Karnataka to simplify the process of registration.
  The main objective of Bhoomi-Kaveri integration is to bring synchronization between Kaveri (Registration software) and Bhoomi by reducing time lag between registration and initiation of mutation process. It reduces the rejection of mutations in Bhoomi due to wrong data entry.

Benefits

- Kaveri takes bhoomi data from the Bhoomi database during the registration process itself for registration of all agricultural properties.
- No sale, pledge/mortgage transactions allowed on government land.
- Only the current owner can sell the land.
- Transacted extents of the seller should be less than or equal to available extents.
- No sale transaction allowed on PTCL lands.
- Govt. restrictions like land grant conditions are checked before performing transactions.
- Mutation transactions initiated automatically.
- Substantial reduction in the average days taken for disposal of mutation in Bhoomi.
- There has been reduction in time taken for land transaction (Sale and Mortgage).

Bhoomi integration with Sakala

- Sakala – Karnataka Guarantee of Services to Citizens Act 2011
- Bhoomi mutation transactions have been integrated with Sakala online system.
- Even Bhoomi transactions have been brought under Sakala.
- Citizens can monitor the status of the request/transaction and claim compensation for delay in disposal of request over and above the time period as prescribed under the Act.
- In time push of sakala data using sakala push web service

- *New additions in Bhoomi*
  Linking of AC/DC revenue courts, purchase/conversion of land through software, extending issue of RTCs through GPs, SMS alerts for mutation transactions, Aadhar integration are some of the new additions.
- *Training and capacity building plan implemented for employees*
  Series of training programmes were conducted to train the Bhoomi operators, Bhoomi Consultants, Sub-Registrars and District Registrars for Bhoomi-Kaveri integration, similarly all Land Acquisition Officers and their staff were trained for Bhoomi-Bhooswadeena integration. In case of Bhoomi–Bank integration, a series of training programmes were held to train officers from different banks, master trainers have been trained by Bhoomi Monitoring Cell. Problems/issues faced at various stages
- *Future Initiatives on Modern Survey*
- Handling of simultaneous transactions
- Split the database into agricultural and non agricultural
- Handling of different land class (Nine fold classifications)
- Updating of trees against owner
- Handling of different category Government lands
- Land data Hub
- GIS capable
- Revenue service café
  - Tenancy/No tenancy certificate
  - Small/Marginal farmers
  - Permission to buy lands
  - Land availability list
- Updating of EC after mutation of registered lands
- Land Records to LIS System: Complete Data Hub
- Linking with EPIC, UID and Ration cards
- Eliminate Impersonation
- Family based regulation

- Linking with Birth and Death Database
- Automating updating of Land Records
- GIS based Land Records System – Decision Support System and Linking with Census Data and Khatha number
- Integration with Judiciary
- Field reports using handheld devices
- Bhoomi as land admin tool
- Land consultancy

References

1. *The Karnataka Revenue Survey Manual*, Volume 1 and Volume 2 (1984), The Government Press, Bengaluru.
2. *The Mysore Revenue Manual*, Volume 1 (Revised Edition 1931), The Government Press, Bengaluru.
3. *The Bombay Survey and Settlement* by R. G. GORDON, Volume 1 and Volume 2
4. Website of the Department of Revenue, Government of Karnataka
5. Annual Report 2020-21, Department of Survey Settlement and Land Records, Government of Karnataka.
6. Reports of Survey Training Institute, Mysuru
7. Karnataka Land Revenue Act 1964

2.7

Kerala

Dr. Anishia Jayadev

A Brief History of Survey in Kerala

The system relating to the maintenance of land records in Kerala is the result of a process of evolution which is complex and varied and differs in nature in different parts of the state and also is a result of political and historical factors. Kerala was formed as a result of the merger of height of the erstwhile Travancore Cochin state and Malabar district in Madras presidency. The Travancore Cochin state itself had been formed a few years earlier by the merger of the princely states of Travancore and Cochin. The three constituent units or Kerala had their own district administrative styles and systems which continued to cast their shadow on its administrative systems of unified Kerala. Due to the political separateness which the component part of Kerala viz, Travancore, Cochin and Malabar enjoyed prior to the merger, the system of revenue administration was not uniform. The settlement system of Madras was an elaborate one and was based on:

1. Classification of Soils.
2. Assessment of grain output of each class, cultivation, expenses and the cultivators and proprietor's shares.
3. Fixation of commutation rates, and conversion of grain output into money.

In the Malabar region, settlement was done between 1926 and 1934. The procedure followed was the one, which existed in the (Malabar) system in accordance with the Madras Survey Act. Where lands were classified into wet, dry and garden. This system resulted in the maximum possible revenue for the state. Settlement operations in Travancore were completed between 1886 and 1911 and in Cochin between 1905 and 1909. The state of Travancore-Cochin was found in 1949 by merging the Travancore State and Cochin State. The state of Kerala was found in 1956 by adding the Malabar district, Kasargod area, former Madras State and Travancore-Cochin State. Each of this area had its own Survey and Settlement methods.

Table *Brief history of Survey and Settlement*

Year	*Survey and Settlement Operations in Kerala*
1712	Kettezhuthu (what is heard) survey and settlement conducted based on the discussions with landholders, Pattas were issued.
1738-1748	This settlement was confined to the lands belonging to Sree Padmanabha Swamy Temple. No measurement of land was conducted.
1775	Ramayyan Dalava conducted a complete Survey and settlement. Holders were issued pattas. The nature of survey is not known.
1801	A complete survey was conducted. This was a 'Kandezhuthu'. (Record of what is seen). The tenures were similar to the previous settlement. Pattas were also issued after the settlement.
1817	This was only a settlement of garden lands. Pattas were issued subsequent to the settlement.
1836	A complete resurvey of garden lands was conducted. Side measurements were made with a '10' Feet Rod. Rough Pattas were issued after the settlements.
1882-1909	This is the latest settlement record.

According to the Resettlement Manual, 1930, the last settlement was conducted in Cochin during 1905-1909 following the settlement proclamation of 1905 and in Malabar during 1926-1934. In all the three regions, settlement was conducted after conducting a land survey. The survey records in all the regions were maintained according to the Land Records Maintenance Rules in the respective regions.

The Survey and Boundaries Act, 1961 came in to force on 01 September 1964 by repelling three Acts.[39] Though the acts were repelled, the customs in administrative procedures were continued in accordance with the repelled Acts in that region. Therefore, to bring into in uniform standards throughout the state, Government has published Survey Manual. This manual is designed in such a way that to help the officials of all the Revenue and Survey officials in their duties.

Subsequently, a survey of Edavakas[40] namely Kilimanoor, Vanjipuzha, Poonjar, Nediyiruppuand a resurvey of Nedumangad taluk was also conducted. The resurvey records of Nedumangad Taluk were not finalised due to large number of complaints. By and large, these records were prepared prior to

[39] a) The Madras Survey and Boundaries Act, 1923 (Madras Act VIII of 1923) as in force in the Malabar District referred to in sub section (2) of section 5 of state Reorganisation Act, 1956 (Central Act 37 of 1956),

b) The Travancore Survey and Boundaries Act of 1094 (Act X of 1094) as in force in the former Travancore area, and c) The Cochin Survey Act II of 1074 as in the force in the former Cochin area.

[40] Edavaka – The place or area of old Thiru-Kochi region. These are not included in the ayacut of government, Also excluded to pay tax to Government. These lands are considered as Government land. There are four Edavakas, namely Kilimanoor, Idappalli, Vanjippuzha and Poovar.

independence, but still in use in the state till the resurvey records, prepared from the year of 1966 was put in use in many of the villages of the state. The methods used for the survey records existed prior to the resurvey, which was conducted in 1966, are enumerated below:

(i) *Tak System or System of Simple Triangles*: In this system, each Revenue field was split into a number of triangles and the sides of the field forming the arms of the triangle. This system was simple for practical, but some defects found in the result. This system was adopted in Karthikapally, Karunagapally, Kollam, Chirayinkeezhu and Thiruvananthapuram taluks.

(ii) *Plane Table System*: Under this system of survey, field observation and plotting are done simultaneously. After entering the plane table, radiating lines are drawn from the fixing to the various points with the help of sight Rule, measurements to these points are taken and plotted to scale along the radiating lines. This system was adopted in north Wayanad and South Wayanad.

(iii) *Base Line and Offset System*: Theodolite stations were fixed at Village and Khandom[41] boundaries to form blocks of about 50 hectares. The blocks were divided into large triangles and the boundaries of survey fields and subdivisions fixed by offset taken from the sides of triangles. Revenue fields were clubbed to form survey fields of approximately two hectares in wetlands and four hectares in dry lands. All the measurements taken were entered on the block sheets. This system was adopted in the following taluks: Mannarkad, Perinthalmanna, Ottapalam, Palakkad, Alathur, Aluva, Devicolam, Paravur, Kunnathunad, Kothamangalam, Muvattupuzha, Cherthala, Vaikom, Kottayam, Changanasseri, Ambalapuzha, Kuttanad, Kanjirappally, Thiruvalla, Chengannur, Pathanamthitta, Mavelikkara, Kunnathur, Pathanapuram, Kottarakkara.

(iv) *Diagonal and Offset System or Triangle and Offset System*: This system is being adopted for survey since 1902. Each field trijunction is connected with the next field by a line called G line and selecting convenient diagonals completes the triangles. Independent framework is provided for each survey field. Field and subdivision bends are offset on the G lines and diagonals. The diagonal and offset system affords an independent check of a substantial amount of fieldwork done by the surveyor. The up-to-date diagonal and offset system is more accurate, less costly and quite easy for maintenance of framework of survey and land records. This system was adopted in the following taluks: Kasaragod, Hosdurg, Taliparamba, Kannur, Talasseri, Vadakara, Koyilandi, Kozhikode Eranad,

---

[41] The principle of survey is whole to part. To follow this principle, a Taluk is divided into Blocks and Blocks are further divided into Khandoms. The outer boundaries of these Blocks and Khandom are surveyed and fix the outer measurement. So that if any error occur in the field-survey, it never crosses that khandom/block boundary.

Tirur, Ponnani, Talappally, Chavakkad, Trissur, Chittur, Mukundapuram, Kodungallur, Kanayannur, Thodupuzha, Meenachil and Nedumangad.

Revisional Survey in Kerala: why it was felt necessary

In Cochin and Malabar areas, the mutation (Pokkuvaravu/Jamathiry/Transfer of Registry) was effected in the revenue records only after surveying the new sub-division. This work fell in arrears after the independence. The village officers whose primary responsibility was the maintenance of land records were deployed for poverty alleviation schemes and hence the land records maintenance was neglected to a great extent. In the Travancore area, the transfer of registry was up-to-date to a great extent. But corresponding changes were not effected in the maps. Further in the state; various legislation towards agrarian reforms was introduced after independence. Due to the above legislations, the tenants and sharecroppers became absolute owners of the land. When these reforms were introduced on a war-footing basis, the corresponding changes were not effected in the survey records. Hence, a total resurvey of the state was required and Government had ordered for the complete resurvey of the state on 25 May 1966. The following steps have been taken during resurvey:

- *Legal Notices in the Resurvey*: The individual notices under section 6 & 9 of the Survey & Boundaries Act were dispensed with as per the following amendment of the Survey & Boundaries Act. No. 11611/ Leg/ A1/ 86 Law (Legislation-A) Department. Now, according to Survey & Boundaries Act, there is no individual notice is required prior to the resurvey or prior to the finalisation.
- *Demarcation*: Each taluk is divided into main circuits with an approximate area of 150 kms. And each main circuit is connected with the G.T. Stations established by Survey of India so as to provide geographical co-ordinates to all survey points. According to present system of survey, each taluk is divided into blocks of approximately 1000 hectares. Then each block is divided into Khandom with area of 25 to 40 hectares. Each Khandom is sub-divided into Survey numbers of approximately four hectares in dry land and two hectares in wet land.
- *Survey of Block and Khandom*: The block and Khandom boundaries are surveyed by traverse methods.
- *Survey of Holdings*: Normally survey fields are formed by clubbing 10 to 20 holdings and with an approximate area of two hectares in wet land and four hectares in dry land. The boundaries are demarcated generally according to the physical possession as seen on ground except where they are the valid documents to prove that it has to be demarcated otherwise. But Government lands are demarcated as per the previous records so as to detect all subsequent encroachments.
- *Survey of Poramboke*: The Government lands even if they are under unauthorized occupation, are surveyed and recorded as Poramboke.

- *Nallathu Poramboke*: Certain private lands, which are now being used by public for the following purposes, are surveyed as Nallathu Poramboke.
    - Roads, Streets
    - Thodu, Streams.

The propriety rights of these Nallathu Poramboke shall continue to be vested with the respective landowners. The roads, streets etc. are surveyed as subdivision in the sketches only if it has got more than two meters width. The other roads, streets etc. are shown as topo details in the respective sub division. No tax is collected in respect of Nallathu Porambokes.

- *Variation in Area from the Previous Settlement*: In many cases there is variation in extent in the resurvey records from the previous survey and settlement records. After the finalisation and implementation of the resurvey records, basic tax is collected according to the area in the resurvey records and no separate pattas are required in cases of excess areas. For registration of title deeds and all other transactions, resurvey number, subdivision number and extent should be followed.
- *Supply of Records*: The not final records are issued to the landholders on payment from the Office of the Assistant Director of Survey & Land Records concerned. The landowners can obtain the above sketches and satisfy themselves that the boundaries are properly determined. The copies of the details of Landowners recorded during resurvey in the form of field register are also available in the resurvey office on payment.

The Kerala State consists of old Travancore State, Malabar and Kasargod areas of old Madras State and old Cochin State. The original survey of former Travancore State was conducted during the period 1883-1912 and that of Cochin area during the period 1899-1909. After that no resurvey has been conducted in these areas. In Malabar areas, though a resurvey was conducted during 1923-28, it was found necessary that the sketches in the field measurements books and other survey records had to be completely re-prepared afresh or a resurvey conducted. This is mainly due to want of systematic maintenance of land records and also due to insertions of numerous sub divisions in the original measurement sketches. Arrears had also accumulated in carrying out mutations in land records. With the introduction of metric system in land records, necessity for re-preparation of land record under that system also arose. Resurvey of the State and preparation of land records based on the existing limits of occupations would also facilitate the speedy implementation of land records and collection of agricultural statistics. Considering all these aspects, it was decided that a resurvey of the entire State would be attempted.

The resurvey is done under the provisions of the Survey and Boundaries Act (Act 37 of 1961). According to the provisions in the Act, individual notices are to be issued to the landholders and their objections, if any, heard and disposed of before the survey records are finalised. It was found on practice that the service of individual notices is a time consuming and laborious process, employing a large number of staff without any resultant advantage. Therefore, the Board of Revenue suggested to amend the Survey and Boundaries Act as early in 1971 dispensing with the issue of individual notices. After detailed correspondence between Government and Board of Revenue for 1971-1983 and discussions at various levels, an ordinance amending section 9(2) of Survey and Boundaries Act was issued by the Government in November 1983. According to the ordinance, the decision under section 9(2) of the Act is to be published in two leading local dailies, the records will be exhibited at a public place like Village/Panchayat office etc. and the parties who are interested in the boundaries may verify the resurvey records and prefer complaints about the survey, if they are aggrieved. These complaints are heard and disposed of by the officers of Survey & Land Records Department not below the rank of Superintendents before the Resurvey Records are finalised and notified under Section 13 of the Act.

Generally, a resurvey is followed by a re-settlement. Since basic tax has been introduced in Kerala State, no further settlement of land revenue seems necessary. The other part of the settlement work i.e. preparation of revenue registers like Basic tax, Thandaper etc. from whom land revenue is to be collected after conducting field verifications is being done by a process called "translation of resurvey records into land records". Since some of the resurvey records prepared date back to the period 1966-67, it has become necessary to update this resurvey records after conducting field verification. For attending this work, 40 Special Tahsildars have been employed in eight taluks (six districts) since 1980. 400 Surveyors, 80 Draftsman, 40 Head Surveyor and eight Head Draftsman from the resurvey parties have been diverted to work under the Special Tahsildars, for updating the resurvey records and preparation of land records. The equivalent posts in the resurvey scheme are kept vacant as per Government orders. From the inspection of this scheme, resurvey records of 170 villages have been handed over to the Special Tahsildars and they have completed the work in all respects only in about 100 Villages. The idea when the scheme was introduced was that each unit could complete the preparation of records of one village within a period of 8-10 months, but due to the non-availability of village officers for preparation of registers, each unit on an average has completed only 2-3 villages so far. This item of work at district level is done under the supervision of District Collectors and the work at State level is reviewed by the Additional Secretary, Board of Revenue (LR).

In respect of the villages where resurvey was done, recently the resurvey records need not be updated since it generally depicts the present state of things on ground. In such cases when the resurvey records are finalised, the services of the Special Tahasildars and the staff under then can be utilised to prepare the land records such as basic tax, Thandaper (revenue record of property) etc. straight away without further field verification.

After finalising the resurvey, the land records such as F.M.B., Village/ Block map, basic tax register, Thandaper register, Poramboke register etc. are to be handed over to the revenue authorities for maintaining them in village and taluk offices. At present, two copies of field measurements sketches and only copy of other registers are prepared. The copies of block maps are printed in the Central Survey Office. Due to the constant use of the F.M.B. in field for the work corrected with the translation of resurvey records into land records and its handling at various stages, most of the sketches in the original and duplicate field measurement books have become unfit for use. It is therefore necessary that copies of these records are to be taken for supply to the Village and Taluk offices. For taking copies of these records, it was suggested to purchase continuous photo copier machines so that the machines can be installed in the respective collectorate and required copies of F.M.B., basic-tax register etc. taken under the supervision of the Deputy Directors attached to the Collectorates. While purchasing of the photo copier machine and taking copies of the records will take time, it is also suggested that the duplicate copy or the F.M.B. and the only copy of the Basic Tax Register etc. prepared may be handed over straight away to each village office though the District Collector from an appointed date soon after finalisation of resurvey records. When resurvey records are handed over, the previous records available in the village office will be taken back by the Collector and kept in his office. The Revenue administration from the date can be carried on in the respective villages based on the resurvey records. This will help to bring the resurvey records up to date by incorporating the subsequent changes in them. As and when the photo copier machines are purchased the records of each village can be brought to the Collectorate and copies taken for supply to Village and Taluk Offices.

Generally, after resurvey and resettlement landholders are issued a patta showing the details of lands under each landholder. It is suggested that the patta to the landholder can be issued as and when resurvey records of each village is finalised and handed over to revenue administration. It is learnt that in the neighbouring Tamil Nadu State, a similar system has been introduced after formulating necessary legislation in the matter. A similar legal system of issuing patta pass book has been introduced in Gujarat State also. It is therefore suggested that when resurvey is finalised and the resurvey records given effect to in each village for revenue administration, a patta pass book showing all the details about the land can be issued to the landholders of this State also after enacting necessary legislation in this regard.

The very purpose of conducting the resurvey is to prepare a land records showing the existing limits of each land holding including the persons for whom certificate of purchase, conferment of title like *Kudikidappu*[42], *Kudiyiruppu*[43] etc.

---

[42] *"kudikidappu"* means the land and the homestead or the hut so permitted to be erected or occupied together with the easements

[43] *"kudiyiruppu"* means a holding or part of a holding consisting of the site of any residential building, the site or sites of other buildings appurtenant thereto, such other lands as are necessary for the convenient enjoyment of such residential building and easements attached thereto, but does not include a *kudikidappu*;

under the land reforms Act was made. It may therefore be seen that the land reforms in its real sense can be said to be complete only after a statutory land records for all the persons benefited by the land reforms is prepared. Apart from preparation of land records, issuance of a Patta Pass Book could also help the weaker section of society to possess a legal document in support of the lands under their possession, who are not capable of documentation.

The following are the basic records prepared on completion of Resurvey of a village/Panchayat:

- Field measurement sketches showing the measurements of each holding including Government lands with necessary data to rely the boundary on ground as and when required. The scale of the sketch is 1/500, 1/1000, 1/2000 and 1/5000 according to the extent of holding.
- Land register/Field register showing the name of present landholder extent, classification, nature of previous landholder, corresponding old survey/sub division number, details of main crops raised in the land etc.

The combined map of each block of about 1000 hectares in extent formed within Village/Panchayat following natural boundaries as far as possible, thus three Revenue Village may consist of one or more of such blocks (scale 1/5000).

Existing Practices of Land Surveying and Recording Systems

a) At present, to expedite the resurvey activities, modern survey method of Continuously Operating Reference Stations (CORS) got approval from government and administrative sanction was obtained to spend an amount of ₹12 crores. For installing CORS network, an agreement was drawn with Survey of India to establish 28 COR stations throughout the state.

b) Along with that, using modern scientific technology, government is trying to provide the people service of the departments of Survey, Revenue and Registration through single window system. For this, the present software 'Bhoonaksha' is being customised by NIC. E-maps or (Effective Mapping Application for Surveying) is an online application prepared by NIC to take care of land related records. This has also started by February 2021. Two villages have been covered by e-maps. The rest of the villages where digital survey has been completed will also be covered.

The milestones reached

- Using modern survey machines, geo-reference digital records are being prepared in WGS 84 systems. In the year 2019-20 work of four villages and six blocks were completed and records were handed over to Revenue administration. Other than resurvey, land record maintenance, land acquisition, land assignment, special surveys etc. are taking place, and hence there is staff shortage. Hence, from resurvey establishment, technical staffs are used to complete the work. As cited earlier, there are 747 villages whose survey is yet to be completed. For this, the department would be adopting for modern technology like CORS and RTK. Currently the work is being done using electronic total station (ETS), Global Positioning System (GPS) and saved in WGS84 system as geo reference digital records.

- To digitise land records, in all the 13 districts except Palakad, there are district digitisation centres and one central digitisation centre is functioning at Trivandrum. In the survey and Land Records Department, all available survey records are scanned and made available online through the project *e-rekha*. The records can be accessed from the web portal www.erekha.kerala.gov.in. Under this project 3,99,999 settlement registers including earlier survey records were conserved and scanning of 3,72,073 records were scanned. Scanning of 838 villages resurvey FMBs and block maps of 792 villages and land registers of 200 villages were completed.
- At present 813 villages FMBs are available in the web portal. Public can view it free of cost and access online by *e-remittance*. Steps are being taken to provide more documents online. Over this, CORS network installation is also being done.

Problems/Issues faced at field level by practising the current survey and land recording systems:

A Case of Torrens System in Kerala

Torrens system is a system which insists the presentation of survey map along with the deed for registration in respect of any transfer or otherwise disposal of land. The above map shall be prepared by a licensed surveyor or by an officer authorised by the Government in this behalf and got approved. Kerala has made a feeble attempt to introduce Torrens's or, to be more precise, a component of Torrens in the villages under the Principal Sub-Registrar Offices of Kottayam & Angamaly since 1995. Due to the strong opposition and court cases this initiative could not be scaled up but somehow still being followed in 13 villages.

The villages where Torrens system exists are as follows:

Kottayam- Kottayam, Aimanam, Chegalam, Nattakom, Thiruvarpu, Peroor, Kumarakom. Aluva-Angamali, Manjapra, Mukkannur, Thuravur, Ayyauzha, Karukutty.

- Licence issuing officer
  The licence issuing officer is The Director of Survey and Land Records or an officer authorised by him.
- Qualifications of Licensed Surveyor
  a) A chain survey certificate approved by The Director of Survey and Land Records. OR
  b) I.T.I Certificate in surveyor trade. OR
  c) Six years military experience in surveyor trade. OR
  d) Not less than six years' experience in Kerala Survey and Land Records Department as a Surveyor

- Application for Licence
  Application in Form No-26 together with the chalan receipt in original towards the remittance of fee of ₹2205/-(Two thousand two hundred and five only), two passport size photos, copy of S.S.L.C front page and copy of qualifying certificate.
- Issue of Licence
  The licensing officer, being satisfied of the suitability of the applicant, shall issue the licence in form No-27 for a period of two years which may be renewed in every two year. Renewel fees ₹1105/- (One thousand one hundred and five only),
- Jurisdiction of Licensed Surveyor
  The area of jurisdiction of a licensed surveyor shall not extend to more than one taluk.
- Power to suspend License
  The licensing officer shall have power to suspend a license for reasons to be recorded in writing.
- Power to cancel License
  The licensing officer shall have power to cancel a license for reasons to be recorded in writing after having given the licensed surveyor an opportunity to defend his case.

For smooth revenue administration and for effective tax collection proper survey records are a must. This happens through resurvey. Out of 1665 villages in the state, resurvey records of 908 villages have been handed over to revenue administration. From remaining 757 villages from different districts, resurvey of 30 villages is progressing. The major issues are as follows:

- ✓ Large number of LRM complaints in the State
- ✓ No land settlement mechanism in place to ensure title
- ✓ No concept of Record of Right (RoR) document in the State
- ✓ Absence of standardization in land records procedures
- ✓ Absence of citizen grievances addressing mechanism on land complaints
- ✓ Absence of single window land records service delivery system in the State
- ✓ paper records are the outcome of digital resurvey
- ✓ No standard software solution for land records in the State
- ✓ Non-updating in the base records
- ✓ Longer duration of resurvey process (two year or more for a single village)

Other than resurvey and LRM, the department provides services for giving patta, forest rights, land for zero landless programme, power grid line, etc. This leads to reduction in staff for the conduct of resurvey. In the year 2016, all the staff was called back from such duties on November, within a few days they were asked to revert to the various duties. But the order was withdrawn and again the survey staff had to leave resurvey and attend to other duties. The district collector was authorized to appropriately get the needed survey staff for such duties.

For completing the resurvey of remaining villages staff deficit was there. Hence, it was explored that survey may be conducted by government approved agency. For this, a team consisting of land revenue commissioner, director survey, additional director survey, and revenue IT cell nodal officer and Kerala Land Information Mission Project Manager visited Gujarat and gave a report to the government. The government approved the report and it was decided to use the survey of government approved agency, those who have technical expertise in survey, and those who have received training from survey school to complete survey. The regular employees of the department would do the validation work. In principle, it was agreed that the digital survey would be conducted by using central funds and any amount exceeding that will be spend by the state.

Improvised Modern Techniques used for Land Survey in Kerala

Continuously Operating Reference Station (CORS) Technology

A continuously Operating Reference Station (CORS) network is a network of Real Time Kinematic (RTK) base stations that broadcast corrections, usually over an Internet connection. Accuracy is increased in a CORS network, because more than one station helps to ensure correct positioning and guards against a false initialization of a single base station. This technology will bring more efficiency, accuracy etc. in the survey works of Kerala.

Procedure and Advantages

The advancement of GPS technology like Real Time Kinematic (RTK) processing techniques paved the way for eliminating the traverse works in today's world. RTK uses a fixed base station and a rover machine to reduce the rover's positional errors. The system will avoid the post processing correction work and which saves considerable time of the surveyors. In other words, the device which is capable of collecting RTK signal will get the correction applied to the GPS value in the field itself. This device can replace the ETS devices in the survey works which may greatly reduce the duration in completing survey works. When CORs set up is established, RTK devices can be synchronised with CORS and bring out quick results in survey works with highest accuracy.

One surveyor can directly measure the parcel bends by using an RTK device without referring to any traverse stations and with less manpower. Since the RTK device gets correction signal from CORS, every bend points will get desired accuracy level. In addition to that the envisaged system will greatly reduce many of the frameworks; preparatory works etc. in resurvey process. In a way, the resurvey of an entire village can be replaced with an updating survey of any piece of land irrespective of its size, boundary etc. without any framework. This may reduce the work load of LRM and resurvey operations and may bring advanced level of GIS data for web enable services.

Action Taken

The Government have sanctioned the implementation of COR Stations in the state in 2019. But, due to delay in the implementation of the scheme, the said amount could not be spent during the financial year 2019-20 and the administrative sanction has been renewed. Out of ₹12 crore, an amount of ₹8 crore is earmarked for setting up of required COR stations in the state and the remaining amount for the purchase of ancillary equipment such as Real Time Kinematic (RTK) Machines. As part of the implementation of CORS technology in the State, Government have accorded sanction to set up the required COR stations in the State through the Survey of India, and approved the terms and conditions of the Memorandum of Understanding. Based on that, the Director of Survey and Land Records authorized to sign the MoU on behalf of the State.

As an initial step, the tentative location of 28 COR stations to be set up in the State has been ascertained by the Survey of India and three suitable locations have been identified for each station and mapping works of these locations are in progress.

Survey of Villages and Mapping with Improvised Technology in Village Areas (SVAMITVA)

The scheme aims to provide an integrated property validation solution for rural India. The demarcation of abadi areas (the abadi area includes inhabitant land, inhabited areas contiguous to Abadi and wadis/basties in rural areas) would be done using Drone Surveying technology, with the collaborative efforts of the Ministry of Panchayati Raj, State Panchayat Raj Department, State Revenue Departments and Survey of India.

This would provide the "record of rights" to village household owners possessing houses in inhabited rural areas in villages which, in turn, would enable them to use their property as a financial asset for taking loans and other financial benefits from banks. Further, this would also enable updating of property and asset register to strengthen tax collection and demand assessment process of Gram Panchayats. Thus, the legal record of property holders and issuance of "Property Cards" to household owners based thereon would facilitate monetization of rural residential assets for the purchase of credit and other financial services. This could also pave the way for clear determination of property tax, which would accrue to the GPs directly in States where it is devolved.

Apart from demarcation of individual rural property, other Gram Panchayat and community assets like village roads, ponds, canals, open spaces, school, Anganwadi, Health sub-centres, etc. would also be surveyed and GIS maps would be created. Further, these GIS Maps and spatial databases would also help in preparation of accurate work estimates for various works undertaken by Gram Panchayats and other departments of State Government. These can also be used to prepare better-quality Gram Panchayat Development Plan (GPDP).

In order to implement the scheme SVAMITVA in the State, Director, Department of Survey and Land records has been appointed as the Nodal Officer for the same from the Government and the willingness to enter into an agreement with Survey of India for Drone survey in *abadi* areas has already been intimated to the Government of India.

Issues and Way Forward

- In Kerala, Revenue, Survey and Registration departments are handling land related matters. Revenue and Survey Departments are under one ministry and Registration Department is under another ministry.
- Registration of land is happening without an approved sketch. After registration the application will be submitted to the Taluk office for Pokkuvaravu (Mutation). But many of the landholders will not show interest to apply for the pokkuvaravu (mutation) after registration. They will apply when they want to take a loan or want to sell, then only they will come for the mutation. So the land records could not be able to update properly.
- While register a documents, it is not verifying the survey number, subdivision number and area scientifically. Register the document with the information that provided by the client. It will cause difference in survey number, subdivision number and area after resurvey with the document they registered. This lead to resurvey complaints.

There are three different departments (Survey, Revenue, and Registration) involving in the land record management activities of the State. There is no unified/standard system or practice in place wherein single window operation of land transaction is followed:

- Dearth of staff, dearth of modern survey equipment and non-availability of customised software are the challenges faced by the department.
- For taking care of lack of equipment, it was decided to utilize 12 crore of rupees to establish CORS network and to digitise survey by Real-time kinematic (RTK) equipment. Lack of instruments is also a factor to not to achieve the progress in resurvey activities.
- Very limited ETS machines are available with department.

Hence, it is planned to expedite the survey activities using RTK machines with the help of CORS network.

- Another issue faced by the Department is that even though resurvey is done by Survey Department alone, land related issues are taken care of by Registration, Survey and Revenue Departments. Since the other two departments have no role to conduct resurvey, it becomes difficult in taking decision on real ownership of land records. The current practice is that once resurvey is completed the records will be given to Revenue administration and then they are the custodian of that record. But since they have no responsibility on resurvey, they find it very difficult to maintain the records and it results in complaints regarding resurvey. Since there is no coordination between the three Government Departments, the resource usage is not optimum that leads to complaint.

The Way Forward

If the resurvey activities of a district will be carried out under the administrative control of the District Collector, and coordinate the activities of Revenue and Survey Department, then the human resource will be utilised optimally, and better service could be delivered to the public. Under this premise, it has been under the active consideration of the Government that on the basis of importance, the conduct of survey in Districts be given to District collector's administrative control. On the basis of the survey, Superintend Offices will be initiated and resurvey, land acquisition, land assignment and all other survey duties be conducted under a Taluk Survey Superintendent.

Annexure 1 *Resurvey Progressing Villages*

Sl. No.	*District*	*Taluk*	*Village*
1.1	Thiruvananthapuram	Thiruvananthapuram	Vanchiyoor
1.2	Thiruvananthapuram	Thiruvananthapuram	Pettah
1.3	Thiruvananthapuram	Thiruvananthapuram	Kadakampally
1.4	Thiruvananthapuram	Thiruvananthapuram	Muttathara
1.5	Thiruvananthapuram	Chirayinkeezhe	Attingal
2.1	Kollam	Punalur	Alayamon
2.2	Kollam	Punalur	Channappetta
3.1	Pathanamthitta	Pathanamthitta	Pathanamthitta
4.1	Alappuzha	Kuttanad	Edathuva
5.1	Kottayam	Vaikom	Kaduthuruthy
5.2	Kottayam	Vaikom	Muttichira
6.1	Idukki	Peerumade	Elappara
6.2	Idukki	Peerumade	Peerumade
6.3	Idukki	Thodupuzha	Thodupuzha municipality
7.1	Ernakulam	Kanayannur	Edappally north
7.2	Ernakulam	Kanayannur	Edappally south
8.1	Thrissur	Thrissur	Kozhukulli
8.2	Thrissur	Thrissur	Thanniyam
8.3	Thrissur	Thrissur	Killannur
8.4	Thrissur	Thalappilly	Nelluvai
8.5	Thrissur	Thalappilly	Kiralur
9.1	Palakkad	Palakkad	Palakkad-2
9.2	Palakkad	Palakkad	Palakkad-3
10.1	Malappuram	Tirur	Tanalur
10.2	Malappuram	Eranad	Payyanad
11.1	Kozhikkode	Vadakara	Edachery
11.2	Kozhikkode	Koyilandi	Payyoli
12.1	Wayanad	Sulthanbathery	Nenmeni
13.1	Kannur	Iritty	Ayyankunnu
14.1	Kasargod	Hosdurg	Thimiri
14.2	Kasargod	Hosdurg	Puthukkai
14.3	Kasargod	Hosdurg	Balla

Annexure 2 *Resurvey Progress as on February 2021:*

Sl. No.	*District*	*Total Villages*	*Resurvey Completed*	*Balance*
1	Thiruvananthapuram	124	113	11
2	Kollam	105	88	17
3	Pathanamthitta	70	58	12
4	Alappuzha	93	76	17
5	Kottayam	100	87	13
6	Idukki	68	37	31
7	Ernakulam	127	75	52
8	Thrissur	255	72	183
9	Palakkad	157	115	42
10	Malappuram	138	56	82
11	Kozhikode	118	16	102
12	Wayanad	49	36	13
13	Kannur (Inc.Desams)	132	56	76
14	Kasargod	129	23	106
	Grand Total	**1665**	**908**	**757**

Annexure 3 *Achievements made by the Department of Survey and Land Records during the period from 01-04-2020 to 26-02-2021*

1. **Resurvey**
   a. Resurvey completed and handed over the records for the revenue administration – **3 Villages (Part)**
   b. Resurvey field work completed and notified as per section 9(2) of Survey and Boundaries Act – **2 villages**
   c. Resurvey field work, Office process and Appeal against land complaints completed and notified as per section 13 of Survey and Boundaries Act – **1 Village**
   d. Resurvey of **30** villages and updating survey of **3** villages are in progress.
2. **CORS (Continuously Operating Reference Stations)**
   In order to facilitate the survey activities of State, action has been taken to introduce and establish modern technologies in this domain. As part of it, an MoU has been executed with the Survey of India for establishing a required number of (28) Continuously Operating Reference Stations across the state on **18/01/2021**. The estimated amount for the above project is **₹8/- Crore.** As an advance ₹3.2 Crore has been released on 30/01/2021.
3. **e-Maps (Effective Mapping Application for surveying)**
   The department didn't have adequate software to prepare survey maps for the land management through online. In order to achieve this, new application, e-Maps, has been developed by the National Informatics Centre (NIC) and launched in **two villages** (Vanchiyoor village in Thiruvananthapuram and Kaduthuruthi village in Kottayam District) on **18/02/2021**.
4. **Survey Training Institute**
   Construction of a new building for the Modern Government Research Training Centre for Survey (MGRTCS) at ILDM Compound in Thiruvananthapuram has been completed and started functioning from 10/02/2021 onwards. The total estimated cost for the project was **₹2.19 crore.**

2.8

Madhya Pradesh

Ashutosh Tiwari

Introduction

Survey is the activity in which measurement related attributes of an area are collected with the help of man and machine. It is an essential and important requisite for Land management and includes three activities namely field work, mapping and computation. For preparation of land records, fieldwork is the first step. Historically fieldwork in Madhya Pradesh has followed the steps of technological advancement starting with jarib (chain) survey, plane table and theodolite; it has now evolved to Electronic total station machine (ETS) to Drone survey. For mapping, at different times, aerial survey to satellite imagery purchased from National Remote Sensing agency has also been used with their limitations.

Legal Framework

The Madhya Pradesh Revenue Code 1959 (Code No.20, Year 1959) had been enforced through Gazette notification dated 21 September 1959. The original Revenue Code of 1959 had been comprised of 19 Chapters, 264 clauses and three schedules.

The Madhya Pradesh Revenue Code 1959 was later amended as Madhya Pradesh Land Revenue Code Act, 2018 (Code No.23, Year 2018) that was enforced from 25 September 2018 and its Gazette notification was published on 12 February 2020.

Section 66 and Section 68 of Chapter 7 under the Madhya Pradesh Revenue Code 1959 defines the process regarding the survey for revenue assessment.

- *Section 66*
  1. Division of Land survey numbers along with clustering of such numbers – village-wise; validation of existing survey numbers; restructuring of existing old survey numbers and christening of new survey numbers related operations incidental to them.
  2. Classification of soil.
  3. Preparation of field maps or revision or improvisation of existing maps as the case may be.
  4. Development of proper Record of Rights (RoRs) for updating of land records in the local area.

- *Section 68: Composition of Survey Numbers and Villages*
  All rules made thereto towards non-official settlement subject to regulations under this Code shall hold for:
  1. Lands subject to the guidelines under survey be measured and in such survey numbers, survey marks shall be referenced for all those necessary thereto;
  2. Such lands that shall be partitioned into survey numbers, followed by grouping them into villages of such survey numbers; and
  3. Survey numbers that shall be accredited by experts and figures under those survey numbers and reclassified/restructured or christened after conducting a new survey.

But included within the above, other than foregoing provisions; all lands to be surveyed for agricultural purposes shall not hereafter be less than the minimum expanse as ordained for under different predefined land size categories. But all guidelines and restrictions subject to the aforesaid and all foregoing shall NOT apply to the survey numbers existing prior to the date of notification of Section 67 subsection (1).

Land revenue settlement has been defined under Section 75 of Chapter 7 under the Madhya Pradesh Revenue Code 1959 as follows:

The outcome of the operations undertaken towards determination or revision of land revenue payable on lands in a local area while the revenue survey is in operation is called "settlement" and the period during which the revised land revenue so assessed shall be 'in force' is called as the 'settlement period'.

But according to the Section 64 of Chapter 7 under the Madhya Pradesh Land Revenue Code (Amendment) Act, 2018:

1. The proposal towards initiating a survey in any tehsil shall be done only after a Gazette Survey notification to that effect is released by the Commissioner, Land Records in that area concerned.
2. The proposed survey shall be undertaken in all such areas or only those areas that the Commissioner, Land Records as under Section (1) shall notify.
3. The proposed land survey as notified under sub-section (1) shall continue in the notified areas till a subsequent notification regarding the termination/closure of such survey process is subsequently declared.

Current Survey Methods
(Adopted by the State Government)

Chain (Jarib) Survey

Survey by chain is a very old method of survey. In ancient times, when technology was not developed, chain survey was the purest method of survey. With the help of chains in a chain survey, the available field (area) can be measured and a map of that area can be prepared. The most important point for keeping information of any area is a map. The map provides information about the actual location of that area like river, drain, khanti, hill, pond, meds etc.

The chain survey takes only measurements on the area and map generation work is done in the office. With the help of chain survey we only do Linear Measurement. For angular measurement, other tools such as compass etc. are used. Chain survey is the most commonly used method for limited area survey. If a precaution is taken while conducting the survey, it provides a pure area. In pre-independence India, different states used different jaribs. In British India, mostly Günter jaribs were used. Madhya Pradesh formed in 1956, an agglomeration of various subsection of different states, had initial maps of those areas formed on that old particular jarib.

However, post measurement Act, 1957, only metric scale instruments are in use, one must have an idea of these jaribs for better appreciation of the topic.

Sl. No.	*Name of Jarib*	*Length of 1 Kari*		*Length of Jarib in Mt.*			*Unit of Area*	
		Inch	*cm*	*Gaj/Yard*	*Mt.*	*Ft.*	*Part*	*Total*
I.	II.	III.	IV.	V.	VI.	VII.		
1.	Shahjhani	19.80	50.29	55.00	50.29	165.00	Biswa	20 Biswa =1 Bigha
2.	Farukhabadi	18.90	48.01	52.51	48.01	157.52	Biswa	20 Biswa =1 Bigha
3.	Saharanpuri	18.30	46.48	50.83	46.48	152.50		
4.	Gwalior	18.00	45.72	50.00	45.72	150.01	Biswa	20 Biswa =1 Bigha
5.	Fathepuri	15.84	40.23	44.00	40.23	131.99		
6.	Engineering	12.00	30.48	33.33	30.48	100.00		
7.	Metric jarib (30)	11.81	30.00	32.81	30.00	98.43		
8.	Metric jarib (20)	07.87	20.00	21.87	20.00	65.62	Are	100 Are = 1 Hectare
9.	Gunter jarib	07.92	20.12	22.00	20.12	66.01	Decimal	100 Decimal = 1 Acre

Process of Land Measurement (Traditional)

1. Traversing: Prior to land measurement in any area in general; the area is traversed and surrounded by masonry stones and the entire area is inspected and prepared and laid out in a convenient manner.
2. *Murabbatarasi*: After the inspection of the site, the Murabba is made. Murabba should not be more than 20–20 or 20–15 jarib. The land measurement work is done correctly and conveniently by the Murabba. Murabba also prepared in the map according to the area in which the possibility of any kind of mistake in measuring the land does not last. The survey work is done by dividing the entire area into triangular blocks and Murabbas, so that the fault is confined within the block (Murabba).
3. Land measurement: First the boundary of the area is measured, followed by the measurement of the Murabba lines, thus all the Murabba is drawn on the map. After this, detailed land measurement is completed by preparing field-book, which is not more than two km long. The bends of

the corners of the fields on both sides of the lines are written according to the location in the field-book. Offset should not be taken more than one and a half jarib (chain) distance.

4. Plotting: Plotting work of day-to-day geo-measurement is completed, which makes the plotting work perfect as the memory of the geo-measuring employee remains fresh. If a mistake is made, it is corrected on the second day. Any line is drawn as base line. With help of diagonal, all jarib lines are drawn. This task is also called framework. Each jarib line is drawn with the help of dividers. By dissecting the arcs, desired points are obtained.
5. Boundary matching: After preparation of map, boundaries of border villages are matched. This is called "med-milaan". In case of discrepancy, boundaries are kept on the basis of Patwari map.

Process of Land Measurement (Modern)

(i) Detailed Geo-Measurement with ETS machine

ETS machine is an electronic device used for surveying natural and man-made topographies, structures on the ground. It performs linear and angular measurements simultaneously. Both detailed geo-measurement and garland line measurement are done with the ETS machine. Under the "working whole to part" principle of survey; the area which is measured in detail is measured using the line measurement, i.e., measuring the village boundary, and with the help of these points, the detailed land is measured. Once the measuring is done, the whole work is done under garland measurement, while part work is done under detailed geometry.

Steps for linear or detailed geo-measurement with ETS machine:

1. Centering and Levelling – The machine is mounted on a tripod with the help of a try-bench and at a given point adjusts/installs at the centre with the help of the optical eyepiece mounted in the trivet, then the air bubble in the try-bench is adjusted so that it comes in the middle of the circle. The centering levelling process consequently known for linear distances and angular measurement precision.
2. Survey – Under the survey operation, with a prism on the various corners, Meda, Timera, Alamat offset points located on the ground, focus with the telescope and measured all offsets one after the other. In this way, all offset points are stored in the form of data along with point ID and other attribute. All the measurement offset points appear on the map page. After that, by creating a new area in the Area page, we add the drawing of all the fields according to chance. In this way, the four boundaries, area, perimeter of each field are obtained and the map is prepared on a scale of 1:1. The said survey data is copied into the pen drive.
3. Generating field book and Scaling Map – The computers process the copied data into various software and print the field-book, field-sheet and

scaling map. With Leica Geo office software, the field-book prints the map and field sheets at 1:1 and the Scaling Map from the AUTOCAD software.

In this way, the map, field book and other necessary data of the surveyed area are obtained as soon as possible with the ETS machine. Linear measurement, detailed land measurement and population survey are very easy and convenient with the ETS machine. Also, all data is saved in the internal memory of the machine. At the time of survey, the machine's data should be periodically crosschecked so that human and mechanical errors can be detected. Apart from this, there are many options available in the machine, with the help of which the distance angles between different points are detected. It is possible to be stamped in the Area Division Option. Also different points can be created in the machine as per Triangulation method.

(ii) Satellite Imagery based geo-measurement

In this method field bunds are digitized based on high resolution satellite image and map is prepared after field verification. In this system DGPS (Differential Global Positioning system) is a very important element. Geo reference is prepared by using exact ground control points (GCP). Each GCP is processed accurately by collecting the GPS coordinates and ortho image is prepared with high resolution in systematic way with different procedures of photogrammetry.

Steps involved are:

1. Control Point Establishment
2. Satellite Data Acquisition
3. DEM (Digital Elevation Models) Generation
4. Ortho Product Generation
5. Feature Extraction Using GIS Technology
6. Participatory Ground Truthing of Land Parcels

1. Control point establishment: It is the basic step for this methodology. A geometric control network is constructed and is established on ground, in the area, for which control points are to be made. Certain things to be kept in mind are –
   - Identification of the reference station in the centre of the survey area.
   - DGPS data collection, using dual frequency geodetic DGPS receivers, for 72 hours
   - Determining the reference station coordinates with reference to International geodetic survey (IGS) stations.
   - Identification of GCP locations in the satellite image.
   - Collection of GPS data at GCP locations for three hours.
   - Determining the GCP coordinates, with reference to the reference station, in DGPS mode
   - Where multiple overlapping is taken and control points established, all images can be adjusted for parallax simultaneously. This process is known as bundle block adjustment. Digital photogrammetric bundle

block adjustment of multi-resolution and multimode satellite data, altogether.

2. Satellite data acquisition: Satellite images are photos of earth and other planets which are collected by satellite imagery directed by government and other establishments. Quality of satellite imagery is decided by the information fetched by it. It may be evaluated on the basis spatial resolution, spectral resolution and temporal resolution.
3. DEM (Digital Elevation Model) generation: Aerial triangular and block adjustment techniques are performed using a high-end digital photogrammetry system with automatic image matching feature. All aerial photographs/satellite image/Drone images covered are thus associated with first-order points, mass points and tie points in a single block and thus the accuracy maintained is a location accuracy of 20 cm.

   DEMs are generated at a closed interval to the grid points and terrain features are added to obtain a digital field model. These digital terrain models are edited and tested for accuracy. Altitude accuracy is within one meter, which is sufficient to generate cadastral maps.
4. Ortho rectified satellite image generation:
   - Generating an image corrected for terrain-induced distortions for achieving better planimetric accuracy.
   - Ortho-rectification of world view – 2 images for the entire District area physically separate images but virtually seamless.
   - Data fusion-synergistic merging of higher resolution black and white (panchromatic 0.5 M resolution) data with coarser resolution colour (multi-spectral 2 meter) data for getting colour-coded images of high resolution ortho-rectified satellite data.
5. Feature extraction using GIS technology: To access it, a brief idea of vector and raster model is necessary. Data model is a conceptual description (mental model) of how spatial data are organized for, used by the GIS. It represents a set of guidelines to convert the real word (called entity) to the digitally and logically represented special objects consisting of the attributes and geometry. The attributes are managed by thematic or semantic structure which the geometry is separated by geometric topological structure.

   Raster and vector are two very different but common data formats used to store geo-special data. Vector data uses X and Y coordinates to define the locations of points, lines and areas (polygons) that correspond to map features such as fire hydrants, trails and parcels. As such, vector data tend to define centers and edges of features.

   Raster data on the other hand, use a matrix of square areas to define where features are located. These squares, also called pixels, cells and grids, typically are of uniform size and their size determines the detail that can be maintained in the dataset. Because raster data represent square area, they described interiors rather than boundaries, as is the case with vector data.

Vector data are excellent for capturing and storing spatial details, while raster data are well suited for capturing, storing and analyzing data such as elevation, temperature, soil pH etc. that vary continuously from location to location.

For feature extraction, field bunds, natural and manmade structures are delineated with ortho image by plot parcel on available ortho-rectified imagery. Unclear areas are surveyed by using DGPS and ETS. In this way, vector database obtained by remote sensing/DGPS/ETS are integrated in GIS environment so that base cadastral database may be developed for future settlement/title verification. For updating any local characteristic, present cadastral vector data is superimposed over ortho-rectified imagery dataset.

6. Participatory ground truthing of land parcels: The field work shall commence as per the scheduled published. The field team shall mark boundaries of the land parcels on the Bromide/coated paper prints, as shown by the concerned owner in the presence of the owner of the adjacent land parcels. After identifying boundaries in the presence of the owners and marking them in the Bromide/coated paper prints, the survey team should obtain an acknowledgement from the owners/concerned officials that the boundaries and details of the land parcel are recorded in their presence and to their satisfaction. The details of the surveyors, who have carried out the survey, should also be recorded. In case the parcel limits are obscured in the ortho-photo, or the ortho-photo is not available, parcel boundaries, as shown by the concerned owner, in the presence of the owners of the adjacent land parcels shall be surveyed using TS/GPS. In such cases, the survey agency shall generate the land parcel map based on their TS readings and obtain acknowledgement of each plot/parcel from the owners. The tertiary control point should be used as the reference station for DGPS. The tertiary control point and auxiliary point should be used for TS survey. The plot boundaries can also be surveyed using the offset from the details appearing on the ortho-photo, in which case tertiary control and auxiliary points will not be needed.

The survey team should take care that the ridges, which are not actually boundaries of the parcels, are not taken into account for delineation of the parcel boundaries. In case where collective cultivation is done, or where boundaries are not demarcated, the parcel boundaries should be recorded only after their demarcation on the ground has been carried out with reference to the existing land records and as per procedure laid down in the relevant revenue manual in the presence of the concerned owners. Each land parcel should be identified by its owners and should be given a unique ID which shall be used for linking the attributes data collected in respect of the land parcel.

The Landowners who intend to affix stones at their field junctions, may be shown the points where stones can be affixed. The current land use, irrigation status and other land attributes data shall also be collected by the survey team as per data model structure.

Resurvey in Madhya Pradesh

Modernization of land records is being done under the Digital India Land Records Modernization Programme (DILRMP) of the Government of India in the state. The most important part of this scheme is the work of the all-round survey of agricultural lands. Currently the maps are to be updated according to the actual situation under the survey resurvey work. The maps available with the revenue department in the state have become quite old. Due to lack of uniformity in location and maps at the site, processes of mutation, demarcation, etc. are being disrupted due to which there is an increase in land disputes. Therefore, it has become necessary that under the modernization scheme of land records, the map should be updated according to the present situation.

Under the Survey Resurvey Scheme, the revenue records of the respective villages will be purified by the update of the revenue records, on the other hand, the villagers will be benefited due to the correctness of the records. Due to the purification of land revenue records of the villagers, there will be a reduction in mutual disputes, they will also have facility in their demarcation, nomination etc. Presently, due to differences in maps and actual location, there is a situation of mutual dispute among the villagers, which gives rise to crimes over time.

Why Resurvey – Challenges in legacy survey:

1. No timeline for the start and completion of survey activities.
2. Offline and manual survey process.
3. Discrepancy with data reported and actual progress on field.
4. Decentralized database and no real-time monitoring/reporting.
5. Lack of transparency towards the execution of survey activities.

Need for survey: The features of map change over a period due to:

- Change in ownership and merging/subdivision of land parcels
- Changes of land use
- Changes in geography – river changing course etc.

Since map is not static, new maps need to be created to update the changes. Amendments to MPLRC has recognized this need and introduced provisions for survey.

Benefits of the scheme at various levels

1. Ease of nomination and practice
2. Early resolution of demarcation problems
3. Ease of purchase and sale

Benefits to the department

1. Facility to establish decisive and non-discretionary ownership.
2. The administrative unit like Majra Tola will facilitate the construction of revenue village, construction of new tehsils etc.
3. Ease of Land Acquisition.
4. Easy to solve revenue related matters.
5. Convenient for paperless land records

Community benefits

1. Ease of preservation and assessment of public use routes.
2. Ease of conservation of released land/government land, etc.

SVAMITVA (Survey of Village Abadi and Mapping with Improvised Technology in Village Areas) SCHEME

Under the 'SVAMITVA' scheme of Government of India (Ministry of Panchayati Raj) Department of Revenue, M.P. decided to implement the RoR (Record of Right) of Abadi land in rural areas. This ambitious project is to be carried out with shoulder-to-shoulder partnership of Survey of India, Panchayati Raj Institutions and Revenue Department of M.P. Using Drone Survey to get the primary imagery, it is the most modern technology, so far, to be used in survey works in the State of M.P. Districts have been segregated into different stages to carry out survey operations. Right now, notification for the third stage of districts has also been published in the Gazette. Pilot plan has been initiated in the June 2020 first week. District Harda in Madhya Pradesh has been perhaps the first district in India where 100% target has been completed under SVAMITVA and RoRs have been handed over to owners. Entire scheme is expected to be implemented in rest of all districts by 2021-22 and 2022-23.

It is pertinent to mention that technique of Drone Survey has been adopted in this scheme. In modern survey techniques, drone survey is an important name. Drone survey process includes three steps namely establishment of base station, drone flying and feature extraction. Although survey through satellite imagery still in practice, but due to certain characteristics, former is more useful and effective, which are as follows:

1. Surveyor may decide timing and gap of survey at its own.
2. Image resolution is pretty better which facilitates detailed survey of micro level.
3. Satellite image capturing has limitation of minimum survey area whereas for small region drone survey is cheap and useful.

This survey is carried out under sections 65, 67, 107 and 108 (2) and Madhya Pradesh Land Revenue Code (Land Survey and Land Records) Rules, 2020 under Madhya Pradesh Land Revenue Code, 1959 Chapter-7. Under this action, maps and records of land is prepared in electronic form.

Abadi Survey Flow Chart

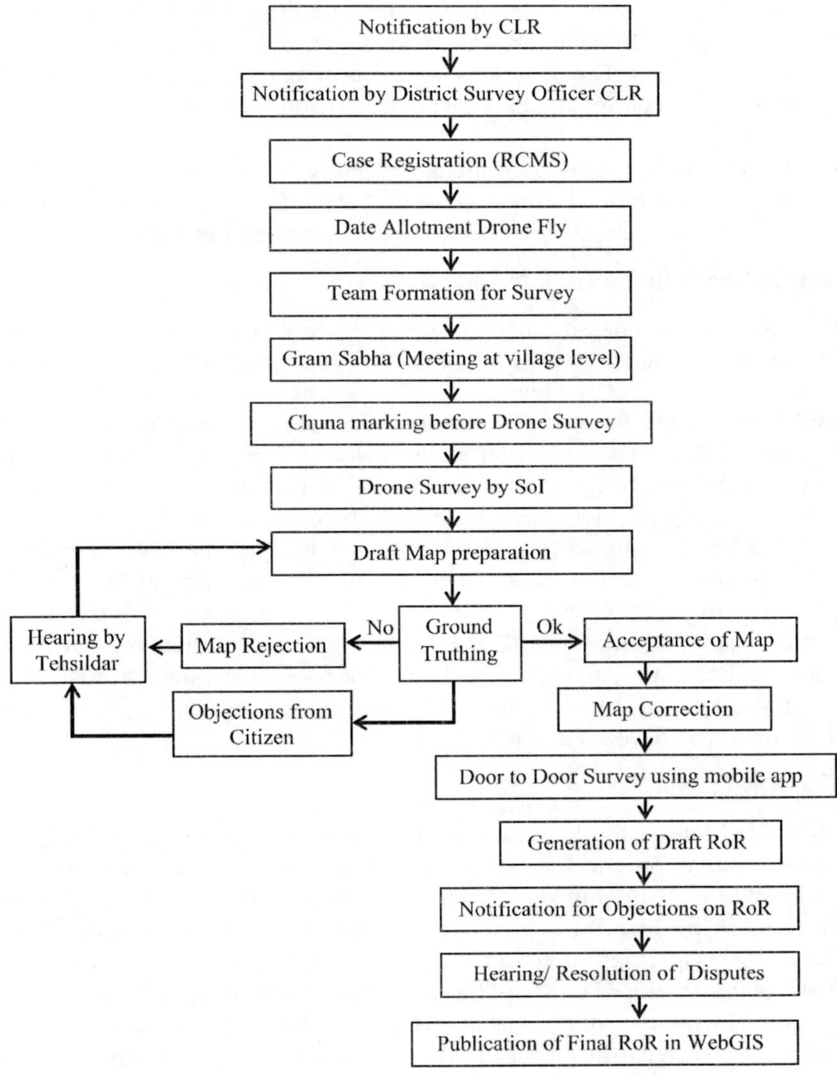

Challenges in Pilot Project:

- Frontline executives of Revenue Department are not very familiar to recent technological advancements of survey field. Hence, training leads a crucial role so as to complete the project.
- People have apprehensions of modern techniques in land record corrections; like a tribal person in interiors of state is stunned to see the use of flying Drone for his land records updating!

- Technique has limitations in correcting complex land dispute issues for survey, a 'land parcel' only is actually a traditional 'mitti' of landowner's family which he, by no way going to lose or exchange in due course.
- Coordination between various government agencies like Survey of India, Revenue Department, Panchayati Raj Institutions and others also has challenges.
- Development of new applications for feature extraction, their first time use by first time trained workforce needs continuous and rigorous monitoring and corrective measures so as to cope up with budding challenges.

New Initiative in the Field of Land Survey

For setting up of control points in survey process, a cutting edge technology of CORS is being adopted in MP. CORS (Continuously Operating Reference Stations) is a Global Navigation satellite system in which control points are established in the form of permanent CORS stations. This system facilitates to conserve the data along with automatically correcting it with GPS/GNSS data as per their precise location and provides it to the end user to locate the exact status of data. More than one control stations work in it because of which mistakes based on distances are minimised at most. It is a fast and economically viable technology for data positioning. Also, the user may amend the data in real time. It confirms the current location with +-20 mm accuracy. This technique is appreciated worldwide for its 3D status. It has huge demand in survey, navigation, construction, mining, agriculture and scientific researches which invariably need exact location and data continuity. This technique is developing continuously therefore it will have a major role in future too.

The Way Forward

Like SVAMITVA for Abadi region, for regions except Abadi in rural areas; survey-resurvey programme has been launched. A pilot project has been launched for tehsil Mho, District Indore. Under this scheme, Maps and RoRs are proposed to be made by Map-IT, a premiere government institution of state of M.P. Government, after ortho-rectification of satellite imagery. A customized GIS tool is being developed by Map-IT and survey data will be extracted by Patwaris, the ground workforce of revenue department in labs itself. In budding stage, this project is expected to be launched as pilot very soon and to be completed in next 3 to 5 years. Very similar project for urban areas is also on cards in near future.

2.9

Maharashtra

Sham Khamkar

Introduction

In a predominantly agricultural country like India, Land Revenue was the major source of income to run the administration. Importance of maintaining records of land holding was emphasized by the Britishers. The state of Maharashtra in its erstwhile form was also swept by land administration wave started during those times.

After the fall of Maratha Empire in 1818, the British succeeded to the legacy of the farming system of the earlier Maratha rulers. Maratha system was Ryotwari but in order to systematize matters, the systematic Ryotwari system which had been introduced in Madras Presidency in 1793, was adopted in the Bombay Presidency. But due to the over assessment imposed during the Maratha period, the economic condition of the people went from bad to worse. So, in order to have a systematic introduction of the Ryotwari system, land survey accompanied by settlement on sound principles was done. Mr Pringle, Assistant Collector, Pune surveyed the lands by Chain and Cross-staff and introduced the English Acre as unit of assessment.

The present Maharashtra State is formed by merging various areas which were earlier the parts of other states. The Vidarbha region of the state was the part of Central Provinces and Berar, whereas Marathwada region was the part of Hyderabad state.

Types of Surveys Carried out in Maharashtra

Cadastral Survey

Cadastral Survey is a field to field survey of a revenue village or an estate undertaken by Government, to ascertain the position of boundaries, area and quality of each field. It provides the data for the settlement of land revenue and the preparation and maintenance of record of rights. In Maharashtra, there were two systems were followed of cadastral survey, i.e., Deccan system and Central Provinces system. Cadastral surveys excluding those in the Central Provinces districts (Nagpur division) were conducted based on the Cross-staff system.

In the Bombay Presidency, original settlements were done from 1840 to 1880 and the revision settlements were done from 1868 to 1930. In Marathwada districts, previously belonged to Hyderabad state, survey was done in 1875, on the lines of Deccan system. From 1904, no new survey activity was undertaken and only maintenance and preservation of survey record is being done.

In Deccan system, the work of revenue survey is divided into two sections. The Traverse section comprises the measurement of the angular and linear distances with the help of Theodolite and Chain which furnishes the Skelton for detailed framework to follow. The cadastral section relates to the measurements of detailed topography on the Skelton provided by the traverse survey by the Cross-staff or plain table. The village map was constructed by laying down the traverse and base lines and then plotting thereupon the separate survey numbers. The scale of these maps is usually 20 chains to the inch. At time of survey, the various types of boundary marks, such as mound, stone, stone cairn, hedge were erected on the boundaries.

All revenue surveys were conducted on foot-pound system. The unit of measurement was a Gunter Chain measuring 33 feet divided into 16 parts, called annas, each measuring 33/16 feet. In some parts of the State, 41 3/4 feet chain was used for the measurements. In Central Provinces districts, the chain used for revenue survey was of 66 feet chain divided into 200 links.

In the revenue survey of old Bombay Presidency districts, Marathwada districts and Berar districts the unit of area is an English Acre which comprised 40 gunthas or 40 square chains viz. 43560 square feet and each guntha = 1 square chain viz. 1089 square feet. The area of each parcel of land surveyed is recorded in Acres and Gunthas. Whereas in the four Central province districts the area is calculated in Acres and cents viz. upto two decimals of Acres (viz. 100 cents = 1 Acre). After the enactment of the Standards of Weights and Measures Act, 1956 introducing the Metric system, the derived Units for recording the areas of agricultural lands are the Hectares and Acres.

In old Central Provinces districts (Vidarbha region) at the time of original survey theodolite framework was done on traverse method and by plane table method detailed cadastral maps are drawn to the scale of 16 inches to a mile or 10 chains to an inch. The map, thus prepared was the only measurement record. The traverse framework was maintained up to date by periodical inspections. There are no boundary marks in the shape of stones to the individual holdings. To bring the Vidarbha region survey records at par with the other survey records of the state and for bringing Record of Rights up to date, resurvey was conducted from 1974 to 1994.

After passing of the Khoti Abolition Act, 1949, Inam Abolition Act, 1940 and Bombay Merged Territories and Areas (Jagir Abolition) Act, 1953, all the unsurveyed and unsettled Inam villages, Khoti villages and Jagir villages were surveyed under the provisions of Bombay Land Revenue Code, 1879. These villages are surveyed by Minor Triangulation measurement system. In these villages, after the index map is completed, the theodolite stations, along with their legs and leg measurements are plotted on the cloth mounted square ruled detailed measurement sheets according to the progressive coordinates worked out in the traverse patrak. By using these theodolite stations detailed measurement was carried out using Plane Table.

City Survey

British Government realized the necessity for the survey of towns and cities as an adjunct to municipal administration and such surveys, as a matter of fact, were undertaken at an early date of British rule. It was pronounced by the then British Government that it is as much the duty of the Government to survey cities and village sites as to survey agricultural lands. In Bombay presidency area, in 1867 Act was passed to make provisions regarding the application of earlier 1865 Act to towns and cities. And under the provisions of Bombay Land Revenue Code,1879 the city survey of towns having population more than 2000 and less than 2000 was done from the first decade of twentieth century.

Objects to carry out City Survey were three-fold and can be described as administrative, fiscal and legal. The area to which such survey may extend was defined as the village, town or city site. The actual operation of the survey falls into several parts. It includes actual measuring and mapping i.e. traversing, detailed mapping and the enquiry to decide the correct limits and frontages of all properties, and their ownerships. Based on this record of rights in the form of property cards were prepared. In districts of Vidarbha region, Nazul land in most of the important towns have been regularly surveyed and settled from 1918 onwards.

In Bombay Island, the first mention of survey was in 1670-71, but this survey is not forthcoming. From 1811-1827 southern half of the island was minutely surveyed and registers showing various details were compiled. The northern half was only topographically surveyed and only the areas held under the different tenures were denoted on the map. Lieut. Col. Laughton conducted next revenue survey of the Island from 1865-1872. In this survey, plans were prepared on a scale of 40 feet to an inch for the southern half of the island and 100 feet to an inch for the northern half of the island, together with the registers showing the area, name of the occupant and the tenure of every holding. Then from 1915 to 1918 cadastral survey of Mumbai City was conducted, because city had undergone vast developments since the survey of island by Colonel Laughton. This record of city survey is now maintained.

Consolidation of Holdings

One of the main reasons for the low productivity of agriculture in India is the Fragmentation of Lands. Owing to the pressure of population on land and the customary laws of inherence, land has been divided and sub-divided into fragments which are so small that they prevent economic use of land. These fragments are not only small in size but are normally scattered in different directions at different places. The productivity of agriculture has therefore, been declining. It is therefore, necessary to improve agriculture to bring the scattered holdings together into compact blocks. A bold move on the part of the then Government of Bombay to introduce by statue compulsory consolidation of holdings in 1947 was taken. Such a measure would not be successful unless steps were simultaneously taken to prevent further fragmentation of land.

Land consolidation was planned for the readjustment and rearrangement of land parcels and their ownership. As per the Bombay Prevention of Fragmentation and Consolidation of Holdings Act, 1947, the consolidation scheme was implemented from 1948 to 1993 in most of the villages of the State. The consolidation process was implemented with an objective to bring together scattered plots owned by cultivators into compact blocks. In consolidation scheme, the survey numbers were converted to Gat numbers.

Existing Practices of Land Surveying and Recording Systems

After the original and revision settlement, no new settlement was conducted in the State. But various types of measurements such as boundary confirmation, sub-division, land acquisition, non-agricultural conversion etc. are done. After measuring the field by using plane table, boundaries of survey number or subdivision of a survey number are confirmed as per the original survey record available in the office. For the boundary of a survey number Tipans (Field Measurement Book) are used. Tipan is an individual land parcel map prepared at the time of original survey by using cross staff and chain. This map is not to the scale, so first scale drawn diagram of survey number is prepared. National Informatics Centre (NIC), New Delhi has developed Collabland software for solving the Tipans. Tipan boundary is superimposed on the field boundary. After new measurement of any land separate maps are prepared.

For the agriculture land survey and city survey, until 2000, only plane table was used. But from 2000 onwards Department is gradually moving towards ETS survey. Now, Department has decided to switch over to CORS (Continuously Operating Reference Station) GPS survey from 2021. For Gaothan (village site) survey, Drones are being used in the State in collaboration with SoI.

Problems/ issues faced at field level by practising the Current Survey and Land Recording Systems

The problems faced while carrying out the survey of any land are as follows:

- *Old survey records*: Old survey records are on paper and due to continuous handling they are getting torn and tattered. Due to shrinkage and elongation of paper, scale of some of the maps are distorted. Some records have folds, so the boundaries of maps cannot be joined.
- *Non Uniformity of maps*: There is no uniformity in the scale and language of different types of maps. Tipan is nothing but sketch of a Survey Number drawn but not to the scale. In Bombay presidency areas, details on Tipan

are in Modi script and in Marathwada districts these are in Urdu script. Prior to 1920, the measurement of newly formed subdivisions was done by cross staff and chain and corrected Tipans are prepared. But after 1920 the measurement of newly formed subdivisions is done by Plane Table method in 1:1000 scale and measurement sheets are preserved. Subdivisions in any already formed subdivision is also measured separately on new sheets. For measurement of non-agricultural lands scale of 1:500 is used. In the areas where Town Planning scheme is sanctioned under the Maharashtra Regional and Town Planning Act, 1966, maps prepared by the Town Planning Department are maintained as Land Records.

- *Method of survey*: For carrying out various types of measurements plane table was used widely. Though it is convenient to carry and measure average fields, for large areas it takes much more time.
- *Violation of Standard area*: As per the Section 5 of Consolidation act, standard areas are determined for each class of land i.e. jirayat (dry crop), bagayat (garden) etc. in local areas. But on the fields small fragments are formed due to heirship, sale etc. As per existing acts, these fragments cannot be measured and mapped, and separate record of rights cannot be prepared.

  While preparing consolidation schemes, some lands of the owners are exchanged as per their consent. But it is observed that in some cases the owners have not handed over the actual possession of the land.
- *Non-updation of records*: Original survey records are prepared a century before, so updating of these records and Record of Rights is a need of time. But landowners are reluctant to some extent for new survey for various reasons.

Any pilot/intervention undertaken in the past/present or any future plan: issues, challenges and learning from such interventions

For the preservation of old records and for improvement in survey techniques various programmes are implemented in the state.

Scanning of Old Survey Records: Land Records Department maintains huge volume of textual records related to survey. At the time of original and subsequent surveys various textual records such as gunakar book, akarphod, kami jasti patrak etc. are prepared. Over a period of time this record have deteriorated due to various environmental conditions and continuous use by the Department officials. Copies of these records are given to the public on demand. For this official staff has to make copy of the original survey record which are given to citizens. So pilot project for scanning of old records was undertaken in Mulshi taluka of Pune distrisct. This project was implemented throughout the State and around 26 crore documents are scanned in this project. Now these scanned records are being made available to the citizens using payment gateway. Scanned data of 21 districts is already uploaded and data of remaining districts will be uploaded shortly.

Use of Compactors: Compactors of appropriate size are supplied to field level offices for storing survey records. In these compactors A and B record, which is to be preserved permanently, is kept. This has saved the space in the record rooms and records can be easily searched.

Digitization of Cadastral Maps: Under Digital India Land Records Modernization Programme (DILRMP) state has implemented the project of digitisation of cadastral maps in six districts, namely Pune, Raigad, Nashik, Aurangabad, Amravati and Nagpur. In this project digitization of survey records such as tipan, phalani maps, gat book maps, triangulation sheets, city survey maps, land acquisition, etc. maps are digitized. This project is completed and shortly digitised maps will be made available to the citizens. The digitized village maps are already uploaded on Bhunaksha portal. These digitized maps are being used by the department staff for various types of land measurement cases. Also, the work of digitization of cadastral maps of remaining 28 districts will be started soon.

Digitisation of City Survey Maps: Digitization of City Survey maps of Mumbai City is complete and these are hosted on Bhunaksha portal. These maps are widely used by the Department, Municipal Corporation of Greater Mumbai and citizens. The work of Digitization of city survey maps in Mumbai suburban district is in progress.

Resurvey: Survey of lands in Maharashtra State is carried out in the British period. Over a period, due to increase in population, urbanisation and industrialization, land holding is being transferred on a large scale. Also, various small fragments are formed as land is getting divided and subdivided after every sale or heirship. Actual possession, maps of Land Records Department and Record of Rights are not matching at several places, resulting in litigations regarding land matters. The speed of mutations is more, but the record of maps is not updated accordingly and therefore we can see names of many holders on a piece of land. As mentioned earlier the survey record is very old and it will be difficult to use in future. The boundary marks erected at the time of original survey are vanished due to various developments undertaken on the ground. Considering all these facts the State Government decided to carry out resurvey of lands in rural areas, by using modern techniques.

Resurvey is one of the most important aspects of Digital India Land Records Modernization Programme (DILRMP) of Government of India. The state of Maharashtra has done a pilot study to do the Resurvey using modern technology in 2012. The primary objectives of pilot project were to study the operations and activities, to understand the challenges and limitations and to understand reactions and response of the public.

Department has undertaken a pilot resurvey of 12 villages in the district of Pune. Out of these twelve, six villages were surveyed following traditional Pure Ground method using Electronic Total Station machine. The other six villages were surveyed by following hybrid model using the Satellite Imagery (HRSI). The results were technically compared and conclusion drawn that using Satellite Imagery is better than Pure Ground method administratively, financially and in the interest of faster completion of the survey.

Then resurvey of 12 villages was done by using High Resolution Satellite Imagery and superimposing the original maps of Land Records on it. Then it was observed that there is vast difference in the boundaries and areas of the lands. So the Land Parcel Map (LPM) was prepared and given to the holders, from which they can compare the area of their land with current area in the record of rights. About 50% of LPM's could be distributed to the landholders. And out of that 45% holders accepted the area mentioned in the LPM. Remaining holders did not accept the LPM's, because of the deviation in area or boundary.

Many issues arise while taking up resurvey. Also there is a difference between survey of British era and resurvey in current times. There are lot of differences between the Government and administrative systems as well as the citizens expectations from the Government. Issues which arise out of all these conditions are faced which have undertaken resurvey.

The current survey system is not able to cope up with the emerging challenges and it is time the State move towards a system which protects the property rights of the people in a better way by digitizing maps and removing discretions in surveying. But there are daunting challenges posed by the various issues. Resurvey touches one of the sensitive issues of an individual and of the society that is ownership rights over the immovable property. Disputes related to land is the cause of many civil litigation and criminal cases. So any process affecting the property right either positively or negatively needs to be supported by legislation passed by the competent legislature.

For resurvey, so many modern techniques are available, such as ETS, GPS, satellite imagery, aerial photography etc. Use of Hybrid method instead of Pure Ground method is generally considered with the view to expedite resurvey. But the earlier survey records are prevailing and there are deviations in factum of possession, hence it becomes difficult to decide the method of resurvey and technology to be used. Acceptance of the people is also a main hurdle in resurvey.

Current Initiatives on Land Survey

Use of ETS machines and GPS

The original survey was carried out by using Cross Staff and Chain and Tipans (FMB) of Survey numbers are prepared. For the measurement of sub-divisions in Survey Numbers Plain Table was used. After independence, for all types of measurement works Plain Table is used widely in the State. Though the plane table is a handy instrument, the process of measurement is bit cumbersome. And for the measurement of large area, we have to spend more time.

So for getting more accuracy and speed, from 2000 onwards State has decided to replace Plain Table Survey by Electronic Total Station Survey. Gradually the use of ETS amongst the surveyors is enhanced and they are now conversant with the ETS measurement technique. State receives around two lakh applications for the measurement of land in a year. Use of ETS machines for survey has improved the disposal of cases.

E-mojani-Management of measurement cases

E-mojani application help Department officials in managing survey request in an efficient and effective manner. It also helps Department officials to process the survey request accurately and provide citizens with vital information like date of survey, name of surveyor, measurement fees etc. This application also helps the Department officials in generating challans of measurement fees. Online MIS generated through this application helps the Department officials in understanding the overall status of this project like number of cases, number of pending cases, revenue earned etc. On an average, the application handles more than 1.75 lakh measurement requests per year.

In Version-2.00 of E-mojni Software, citizen portal is made available for the public. Also, the public can view the stage of their measurement application. The citizens can pay the measurement fees online and they can upload the documents. State has started developing a mobile app on the lines of Dishank app, developed by the Karnataka, for guiding the surveyor for going on the site of the measurement. In this app, surveyor can upload the photographs of the site he has measured by geotagging facility. It is proposed to have the area reconciliation facility in the software so as to avoid further disputes.

It is also proposed to develop GIS portal, which will be a central repository for storing all the data related to measurement cases. The measurements carried out using Rovers will be uploaded automatically on this portal, which will lead to create a grid of all land parcels in the state. In this grid co-ordinate based map will be stored, so individual georeferenced land parcel and village maps will be available to the citizens. The maps uploaded in this portal can be used by other Government Departments for planning and other purposes.

Use of CORS

CORS (Continuously Operating Reference Station) is an advanced infrastructure that can solve the problem of accuracy and real time data acquisition. Looking at the importance and usefulness of the technology, the Survey of India has started an initiative of establishing nationwide CORS network. CORS is a geo-positioning infrastructure that provides seamless, consistent and uniform framework of the country. It offers highly accurate DGPS service that also improves the speed, efficiency and simplicity of in-house data acquisition process. CORS takes the overall productivity to the next level by overcoming the limitations of the current RTK technique.

Survey of India (SoI) is going to establish around 200 CORS network in Maharashtra, Uttar Pradesh and Karnataka. Out of these 77 CORS stations are established in the State. These stations will receive signals directly from the satellite. As the system of CORS GPS is RTK, the reading of coordinates of a particular point can be recorded within 15-30 seconds with a horizontal accuracy of 5-10 mm. And auto corrections in the coordinates to precise pointing of a particular location will be done. Installation of 77 CORS is complete and testing of the instruments is in progress. Once the system is functional it will be a 'game changer' of survey scenario, because of its accuracy, speed and capacity to cover large area. With CORS, measurements will be paperless and will have minimum human interference.

In CORS survey, Rover will be used for the measurements, which will give accurate reading within 30 seconds. Surveyors will be having tab which is configured with Rover and CORS system. So map is generated on tab. For CORS survey, about 400 Rovers are available in the Department, by using these Rovers land measurement is being done.

Use of Drones for Gaothan (Abadi) survey

In Maharashtra out of 43,665 villages city survey of only 3,800 villages completed. Day by day urbanization of villages is going on and valuation of the properties is increasing. Due to unavailability of authentic records of the properties falling under Gaothan (Abadi), it becomes very difficult to define the boundaries, area, ownership and giving building permissions. Rural Development Department of the Maharashtra state has decided to prepare a updated GIS based Property Tax Register using modern technology. So, it is decided by the state to prepare GIS based maps and Property Cards of the properties falling under gaothan (ABADI).

Considering the time taken using current methodology for survey, Settlement Commissioner and Director of Land Records (Maharashtra State) discussed this issue with Surveyor General of India, Dehradun. Surveyor General of India suggested a new emerging modern technology that is use of Drone/UAV for mapping properties falling in Gaothan (Abadi) area. Before starting the project, a pilot project was carried out with the technical support of Survey of India to check the accuracy, output and results of drone-based survey at Sonori village of Taluka Purandar, District Pune. It was successfully completed. Based on the experience of this pilot project to maintain the uniformity in methodology for carrying out the work of all villages of entire Maharashtra and to complete the project in stipulated time period Standard Operating Procedure (SOP) is prepared. So far, in 24027 villages drone flying is completed and the entire work of 4175 villages is complete.

In the first phase of the project, only Gaothan (Abadi) area is taken. But there are lot of inhabitations in the area which is outside Gaothan boundary. People having houses in this area are also keen in getting their properties surveyed. At the time of drone flying images of Gaothan and the adjacent properties in village are to be captured, which can be used for doing city survey of this area in phase II.

The idea of Maharashtra using Drone/UAV for mapping was accepted at National level. Government of India has decided to implement the central sector scheme 'SVAMITVA' (Survey of villages and mapping with improvised technology in village areas), Drone survey of rural habitations to enable property validation. It is basically using photogrammetry to create survey grade maps. In this process actual survey on ground by using Electronic Total Station machines is not necessary. People get accurate map, based on the factum of possession.

References

1. The Bombay Survey and Settlement Manual, Volume I and II, Gordon R.G.
2. Manual of Land Surveying, Gordon R.G.
3. City Survey Manual, Anderson F.G.H.
4. The Bombay Prevention of Fragmentation and Consolidation of Holdings Act, 1947
5. Maharashtra City Survey Manual for Large Scale Mapping of Gaothan Areas Using UAVs
6. The Maharashtra Land Revenue Manual, Volume I

2.10

Rajasthan

Dr. Shashi Jain and Krishna Singh Shekhawat

Land Survey System in Rajasthan

The Government of Rajasthan is moving towards the adoption of more sophisticated e-governance offerings, moving from information to transactions to integration and ultimately to transformations. We all know that land records constitute vital element, both in anti-poverty strategy and for modernization. Good land records are essential for a well functioned land market. Historically, land records administration was under one of the oldest and traditional Government departments in which the Patwari at village level maintained record of land ownership. With the traditional way of working and record storing, it was becoming difficult to cope with the people's demand for searching and updating of records. The people at large used to go to Patwari many times for either getting a copy of the Jamabandi, Nakal or registration purpose. Moreover, for every legal transformation of land taking place, the Jamabandi used to be updated at regular intervals which was quite cumbersome and time consuming. There was also heterogeneity in maintenance of manual records. Since the land record data was perceived to be valuable records, so for malicious reasons, the filed functionaries did not also want this data to be compromised into a standard data format. Keeping all these things in consideration, an attempt has here been made to facilitate the preparation of new cadastral maps and new records of rights which are precise, accurate and high on integrity.

History of Survey and Land Settlement Operations

The Afghani Ruler, Sher Shah Suri, after seeing the deplorable condition of farmer, was the first one who tried to decide the land revenue according to the Land Classification in 1540-45 A.D.

Todarmal, one of the distinguished *Navratan*a from the Navratans of King Akbar, and the Diwan-e-Ashraf, invented in 1582 Metal Chain (*Jarib)* and first of all started survey of the land in which the land was measured in Bigha, Biswa, Biswansi. At that time, Metal Chain (*Jarib)* was of 80 hands. After classification of land, Todarmal assimilated the details regarding land revenue from the year 1570-1580. This practice continued up to the British era.

In 1822, Colonel James surveyed and mapped the vast area of Rajasthan, thus laying the foundation of Land Settlement in Rajasthan. As a result, the princely State of Bharatpur was the first to start the process of Land Settlement in 1855, but systematic land settlement operations could be done only after 1901. Alwar was the second State in which Land Settlement was done in 1899-1900 and after that other princely States like Jaipur, Marwar, Mewar etc. also started Land Settlement process. According to the land classification, rent rate was fixed on per bigha basis culminating into increased area of agricultural land and also an increase in the agricultural production. But during British time this system proved to be harmful as the rulers started doing land settlement at small intervals and after every land settlement, the rates of rent were increased and it became impossible for the farmers to pay the rent and once again the farmers started getting distracted from agricultural work.

Recent History of Survey Operations in Rajasthan

Before Independence, out of the 22 princely states of Rajputana, only a few large princely states used to administer the measurement and settlement of agricultural land through their own Settlement Departments.

First Survey and Settlement Operation was started in the year 1876-77 in the princely state of Hadauti (Kota). After the creation of the Settlement Department in 1949, the first survey work was started in the state. In 1978, six Settlement Offices and seven other Settlement Offices were formed in 1979-80.

The last survey work in the state was done in the year 1994. At present, 11 Settlement Offices are working in Jaipur, Jodhpur, Bikaner, Sikar, Alwar, Bharatpur, Kota, Tonk, Bhilwara, Ajmer and Udaipur. Settlement Department surveys the villages of Rajasthan and prepares maps of the Land and Record of Rights (*Misal Bandobast*) under the legal provisions and handovers the entire record to the concerned District Collectors. Traditionally, the survey/resurvey and record operations were carried out as per the provisions of Chapter 7 of the Rajasthan Land Revenue Act, 1956, together with the Rajasthan Land Revenue (Survey, Record and Settlement-Government) Rules, 1957.

Traditional System of Survey Operations

After independence, Rajasthan was carved out on 01 November 1956 by unifying the princely states in several stages. In 1949 (Samvat 2006), the present Land Settlement Department was established in United Rajasthan. At that time, there were very diverse and adverse conditions before the department, as all the princely states had different Metal Chain (*Jarib*)[44] for measurement

[44] The Metal Chain (*Jarib*) consisted of 100 strings (*Kadi*) or 10 *gatthas*, 1 *gattha* was equal to 10 strings (*Kadi*). In the record of right the area was written in *Bigha*

of land, scattered, unorganized and incomplete records. The different units of measurements of Bigha-Biswa at that time were as follows:

S. No.	*Jarib Name*	*Area*	*Bigha (in sq. yards)*	*Area of use*
1.	Akbari	110 × 110 ft	1344.44	At present in Chittorgarh.
2.	Shahjahani	165 × 165 ft	3025	At present in most districts of Rajasthan
3.	Gantry	132 × 132 ft	1936	In some districts such as Bharatpur, Ajmer, Nagaur etc.
4.	Farrukhabadi	157.5 × 157.5 ft	2756.25	In some tehsils of Chittorgarh
5.	Dhaulpuri	150 × 150 ft	2500	In early princely states of Karauli and Dhaulpur
6.	Mewari	152.5 × 152.5 ft	2584.03	In early princely states of Mewar

Currently, Metric Jarib is being used for survey, which is 20 meters in length. *Jarib* consists of 100 *kadiyan*, 10 *kadi* which is 2 meters in length. In the metric system, the unit of area is in square meters, in which 100 square meters = 1 acre and 100 acre = 1 hectare and 100 hectare = 1 Sq. km.

Major changes observed at field level from practising the traditional to existing survey and land recording systems

The existing survey-resurvey is the largest exercise of its kind after a period of almost 100 years when all the land was originally surveyed and cadastral maps prepared for the first time in the State of Rajasthan. At that time, survey and settlement operations were mainly carried out for the accurate assessment of the

---

and its small unit was *Biswa*. There are 20 *Biswas* in 1 *Bigha* and 20 *Biswansi* in 1 *Biswa*.

Length	**Area**
1 Furlong = 220 yrds	1 Bigha = 20 Biswa
1 Mile = 8 Furlong	1 Biswa = 20 Biswansi
	Ghatta × Ghatta = 1 Biswansi
1 Furlong = 8 Jarib (Shahjani)	Gatta × Jarib = 10 Biswansi
1 Furlong = 10 Jarib (Gantry)	Jarib × Jarib = 100 Biswansi
1 Furlong = 12 Jarib (Akbari)	Jarib × 10 Jarib = 1000 Biswansi
1 Jarib = 100 Kadi (links)	1 Standard Acre = 1000 Biswansi (Gantry)
1 Jarib = 10 Gatta	Gatta × 2 Jarib = 1 Biswa
1 Gatta = 10 Kadi	2 Jarib × 2 Jarib = 1 Bigha
Shahjahani Jarib	**Gantry Jarib**
Length – 82.5 feet = 27.5 yards	Length - 66 feet = 22 yards
Area - 55 × 55 Yards = 3025 Sq. Yards = 1 Bigha	Area - 44 × 44 Yards = 1936 Sq. Yards = 1 Bigha
1.6 bigha = 4840 Sq. Yards = 1 Acre.	2.5 bigha = 4840 Sq. Yards = 1 Acre.
1 Acre = 1 Bigha 12 Biswa	1 Acre = 2 Bigha 10 Biswa

land revenue to be collected from the peasants. However, the following major changes have taken place over the years:

- *Land has become more valuable than land revenue:* Since last 4-5 decades the value of land per-se has gone up by orders of magnitude. Earlier, the value of land used to be only about 10 times its annual rent or even less, whereas with the advent of urbanisation, industrialisation and development, the value of land has now become 1000 to 100,00,000 times compared to the land revenue rates. Land revenue has become almost insignificant as a source of income for the Government. In fact, in many states, including Rajasthan, collection of land revenue has been put on hold indefinitely.
- *Smaller size of land parcels:* Sizes of land parcels have been reduced considerably with increase in population and division of land holdings and also due to land being put to non-agricultural use.
- *Evolution of Technology*:
    1. Traditionally, survey operations were carried out using the manual plane table survey, the traverse method, the *murabbabandi* method etc. In these methods, the distances were measured using metal chains; theodolite and angles were measured using the right-angle instruments. These methods required greater resources in terms of time, cost and manpower. Moreover, they were prone to both systemic as well as random human errors besides the fact that possibility of manipulation of measurements due to various pressures was omnipresent.
    2. With the advent of newer technologies like Electronic Total Station, Differential Global Positioning System, Satellite Imagery and Internet etc., it has now become technically and financially feasible to generate highly precise and accurate maps with improved accuracies with an error ranging from 1 to 40 cm. Modern maps are geo-referenced and contain a lot more information than the traditional cadastral maps.
- *Non-agricultural use of Land*: Use of land for purposes such as industrial, residential, commercial and institutional etc. has become more pronounced with development. Thus, it has become important to keep track of these converted land parcels. Sizes of these also tend to be much smaller than agricultural land parcels.

Problems/Issues faced at the field level while conducting traditional survey operations

a) The maintenance and regular updating of old records is cumbersome and time consuming.

b) The records do not portray the correct picture on ground regarding the ownership and boundaries.

c) Current Khasra maps are flawed due to the difference in the area of Jamabandi (Annual Register) and Khasra maps due to the wrong *Tarmeem* (division). In cases of land allocation, division and decree, numbers are inserted in the Jamabandi without any *Tarmeem* (division) modification in the maps.

d) Traditional survey system based on bundle (*gatta*) and chain (*Jarib*) is highly delaying, expensive and flawed and due to this, the area of the Jamabandi (Annual Register) and the map is different.
e) There is difficulty in updating the map according to the present situation and the Jamabandi (Annual Register).
f) Notwithstanding the credibility and accuracy of the records prepared by the traditional methods, Section 140 of Rajasthan Land Revenue Act, 1956 stated that the current record is considered to be a presumptive record.
g) Hence, when the existing record is converted into digital format, the digitized version reflects the same errors and as a result it may vary from the ground reality.

Present System of Land Survey and Settlement Operations (Resurvey)

Considering the diverse topography and the geographical area of the State, the survey-resurvey work is at present being carried out using High Resolution Satellite Imagery supplemented with Differential GPS and/or ETS instruments. High Resolution Satellite Imagery brings a high level of integrity to the whole process – it allows for an ex-post-facto re-validation of maps with the help of satellite images. This makes it possible for any person in the hierarchy from the Settlement Commissioner down to the *Amin/Patwari* to ensure the accuracy of the prepared map by using DGPS-RTK instruments. It also enables the common man or a khatedar to measure his land himself and compare the prepared map with the satellite image of his land parcels. In fact, once the cadastral layer is superimposed on the satellite imagery, most of this work can be done on a desktop computer.

Criteria to carry out Resurvey

A decision was taken to carry out record or survey/re-survey operations only in places where record of rights or *field book* or maps are not available or have been destroyed/damaged/outdated etc.

Under the existing law, the Government can declare resurvey without re-calculation of assessment in below mentioned conditions *(legal provisions for carrying out resurvey see Box-1).* In village where cadastral survey has already been done in the past, de-novo survey shall not be undertaken except with the provisions/sanction of the Director on any of the following grounds:

a) A large scale variation since the last survey in the total area of the village under orders of a competent authority, or
b) Extensive changes in cultivation and other features of the area, or
c) Old maps becoming un-serviceable or requiring large scale corrections, or
d) Acquisition of land for canals/roads and public utility works by the Government.

e) Desirability of change in the length of the chain used at the last survey.

f) > 30% difference found between original land record and the ground realities, or

g) > 25% of land record become torn or destroyed, or

h) > 40 years completed of original survey or even before of it, if required or

i) During the original survey, accurate geo–referenced maps were not there due to which the problem of gaps and overlaps arose between the boundaries of any two adjoining cadastral village maps.

Box 1

Legal Provision for Survey/Resurvey and Record Operation

(1) Section 106:- Survey or resurvey (De-novo Operation).-The State Government may direct, by notification in the Official Gazette that the survey or resurvey of any local area shall be made and every such local area shall, from the date of the said notification

(2) Section 107:- Record Operations (Revision Operation). - In respect of any local area which has already been surveyed, that a general or partial revision of the records of such local area shall be made and thereupon.

(3) Section 108:- Record Officers. - The State Government upon the issue of a notification under section 106 or 107, shall appoint an Additional Land Records Officer to be in charge of the operations referred to therein.

(4) Section 109:- Mode of conducting operations.

(5) Section 110:- Assistance in survey of Boundaries.- Under Section 106

(6) Section 111:- Decision of disputes as to boundaries.:- Under Section 106 Notification

(7) Section 112:- Preparation of map and field book:- Under Section 106 Notification

(8) Section 113:- Preparation of record of rights.:- Under Section 106 Or 107 Notification

(9) Section 114:- Contents of record of rights. - The record of rights shall be prepared in such manner as may be prescribed by the State Government and shall consist of the following, namely —

(a) a Khewat, that is to say, a register of all estate-holders

(b) a Khatauni, that is to say, a register of all persons cultivating or otherwise holding or occupying land in such area, specifying the particulars required by section 121;

(c) A register of all persons holding land in such area free of rent or revenue; and

(d) Such other registers as may be prescribed.

(10) Section 115:- Inviting claims to land appearing to have no owner.

(11) Section 116:- Procedure when unclaimed land is used for common purposes

(12) Section 117:- Procedure when limited right over land is established

(13) Section 118:- Determination and record of Kudkasht land

(14) Section 119:- Determination of the Abadi of a village.

(15) Section 120:- Register of villages:-The area liable to fluvial action, precarious cultivation, either wholly or in part been released, remitted, redeemed, assigned or compounded specifying the authority therefore, and the conditions thereof.

(16) Section 121:- Particulars to be stated in Khatauni. Form No. 9 and 10

(17) Section 122:- Attestation of entries. - All undisputed entries in the record of rights shall be attested by the parties interested
(18) Section 124:- Procedure when rent or revenue payable is disputed.
(19) Section 136:- Correction of errors: - The Land Record Officer may, at any time, correct or cause to be corrected in the prescribed manner any clerical errors and any errors which the parties interested admit to have been made in the record of rights or register, or which a Revenue Officer may notice during the course of his inspection in any Register
(20) Section 126:- Existing records to be acted upon
(21) Section 127:- Proceedings pending upon close of survey and record operations

(Section 128-140 are for maintenance operation)

Technology adopted for Resurvey

Three technology options are available for Survey/Resurvey work:

1. Ground Survey Methods using DGPS-PPK/DGPS-RTK/ETS system – Each and every parcel of land shall be surveyed using either through DGPS-PPK, DGPS-RTK ETS system.
2. HRSI and ground-truthing system using DGPS-RTK/DGPS-PPK/ETS system – Through this method, new cadastral maps shall be prepared using HRSI and then verified for accuracy and correctness on the ground using DGPS-RTK/DGPS-PPK/ETS System.
3. Aerial Survey and ground-truthing system using DGPS-RTK/DGPS-PPK/ETS System – Through this method, new cadastral maps shall be prepared using images obtained from aerial survey of the land and then verified for accuracy and correctness on the ground using DGPS-RTK/DGPS-PPK/ETS system.

As per the decision taken by the Government of Rajasthan, the Survey/Resurvey work in the first phase will be carried out with the aid of High Resolution Satellite Imagery in conjunction with the modern survey equipment's like DGPS/ETS.

Pre-Survey Activities

The following survey activities are completed before Survey/Resurvey and Land Record Operation work commences in a district/tehsil/revenue village:

a) Notification and Publicity: Publication of Notifications under Section 106 & 108 of Rajasthan Land Revenue Act, 1956
b) Opening of a Publicity Cell at the District Level. The establishment of the Publicity Cell shall be the responsibility of the Land Record Officer of the District.
c) The publicity cell sensitizes the functionaries concerned and generate awareness among the Tenants/Enjoyer(s) in the area notified for survey

by conducting village level meetings, emphasizing the need for them to be present at the time of visit of the Survey Team, participate in the Survey and Land Record operation and to show the boundaries of their Land-Parcels under section 110 RLR Act, 1956.

Survey Plan:

a) Survey Team submits detailed Programme for survey including number of Survey Team to be engaged after being supplied with existing Cadastral Maps from the Director, Land Records and Surveys.
b) A meeting at the level of Village (Gram Sabha)/cluster of villages is arranged by the local Tehsildar. Local officers of the land owning Departments such as Forest, Water Resources, etc. and the Panchayat level representatives are invited to the meeting.
c) The details of the schedule of the visits of the Survey Team are circulated among the local officials of the land-owning Departments, so that the officials from those departments help the survey agency in the identification of the boundaries of the Land-parcels owned by those Departments.
d) Tehsildar maintains record of meetings held in different villages/cluster of villages.

Series of Components for Survey activities:

- Establishment of Ground Control[45]
- Photogrammetric Process – Aerial triangulation, DEM editing, contour generation and ortho-rectification of high resolution satellite images
- Geo-Referencing of Khasra Maps with reference to ortho images
- Digitization of Land Parcels using Ortho Images
- Field operation (Ground truthing of village boundary and Land parcels, soil classification and other Information)
- Generation of Land Parcel Map (LPM) and notices
- Conduct public interaction session and publicity
- Distribution of Draft LPM and objection hearing if any
- Resurvey and convincing the issue raised by person
- Preparation of Encroachment and Disputed Register
- Promulgation of survey and Land Records

[45] Establishment and observation of ground control points: Five Types of Ground Control Points are established

S.No.	*GCP Type*	*Location/Density*	*Monument Size*	*Time Duration*	*Observations*
1	Iconic	District HQ	25x25x120 cm	72 hour	Static
2	Sub Iconic	Tehsil HQ	25x25x120 cm	12 hour	Static
3	Primary	16x16 km network	25x25x120 cm	4 hour	Static
4	Secondary	4x4 km network	23x23 x 75 cm	1 hour	Static
5	Tertiary	2x2 km network	15x15 x 45 cm	45 minute	Static

Steps followed during Resurvey

I. Processing of High Resolution Satellite Imagery and Generation of Ortho rectified Satellite Imagery:

- Pre-pointing of Ground Control Points has been made prior to obtaining High Resolution Satellite Image.
- Stereo Satellite images with ground resolution of 40 cm or better have been procured for the entire area of interest.
- Pre-processing of Satellite Images and removal of Geometric/Radiometric errors
- The images are adjusted for parallax based on the Ground Control Points through Digital photogrammetric bundle block adjustment.
- The final adjusted block is seamless. The photogrammetric processing ensures perfect one-to-one correspondence between different data sets facilitating optimum utilization of Satellite Data set.
- DEM Generation using the primary and secondary control points
- Ortho-rectification of Satellite Images, Mosaicking and Creating Tiles 2x2 km.
- Tie-line measures are made using DGPS/ETS for checking Ortho-image accuracy.

II. Preparation of Seamless Ground Reality Digital Land Parcel Map for entire district under section 112 of R.L.R. Act, 1956:

- Features visible in satellite imagery are captured through Heads-up digitization using any industry standard GIS software with respect to Ortho rectified images
- Features those are not visible or unclear are captured using ground methods DGPS and/or ETS.
- Vectors generated from Ortho-Image & DGPS/ETS survey are integrated to prepare Ground Reality Draft Land Parcel Map from Solid line 1 and built up topology.
- The administrative boundary is generated from the new cadastral map after dissolving all individual parcels in the GIS.
- Each area feature base on centre Id coordinate x, y second and third Value digit

  Assign Unique Land parcel Id in four digits (xxyy) number, that is, its khasra number.
- Assign village code (xxxyyy) from village polygon.
- Sheet Indexing 2x2 km Tiles
- All maps are to be prepared at a scale of 1:4000 unless the Additional Land Records Officer allows the use of a different scale in those cases where the sizes of the land parcels are too small to be seen properly on 1:4000 scale.

III. Ground Truthing of Land Parcel Maps

Since these survey records form the basis of the conclusive titling system, they must be prepared with utmost care and accuracy. Hence, the Department concerned with survey and settlement will be responsible for ensuring 100% quality check at each stage of the preparation of the survey records and the responsibilities for this checking are clearly spelt out among the Departmental officials. The patwari shall carry out 100% checking, and the Revenue Inspector, tehsildar or an officer of the equivalent rank, the SDO and the Deputy Commissioner/District Collector should randomly check 50%, 10%, 3% and 1%, respectively.

- Ground Truthing of Draft Land parcel map tiles by spot visualization and DGPS/ETS.
- Check for feature matching land parcel boundaries, polygon shape, central line, high tension line and parcel attributes.
- The newly created village boundary and area is authenticated by competent authority.
- The features to be checked are: Permanent, temporary, paddy bund, forest boundaries, drainage and water body, road, rail network, cross drainage, vegetation, amenities details, historical, religious places, etc.

IV. Preparation of Record of Right under section 113 of R.L.R. Act, 1956

(1) The Old Cadastral Map is superimposed on the New Village Land Parcel Map. This super imposition shall enable the generation of Parcel 1, 2 & 3 lines, as revised after ground truthing and as mentioned below:
   a. Parcel 1 : Solid Lines – All those lines which exist on the ground
   b. Parcel 2: Chain Lines (dash-dot-dash lines….) – All those lines which need to be shown on the map for the purpose of honouring legal ownership boundaries, however no physical features exist along that line.
   c. Parcel 3 : Dash lines (--------) – All those lines which do not depict any Land parcel *(Khasra)* but which represent significant physical features on the field such as – pathways/high tension line/central line of road, Nallah, River, significant gas or water pipelines etc. and which shall be depicted in the map by symbols specific to these categories.

(2) The information compiled in Form 4 shall be compared with the above superimposed map and read along with the existing *Jamabandi* to prepare the new cadastral map and record of rights. The mirror principle must be followed scrupulously in this exercise.
   - All agricultural areas on your holding which are 0.0100 hectares or larger.
   - Decision on inclusion/exclusion of disputed plots on the village boundary is based on the Sabik map/record.
   - Integration of Sabik RoR, Mutation Data, etc. with Parcel ID.
   - Tehsildar shall provide the RoR data to the survey team for linking with the New Cadastral map (NCM).

- Khata No., Parcel numbers and Area from Sabik map are transferred to the NCM map attributes adopting GIS process.
- Parcel 2: Chain Lines (dash-dot-dash lines....) – All those lines which need to be shown on the map for the purpose of honouring legal ownership boundaries, however no physical features exist along that line.
- The NCM plot area is to be computed in GIS for each land parcel and statement is prepared in Form No. 4 and 5. In Form No. 5, area difference sheet is prepared for each land holding.

V. Issuance of a draft land parcel notice of under section 114 of RLR. Act, 1956 for each holding/Khatedar, Filing of Objections, Incorporation of Dispute Settlement Order

- Generation of draft Land Parcel Map (LPM): LPM of present plots are generated and supplied to the Landowner in Form No. 7 with proper receipt.
- Objections redressal/adjudication
  (a) Individual notices in the prescribed format, as per the provisions of the applicable revenue manual, are given to all recorded owner(s)/ enjoyer(s) with a copy of the land parcel map and measurement details, marked on the same notice.
  (b) If any objection is raised by the owner(s)/enjoyer(s), it is recorded in the Objections Register.
  (c) The survey team assists the Government officers in resolving the objections. The survey team resurveys the field of the owner(s)/ enjoyer(s), if required and incorporate the necessary changes and generate the revised LPM.
  (d) The survey team maintains the Objections Register. The objections shall also be tracked in the DTDB in GIS form.

Any dispute on Survey Records is filed by the Landowner/Tenant/any Person/ Government Officials having interest in the same Land to Camp Officer/ Tehsildar within thirty days from the date of receipt of the LPM.

After disposal of objection case, the map and record of the concerned plot are corrected as per the orders of the Camp Officer/Tehsildar.

VI. Proclamation for Government land under Section 115, 116, 117 of Rajasthan Land Revenue Act, 1956

An analysis of the following types of lands, which are covered under Section 115 of the Act:

(1) Previously unsurveyed lands**:** A parcel of land which remained previously unsurveyed will have no owner as per the existing *Jamabandi*

(2) Abandoned lands**:** A parcel of land whose owner, as per the existing Jamabandi, is dead or not traceable and no legal heirs are traceable either.

This land could either be lying fallow or possibly be cultivated/used by another person who has no legal title over the land.

(3) Land currently under use for public purposes: That land, which is owned by a tenants (*Khatedar*) as per the old cadastral map (OCM) and the *Jamabandi,* but is being used for public purposes such as school, College, *Anganbadi* Centre, roads, rasta, canals, water tanks or any other such public purpose

(4) A proclamation listing all such lands are issued in Form No. 6 through publication in a reputed daily Hindi newspaper with wide circulation in the area and also displayed in the offices of the Patwari, Gram Panchayat, the Tehsil and the Assistant Settlement Officer

VII. Promulgation of Maps, Field Books and Records of Rights under section 121 and 122 of RLR Act, 1956

Before the final draft of maps, field books (in Form 10) and records of rights is prepared for promulgation – old records of rights and the old online cadastral maps are locked by the Assistant Land Records Officer on the e-Dharti and the Bhu-Naksha web portals. All pending mutations are decided by Tehsildar subsequently and the final version of the *Jamabandi* and the map are made ready for download.

a. It is ensured that all changes that take place in the online version while the Survey/resurvey activity is being conducted shall be incorporated into the version being prepared for promulgation.
b. Before promulgation of the map, the field book and the record of rights, soft copies of these are to be electronically signed by the concerned *Amin/ patwari*, the inspector and the Assistant Land Records Officer and then presented to the Additional Land Records Officer. It will be considered legally valid only upon approval of the Additional Land Records Officer.
c. A paper copy of the same is also prepared, signed and approved as in (b) above which is kept as permanent record in the office of the Additional Land Records Officer.
d. Hard copies of these records are displayed on the notice board of the concerned Gram Panchayat Office/Patwar Ghar for 15 days before they are considered final and legally promulgated.
e. The newly promulgated maps and record of rights are made available to the concerned *tehsildar* on a specified web portal on the same day of approval by the Additional Land Records Officer.
f. The complaints received are verified and necessary corrections, if warranted, are carried out. The survey agency carries out the resurvey of the land parcel, if required.
g. As soon as the disposal of objections is completed, a final notification under the relevant Acts/rules/regulations is published as per the prescribed procedure, completing the process of survey.

h. The land parcel register is updated by the survey agency as per the information received from the adjudication team, after the latter has redressed the objections.

i. Where to find your digital maps
   - Go to: Error! Hyperlink reference not valid. Bhunaksha Portal Web service. From the 'open source overview' screen, click 'Land' then 'View land'. You can download and print your digital maps.

Case Study of Chomu Tehsil in District Jaipur

At present, Survey/Resurvey operations are being carried out simultaneously across 134 Tehsils in 12 districts of Rajasthan in the first phase. One tehsil in each of these 12 districts were taken as model tehsil for conducting the resurvey work. Survey/resurvey work of Chomu Tehsil of Jaipur district is presented below:

Tehsil Chomu	*Data*
Total area	685.40 sq.km.
Land parcel count	133040
Inspector Land Records Circle	11
Patwar mandal	46
Village	136
Sheet (2x2 km)	370

In Chomu Tehsil, 01Sub Iconic, 02 Primary, 46 Secondary and 173 Tertiary, Ground Control Points were established.

Preparation of up-to-date GIS compatible land parcel maps were prepared by hybrid method involving use of stereo high resolution multi-spectral satellite images, Pan sharpened to have 40 cm or higher resolution and DGPS and ETS. Ortho rectified image was vectorised as per ground parcels and parcel to parcel digitization of image with reference to old cadastral map is done. Temporary khasra number was given to all parcels for ground truthing and final layout of Map was prepared. The exercise was conducted for all the villages of Chomu Tehsil and Parcha Notices were also issued. Due to the absence of departmental survey guidelines, the work after parcha notices could not be completed.

- *Gram-Sabha in Village:* Determination and finalisation of village boundary with ground truthing and DGPS RTK, village level parcel map, recording of possession, soil classification and source of irrigation and ground truthing register (Form No. 4).
- *Steps taken for preparation of new village map and record of rights in Chomu:*
  I. Establishment of ground control points
  II. Preparation of Ortho rectified satellite image
  III. Vectorization of land parcel map
  IV. Overlay of Old Cadastral Map on New Village land Parcel Map
  V. Categorization of parcel 1, 2 & 3 lines and polygon
  VI. Preparation of Record of Right for each land parcel (Form No.4)

Creation of GCPs

Gram Sabha

Digitization of land parcel boundary through HRSI

Objections hearings

Distribution of Parcha Notice

Figure 3 *Step-wise activities undertaken during Resurvey*

VII. Preparation of area comparison analysis sheet in Excel (Form No.5)
VIII. Declaration of government land for public purpose (Form No.6)
IX. Parcha Notice (Form No.7)
X. Milan-Khasra (Form No. 8)

XI. Final Khatauni (Form No. 9 &10)

XII. Registers to record Trespasser of Government Land (Form No. 11)

XIII. GIS based query Village land parcel Attribute and classification is updated.

XIV. Final RoR (Misal Bandobast) register is prepared.

XV. After disposal of objections, final notification under relevant rules and regulation are published to complete the process of survey.

Success, Problems and Way Ahead in Land Survey in Rajasthan

Successes

1. With the putting in place the survey/resurvey work, it has been possible to make seamless digital village maps
2. There are no difference in the map and the record of right area
3. With the aid of modern survey instruments like DGPS RTK, the village boundaries are being fixed due to which there will be no need of any control or reference point in future
4. There is no need of regular survey operations
5. It is very easy to identify and demarcate the encroachment area with respect to private to private as well as to private to Government land
6. It has been possible to make digital field book of every land parcel
7. With the aid of decision support system, it is very easy to display any query
8. As this data base is being prepared in GIS platform, it can easily be superimposed on any other layer
9. It is very easy to update any feature related to division of land or any development
10. It is very easy to ascertain the land price and the crop insurance and girdawri can be judged accurately
11. By using high resolution stereo satellite imagery, it is possible to survey areas having steep slopes and having tree cover and high-rise building etc. with accuracy.
12. The records thus prepared by survey resurvey/activity can be stored in soft and hard copies with back up in server.
13. Transparent and accessible data available for the citizens
14. The database is a boon to all natural resource planning and execution activities.
15. 1 M contour interval data generated through actual survey operations is a boon to all engineering applications.

Problems Faced

1. Delay in preparation of guidelines for survey/resurvey activity due to which field activities got delayed
2. More objections related with difference in new and old area
3. Difficulty in identifying the encroached lands
4. Difficulty in mapping due to change in courses of streams, rivers and roads
5. Difficulty in adjudging the public utility lands into Government land

6. Difficulty in removing the gap and overlap between the boundaries of villages
7. Difficulty in making new record of rights due to change in shape of the old khasra parcels
8. Difficulty in fixing the boundaries of urban, forest and mining areas
9. Difficulty in knowing the current land use and land cover
10. Shortage of technical and field staff

The Way Ahead

1) Generation of Unique Land Parcel Identification Number (ULPIN) for every land parcel
2) Linkage with National spatial Data Base (NSDB) as major features are land parcels, water bodies, all types of roads, forest, any infrastructure etc. on 1:4000. May further be synchronized with NSDI/NRIS/NNRMS etc. at national level.
3) Resolving the issues of difference of more than 10% in new and old area
4) Resolving the disputes and litigation cases in a time bound manner
5) Web hosting in public domain
6) Registration and mutation on the basis of new survey records
7) Regular updating of survey records after every five years
8) Collection of all land and property based levies, like Property Tax, Vacant Land Tax, Water Tax, etc.
9) Planning the developmental activities for line department
10) Sharing the database for various government and non-government users
11) Undertaking survey/resurvey work in remaining 22 districts.

Thus, the survey/resurvey activity being carried out in the State involving high resolution satellite imagery in conjunction with modern survey equipment, is playing a vital role in bringing efficacy in survey operations and creation and updating of Land Records with shorter time span with perfection and accuracy as compared to traditional survey method. Not only, accurate and updated land records puts in place a Single Window to handle land records culminating into reduction in land related litigations/frauds but also does real time assessment of property valuation. Thus, due to survey/resurvey work, it has been made possible to make seamless digital village maps which eventually is a prerequisite for social and economic infrastructures required for rapid economic development.

References

(1) Rajasthan Tenancy Act, 1955.
(2) Rajasthan Land Revenue Act, 1956.
(3) Rajasthan Land Revenue (Survey, Record and Settlement), Government Rules, 1957.
(4) Rajasthan Land Revenue (Land Records) Rules, 1957.
(5) Guideline of Settlement Department Rajasthan Government, 2021.
(6) Guideline DILRMP (India).

2.11

Uttar Pradesh

Sunil Kumar Jha

Historical Background

Uttar Pradesh has had a different land system in different centuries. For the first time, land was systematically managed by King Todarmal. King Todarmal-Settlement/land management system is very important in the land system. During this period, Malguzari system was followed according to which rates were fixed on the basis of fertility and area of the land, thus removing arbitrariness in the tax collection. Todarmal introduced Ryotwari system, in which the farmers were the owners of the land. In this system, the head of the village or the tax-collecting intermediaries were given some money in cash, or they were given *Malguzari*-free land (*Maafi Bhoomi*)[46] in return for their services.

After the decline of Mughal Empire and during the establishment of the British Raj semi-zamindars rose in this region. As the state power started weakening in course of time, the security of the property of the people was also declined. Gradually, the rural community began to seek help from the state officials who collected land revenue. As a result, these tax collectors/intermediaries began to take ownership of the land and displaced the rights of the head of the village, and when the British rule was established in the country, they were protected by the Talukdars or zamindars of the British rule and their territories were protected. They were considered to be practical masters/owners.

British Era

Several areas of UP was occupied by the British on several occasion during 1775 A.D. to 1857 A.D. The main objective of British rule was to maximise profit thus various land revenue systems were introduced such as *Zamindari* system, *Ryotwari* system and *Mahalwari* system. The basic objective of all these arrangements was to recover maximum revenue. Due to this, there was an unbalanced distribution of land-ownership, there was a need for land reform to remove this imbalance and to end exploitative economic relations.

[46] The land on which the land revenue or tax of land is exempted or has been waved off by the government.

Independent India

Hence, the objective of land reform in post-independence India was to improve land agricultural productivity and to ensure social justice. In addition, land reform aimed at creating of new job opportunities to promote agricultural participation in economic activities and maximum and efficient utilization of land. Further, to abolish *Zamindari* system Land System Act, 1950 was enacted in Uttar Pradesh.

Over a period of time, there is a need to amend the records and cadastral-maps prepared under the said Act. For this, following procedures were made for revising the records and maps after resurveying the land.

Current Procedure of Land Survey

The work of survey and record operation in Uttar Pradesh government is done by the 06 survey units approved by the state. These surveys units in the state do the survey of village/villages u/s 48 of Land Revenue Act, 1901 before the 11 February 2016 and after that u/s 43 of UP Revenue Code, 2016 and according to the provisions of the Survey and Record Operation Rules, 1978. But if the survey and record preparation notification to start survey procedure in village was made under section 48 of Land Revenue Act, 1901, then after the work is completed, the denotification will also be done under Land Revenue Act, 1901 in Section 48.

The provisions made for the survey process is as follows

1. In respect of an area where revision of maps and of record of rights is considered necessary, the Collector shall made investigations to gather the information relating to condition of land records in such area in Survey Form I.
2. Where the fields entered in Survey Form I for more than 50 per cent of the total number of fields, further inquiry into the condition of records may be made with a view to examine the advisability of revising the map and record of rights.
3. Where on the basis of the investigations and inquiries made under sub-rules (1) and (2), the Collector is of the opinion that maps and records of any of the villages should be revised, he shall cause such villages, together with the information relating to the condition of records, to be entered in Survey Form II.
4. The Collector shall thereafter; send a detailed report about the condition of maps and records together with the information's contained in Survey Form II, to the Board of Revenue
5. (i) The Board may on receipt of the report under sub-rule (4) of rule 4, or on its own motion, arrange to depute an Assistant Director of Land Records or any other officer to examine the proposal of the Collector or give further instructions for the collection of material for report regarding the condition of maps and records.

(ii) The Officer so deputed shall make local inspection and specially scrutinise the area proposed for resurvey. He shall submit the report to the Board wherein he will also suggest, if necessary, the order in which the parganas of the district should be taken up for revision of maps and records.

6. After being satisfied from the report under rule 4 or rule 5, the Board may submit to the State Government the proposal for issuing notification under Section 48 of Land Revenue Act, 1901 before the 11 February 2016 and after that u/s 43 of UP Revenue Code, 2016.
7. Upon the receipt of the proposal from the Board, if the State Government thinks that in any district or other local area, a general or partial revision of record or resurvey, or both, should be made, it shall publish a notification under section 48 of Land Revenue Act, 1901 before the 11 February 2016 and after that u/s 43 of UP Revenue Code 2016 in Survey Form III. Upon the issue of the said notification, the Revenue Records in the custody of regular Lekhpal shall be transferred to Survey Lekhpal.
8. *Boundary Disputes*

(1) Before actually commencing map correction or survey work of the village, the boundaries of contiguous villages should be tallied and if there is any overlapping or gap in the boundaries, tracing of the relevant portions from the maps of the villages should be taken by the Survey Kanungo and the matter be reported for decision through the Survey Naib-Tahsildar. This procedure shall be followed even if any contiguous village is not under record operations.

(2) The Survey Naib-Tahsildar shall make inquiries on the spot after giving sufficient notice to the Pradhans and members of the Land Management Committees and also the general public of the villages involved in dispute and submit his report to the Assistant Record Officer.

(3) The Assistant Record Officer shall soon after the receipt of any such report make inquiries on the spot in the presence of the persons referred to in subrule (2) and pass suitable orders for revising maps of the villages concerned.

9. *Map Correction*

(i) The village map of the area under Survey or Record Operations may be revised either:

(1) By ordinary method of map correction, or chain/jareeb measurement – In starting there was 08 different types of *Shahjahani* jareebs[47]/chains of different lengths werein use in different districts of Uttar Pradesh. After that for a short time *Guntry* jareeb/chain was used in UP before the implement of Metric System. The length of *Guntry* jareeb/chain was 22 yard and area was calculated in Acre.

[47] Jareeb is a fixed length chain used for measurement of the land. Shahjahani jareeb is a type of jareeb used initially.

After the implementation of Metric System a chain or *jareeb* of 20 meter is in use in UP. Now area is calculated in Hectare. In one hectare there are 10000 sq.mts.

In Chain survey measurement of plot or any area is started from a fixed point called "*Sihadda*".[48] Mostly these are the fixed points on village boundaries. Where no-fixed points available, the measurement is started from any well or crosssection/meeting point of four contiguous plots called as "*Chaumeda*".[49] Any measurement should be crosschecked from at least two different fixed points.

(2) By survey or resurvey –

(ii) The Assistant Record Officer after examining the condition of maps shall decide which of the two methods specified in sub-rule (i) should be adopted.

10. For revision of map by survey or resurvey the instructions contained in the book, entitled, "Rules and Instructions for Survey of Villages," shall be followed. This work shall initially be done by Survey Kanungo with the Assistance of Survey Lekhpals.

11. Where the map is to be corrected by ordinary method, it shall be done by the Survey Kanungo with the assistance of Survey Lekhpals and the following procedure may, as far as possible, be followed:

(a) The map to be used for correction shall be the tracing cloth copy of either the map prepared when the village was surveyed for the last time or the map prepared by correction at the time of the last revision of maps and records, whichever is later.

(b) The Survey Kanungo shall first go round the boundaries of the village to find out whether all the tri-junctions/*Chaumeda* and other boundary marks do exist on the spot at the proper place(s) and are shown in the map correctly; and whether the boundary as shown in the map tallies with the position on the spot. If he finds any discrepancy, he will report the matter to the survey Naib-Tahsildar who will examine the position with the help of the maps of the neighbouring villages and report the matter to the Assistant Record Officer for prompt action under section 50. The Assistant Record Officer shall then decide the matter in accordance with rule 8 (3).

(c) The Survey Kanungo shall take up each of the map sheets separately and proceed to correct them from the north-west corner.

(d) The Survey Kanungo shall measure the boundaries of all the plots and record them in the field book in Survey Form IV. The measurements may be carried out either by a measuring rod or by a chain or by

[48] This is the fix point from measurement of land can be started. It situates normally on the boundary of the village.

[49] Cross section/meeting point of boundaries of four contiguous plots

internal survey by quadrilaterals using chain and optical squares where necessary.

(e) The corrections shall be made by taking convenient areas the shapes of which in the map tally with those on the spot. Where the measurements in the map and on the ground do not correspond, it will be necessary to distribute the error, if any, in the plots of Ilia block proportionately without disturbing the relative shapes and position of contiguous plots.

(f) In cases of difference of less than one *gattha* (10 *kari*[50]) where relative position of neighbouring plots appear on the map to tally with the spot, no correction shall actually be made.

(g) In cases of difficulty in which the plot or group of plots cannot be shown in the existing maps correctly, which may be due to error being so large that its distribution in the map would give disproportionate idea of the relative position of different plots or which may be due to the fact that the fields are divided so minutely that their plotting within the map would make it clumsy or indistinct, the area involved should be plotted separately in the margin of the map on the same scale or on a larger scale, if necessary and the portions so plotted should be left blank in the main map with a note showing where it could be seen.

(h) As a rule only boundaries existing on the ground will be shown in the main and Survey Kanungo will not enter private partition among cultivators where there is no physical boundary.

(i) A list of objects along with signs for them with which they will be marked on the village maps where such object exist are indicated in Survey Form V. Objects like roads, masonry, wells, canals, guts, etc. will be marked after actual measurement while those like *kachcha* wells trees *abadi* etc. will be shown in the map at their approximate places.

(j) The correction in the map will be indicated in pencil in the first instance by the Survey Kanungo. The Survey Naib-Tahsildar will check 25% of the corrected plots taking precaution to spread the checking throughout the area of the village, the Assistant Record Officer shall also check some corrected plots in every village with a view to ensure the accuracy of corrections made in the maps. The corrections shall be inked after the checking has been done by the Survey Naib-Tahsildar and the Assistant Record Officer.

12. Where during the course of revision of map, both by resurvey or ordinary methods, it is discovered that area of a plot entered in the record of rights is prima facie incorrect or there is a boundary dispute between two plots, it will be entered in the list of mistakes and disputes in Survey Form VI and it shall be disposed of in the manner as described further in point no. 9.

[50] chain ring, bush, hoop, ring, ringlet

13. Renumbering – After the revision of map, all the plots on a newly surveyed or corrected map will be renumbered, by the Survey Kanungo. The procedure laid down below may, as far as possible be followed:
    (a) The renumbering of plots will be done sheet-wise where the map of a village consists of more than one sheet.
    (b) The numbering will start from the north-west corner, go generally in blocks to the east, come back again to the west taking the plots just below and so on finishing at the end in the southeast corner.
    (c) Where the fields situated in the same village have been plotted on the margin of a map, the numbering will be made in the same continuation as is the main map.
    (d) *Kudan* number[51] should be avoided but if there are any, a note about them will be made on the margin of the map.
    (e) If any plot or plots are left out by an oversight in renumbering, they will be given the number in the same serial starting after the last number of the village as numerator and the number of adjoining plot as denominator so as to trace it out easily.
    (f) If fields or areas of on a village lie within the boundaries of another village, they will be shown in their actual position in the map of the latter village, but no numbers will be assigned to them. Their limits will be marked by a thick line and the name of the village to which they pertain, will be written across them.
    (g) In case of tracts containing very small plots which cannot accommodate the number within them, blocks will be marked of by a thick line, the first one of 99 plots and the latter of 100 plots each and the number of the block will be noted in the centre in a thickly written figure surrounded by a circle, without obscuring any of the field boundaries. The first block in the north-west will be numbered 0 and the field numbers will run from 1 to 99 the second block will be number 1 and the fields it 00, 01, 02, 03, 10,...99, the third block will be numbered 2 and so on. Thus, if a field is numbered 45 in block no. 2 its full number will be 245 which will be entered in all the revenue papers. If some of the fields in the block are large enough, they should contain the fail numbers.
    (h) The renumbering will first be in pencil and will be inked only after it has been checked thoroughly by the survey Naib-Tahsildar.
14. *Area Extraction*
    (i) The area of fields blocks and villages the maps of which are revised, will be calculated by the following methods:
        (a) in case of maps revised by Survey or Resurvey, by area comb; and
        (b) in case of map revised by ordinary method, by *chaumenda* system for regular four-cornered plots and by diagonal system for all other plots.

---

[51] Jump, Kudan number is a number not in sequence. As 1,2,3,4,10,6,7. In this series 10 is Kudan number.

(ii) The area of various plots or block in a village will be added up to find out the total area of the village.

15. *Fard-Mutabiqat*: Immediately after re-numbering and area extraction, the Survey Lekhpal will prepare a list of comparative old and new numbers, known as Fard-Mutabiqat, in the sequence of old numbers in Survey Form VII.
16. *Khasra-Mutabiqat*: The Survey Lekhpal will also prepare a list of comparative new and old numbers, known as the Khasra-Mutabiqat, in the sequence of new numbers in Survey Form VIII.
17. The page totals and village totals of the Fard-Mutabiqat and the khasra-Mutabiqat will be checked cent per cent by Survey Kanungo. The Survey Naib-Tahsildar will also check entries relating to 25 per cent of the new plots and verify them from the relevant records.
18. Test, verification and *partal* (Field verification or ground truthing.) – All the entries of the basic annual register shall be tested by the Survey Kanungo by comparing them with the entries of the previous annual register and connected field book and also the record of rights prepared during the last settlement of the revision of records. Mistakes and disputes detected shall be entered in the list of mistakes and disputes in Survey Form VI.
19. After the test of the annual register has been carried out in the manner prescribed in rule 18, a thorough verification of the entries in the annual register shall be carried out by the Survey Kanungo. This will be done by reading out the record in the village in the presence of as many residents as it is possible to collect and by explaining every entry in this record to the tenure-holder concerned.

    The mistakes and disputes detected or claims made shall be entered in the list of mistakes and disputes in Survey Form VI.
20. After the test and verification of the annual register as prescribed in Rules 18 and 19, field to field *partal* of all the plots shall be carried out by the Survey Kanungo in the presence of as many tenure-holders and other residents of the village as it is possible to collect and the result will be noted by him in Survey *Khasra* in Survey Form IX. The mistakes and disputes discovered during the *partal* will be entered in the list of mistakes and disputes in Survey Form VI.
21. The list of mistakes and disputes in land records in Survey Form VI shall be prepared in two parts. Part I shall contain clerical mistakes and Part II shall contain other mistakes and disputes discovered during the test, and verification of annual register and in the course of the held-to-field *partal*.
22. The Survey Naib-Tahsildar shall check the work of test and verification of the annual register and also the work of field-to-field *partal* to the extent of 25 per cent entries made in the list of mistakes and disputes. The Assistant Record Officer shall also check sufficient number of entries made in the various records with a view to ensure the correctness of the work.

Disposal of Mistakes and Disputes

23. The Survey Naib-Tahsildar shall pass orders in his own signature in appropriate column of list of mistakes and disputes in land records for the correction of all the clerical mistakes entered in Part I of Survey Form VI after consulting the previous land records of the village, where necessary. These orders shall then be noted by the Survey Lekhpal against the relevant khatas of the basic annual register, and shall be attested by the Survey Kanungo. The Survey Naib-Tahsildar shall also satisfy himself by checking that all his orders have been correctly recorded in the basic annual register.
24. i. The Survey Lekhpal shall make necessary number of copies of the notices, containing relevant extracts in Survey Form X *Khatauni Slip (an extract of Record of Right)* in respect of all the holdings in the basic annual register, after the orders of the Survey Naib-Tahsildar mentioned in Rule 23 have been given effect to the Survey Kanungo shall check all the notices and at least 25 per cent of the notices shall also be checked by the Survey Naib-Tahsildar to ensure their accuracy.
    ii. The notices together with the Khatauni slips shall be issued under the signatures of the Survey Naib-Tahsildar to the tenure-holders concerned and persons interested.
    iii. The record of service of notice-cum-Khatauni Slip shall be maintained in the Survey Form XI.
    iv. Notices in respect of land belonging to the Government Departments shall be sent to the Heads of the district offices. Notices in respect of land belonging to or vested in the Gaon Sabha, or other local authority shall be sent to the pradhan of the Gram Sabha or the Chairman of Local Authority, as the case may be.
    v. Any tenure-holder or any other person aggrieved by any entry in any Khata may file an objection in writing the grounds of his Objection to the Survey Naib-Tahsildar within twenty-one days of the service of notice.
    vi. Office copies of the notices issued shall be kept on the common file for so long as they are not made part of separate files.
25. The objections received against the entries made in the Khatauni slip shall he entered in Misil-band Register (register of cases or issues.) in Survey Form XII.
26. (1) The Survey Naib-Tahsildar shall then proceed to make enquiries into all the disputes and claims (other than clerical mistakes) and also objections, if any, received in respect of entries made in the Khatauni slips in the village itself. In deciding disputes on the basis of conciliation under section 54 he shall record the terms of conciliation in the presence of at least two members of the Land Management Committee in the relevant column of the list of mistakes and disputes in Survey Form VI (Part II). These terms shall be read over to parties

concerned and their signatures or thumb-impressions obtained. The members of the Land Management Committee present shall also sign the terms of conciliation. The Survey Naib-Tahsildar thereafter shall record orders in the relevant column of Survey Form VI deciding the disputes in terms of conciliation specifying the precise entries to be made in records. No *ex parte* order or order in default or order in respect of land belonging to the State Government or vested in Gaon Sabha shall be passed by the Survey Naib-Tahsildar.

(2) The cases that cannot be disposed of by the Survey Naib-Tahsildar in terms of conciliation in accordance with the provisions of sub-rule (I) shall be referred by him to the Assistant Record Officer for disposal. While doing so the Survey Naib Tahsildar may fix a date and place for the disposal of the cases by the Assistant Record Officer and communicate the same to the parties concerned before him and issue notices to the parties not so present.

27. (i) The cases received from the Survey Naib-Tahsildar shall be entered in the *Misil Band* Register, in Survey Form XII in the office of the Assistant Record Officer.

(ii) On the date fixed under rule (2) of rule 26 or on subsequent date fixed for the purpose, the Assistant Record Officer shall hear the parties, and decide the objections.

(iii) Any persons aggrieved by the order of Survey Naib Tahsildar made under sub-rule (1) of rule 26 may file, within twenty-one days from the date of order, an appeal before the Assistant Record Officer whose order shall subject to the provisions of Section 219 be final.

(iv) Any person aggrieved by the order of the Assistant Record Officer under sub-rule (2) of rule 27 may file within thirty days from the date of order, an appeal before the Record Officer under section 210 of the Act.

28. The Survey Lekhpal shall note the orders of the Survey Naib-Tahsildar, the Assistant Record Officer and the Record Officer in the basic annual register.

29. (i) The Assistant Record Officer shall cause to be prepared a statement in Survey Form XIII by the Survey Lekhpal, to show the amount of Land Revenue payable on new holdings and apportionment of alternation, if any in the amount of land revenue on existing holding where this may be necessary in view of the orders passed by the Survey Naib-Tehsildar, the Assistant Record Officer and the Record Officer.

(ii) After the entries in Survey Form XIII have been checked by the Survey Kanungo and the Survey Naib-Tehsildar, it will be forwarded to the Assistant Record Officer, who shall examine the same and pass orders for the assessment or apportionment or alteration of the land revenue, as the case may be.

30. Fairing of Records – After the conclusion of enquiries in accordance with the foregoing rules, the Record Officer shall cause to be prepared the following fair records:

1. Village map.
2. *Fard-Mutabiqat* in Survey Form VII.
3. *Khasra-Mutabiqat* in Survey Form VIII.
4. Fair *khasra* in Survey Form XIV.
5. Revised *Khatauni* in Survey Form XV.
6. *Fard-Chahat (A list of wells)* in Survey Form XVI.
7. *Fard-Baghat (A list of groves)* in Survey Form XVIII.
8. *Fard-Tudajat (A list of boundary pillars)* in Survey Form XVIII.

31. Fairing and reproduction of Revised Map – The resurveyed or corrected map, incorporating the amendments where necessary under orders passed during the course of revision of records will be carefully examined by the Survey Kanungo with a view to see that:

(a) it is clear and free from mistakes;
(b) its boundary tallies with the boundaries of the neighbouring villages and reserved forests, if any;
(c) it has been accurately renumbered.

32. After the map has been examined and, if necessary, corrected, it will be traced carefully, compared and checked and then signed and dated by the Record Officer or the Assistant Record Officer whose designation as such will be written below his signatures.

33. The Assistant Record Officer will decide whether the revised maps will be reproduced by the mechanical process or by hand. The first traces of the village map shall be made on sheets of the standard size (28"x20") inside measurement with 1" margin. Two or more small maps for mechanical reproduction will be traced on one sheet after its division into as many oblongs by thick lines across it. Marginal blocks will, as far as possible, be traced on the sheets containing the main map. The heading of the map will also show whether it *was* prepared after resurvey or after ordinary map correction.

34. (i) Whencopies are traced by hand; two copies besides the first shall be traced.

(ii) When maps are reproduced by a mechanical process, the following number of copies shall be obtained:

(a) For revenue and land record purposes –

Two blue prints, six copies on cloth and four copies on paper.

(b) For sale to other departments tenure holders and public –

Four copies of cloth or more copies if the Assistant Record Officer so decides, considering the local requirement's in addition to the number of copies actually asked for.

35. Fairing of Revised Records – The revised records shall be faired out in duplicate with the help of records prepared during the course of revision of records by the Survey Lekhpal. The Survey Kanungo will check all these records carefully and 25 per cent of the entries of all these records shall be checked by the Survey Naib-Tahsildar and five per cent of the entries shall also be checked by the Assistant Record Officer.
36. All cuttings and over writings in the fair records shall be signed dated by the person responsible for such cuttings and over writings. There shall be no erasers. All cuttings and over writings in fair records shall be entered in the *errata* list (list of errors) in Survey Form XIX. This list shall be prepared by the Survey Lekhpal and attested by the Survey Kanungo. The list shall also be signed by the Survey Naib-Tahsildar.
37. The revised records prepared in accordance with the foregoing rules shall be bound and together with the village map they shall constitute the record operations volume. Two such volumes shall be prepared. One of it shall be consigned to the Collector's Record Room and the other shall be sent to the Tahsildar for being handed over to the Lekhpal.
38. On the conclusion of survey and record operations in a district or a part of a district, a Final Report accompanied by map of the tract, shall be submitted by the Assistant Record Officer through the Record Officer to the Board. The report should sum up clearly and concisely all the relevant matters connected with the operations, e.g., purpose of operations, a brief description of the tract, method applied, number of villages, area and plots involved, time taken, difficulties encountered and other special features.
39. On the recommendation of the Board, the State Government may issue a notification under section 48 of Land Revenue Act/Section 43 of Revenue Code, declaring operations to be closed. On the issue of this notification the work connected with the maintenance of land records shall stand transferred to the Collector of the district.

Difficulties and Solutions in the Current Process

It is noteworthy that the current state is in the survey and record the actions of the work is accomplished by conventional methods which includes usage of Jareeb and other manual measurement methods to measure fields, manually calculate area, and maps. Due to the usage of manual methods, there are many problems and challenges seen in the tasks of preparation of survey and record work, which are as follows.

Problems Encountered

1. *Delay in timely settlement of border dispute cases or more-time-consuming process*: Due to manual construction of the map, there is condition of overlap on the boundaries in the land maps of the villages. This overlapping is because of boundary-related issues and regarding this in several cases

are filed in the Courts, etc. Due to boundary related ambiguity, there is a lot of delay in the work of survey and record operations.

2. *Delay in boundary marking or area measurement due to standing crop*: Since manual methods are used, during cropping season with standing crop, work related to boundary marking and area measurement does not remains possible. Thus, time taken to survey and record preparation increases unnecessarily.
3. *Difficulty in demarcation work due to elevation or uneven surface*: If the ground is very low in an area, then there is a lot of difficulty in doing the measurement work in a manual way, it takes more time for survey work. Also, the accuracy of measurement is also low.
4. *Difficulty in demarcation work due to homestead land, gardens, buildings, river etc.*: Due to the homestead land or houses in many places, manual measurement is either not possible or unnecessary dispute arises due to excessive differences and several cases are filed in courts. Due to all these reasons, there is an unnecessary increase in the time taken in the work of survey and record work.
5. Due to the above reasons, there is also a lot of human labour required in survey work.

Solutions

1. *Use of Electronic Total Station Machine (ETS)*: It would be possible to work at any time even when crops are standing on the fields, thus survey work can be completed at good pace. In addition, the electronic total system allows the demarcation to work smoothly even in high-altitude conditions. The measurement done by this is possible with more precision, in a very short time and with relatively less labour.
   But due to different circumstances and different reasons the survey with ETS machine is not successful in UP and at present survey is done by the ancient/old method Chain survey.
2. *Use of GPS etc. to prepare maps and surveys using modern technologies instead of manual methods*: This technique is used to prepare map to be made on the latitude-longitude fixed signs range maps drawn so village/tehsil/district/block boundaries of the state will be fixed forever and border disputes will be settled almost forever.
3. *Survey work by drone:* There was a lot of delay in survey and record preparation when manual techniques are used. Ownership plan by the Revenue Board on behalf of Uttar Pradesh under the direction of the Government of India, with a view to complete the work of survey and record work for a long time, the widespread public interest affected, and to facilitate and expedite the work of survey and record work is being operated. Under which the survey of rural population is being done with the help of modern drone technology in collaboration with Survey Department of India.

Recent Initiatives of Land Survey in Uttar Pradesh

(Survey by Drone - Svamitva Scheme)

Svamitva scheme was inaugurated on 24 April 2020 by the Prime Minister. Under the Svamitva scheme, after the completion of the survey and record work of the rural population through modern technology such as the drone, the rural residential records (gharauni) are made available to the home owners.

Under the Svamitva Scheme, the work of survey and record of the rural population by modern technology is being done by the drone according to the following process –

1. The survey area is notified by the state government before starting the survey work.
2. Subsequently, the concerned District Magistrate publishes the survey area through a public notice. This work of rural population survey is carried out under the constant supervision of the Records Officer, District Magistrate, ensuring the correctness of the records prepared by the Assistant Record Officer.

   Survey teams are constituted to identify individual properties, government property, Gram Sabha land parcels, roads, open plots, etc. and identify boundaries of the property to be surveyed. These teams consist of staff members of Revenue Department and Gram Panchayat. At the time of survey, the presence of police force will be ensured as per the need for maintaining Law and Order.
3. Meetings are held in the Gram Sabha to inform the residents of the village about the schedule of the survey and sensitize them about the survey method and its benefits.
4. At the time of the first survey, the following actions are carried out simultaneously by the survey team –
   - 4.1. Identification of individual properties, government property, Gram Sabha land parcels, roads, open plots, etc. The boundaries of the property areas to be surveyed are identified boundaries are marked by the lime. The disputed assets are represented by a double lime line.
   - 4.2. At the time of lime lining, all the information related to the plot is collected on fixed format. Format-05 and the information are being fed simultaneously on the Board portal.
5. Aerial images are taken using professional survey grade unmanned aerial vehicle drones for mapping the population area in rural areas by the Survey of India and based on these, the population Map 01 prepared by the Indian Survey Department is made available to the Assistant Record Officer/ Deputy Collector.
6. On the population Map 01 provided by the Survey of India, the following actions are carried out by the survey team, in collaboration with the Survey of India, on-site verification.

6.1. In terrestrial verification, if the errors and discrepancies found in the population map – 01 are marked on the prescribed format.

6.2. The population plots will be numbered according to the terrestrial position on the population Map 01 and it is matched with the Format 05. Each plot of population area is numbered sequentially.

6.3. Marking 30 types of structures (viz. Tap, electric pole, office, playground, etc.) found in the population Map 01 at the time of terrestrial verification are also done in relevant formats.

6.4. The new information collected during ground verification, and list of the errors and the proposed amendments in population Map 01 are made available to the Survey Department. Survey of India, after correction of all the errors, incorporating the new information and modifications plot-wise Map 02 provides.

7. Revenue Inspector after verification and modification of Format 07 and population Map 02 it is further verified by Naib-Tahsildar and they also ensure that verification, new information and revisions have been incorporated in the population Map 02.
8. Based on the population Map 02 with the help of software, map of the plot, entry of dimensions of the plot and area of the plot is entered in Format 07 is in. Format 07 (on Board's portal) is prepared.
9. The verified Format 7 and habitation Map 02 are submitted by the Tahsildar/naib-Tahsildar for publication to the Assistant Records Officer, Deputy District Magistrate for inviting objections.
10. The preliminary, rural Abadi Records, Abadi Record Survey. Format 07 and details of the plot in Format 07 and Format 09 on the basis of corrected map "Map 02" will be published by the Assistant Records Officer in the open meeting of the Gram Panchayat, and objections will be invited giving 15 days' time. The minutes of the Gram Panchayat open meeting will be prepared and preserved, and the date of this meeting will be marked in the Abadi Record Survey Form IX as the date of the meeting and resolution of the Gram Panchayat.
11. In addition, regarding rural residential habitation records Formats 07, 08 and 09 will be provided free of cost to the plot owners by Lekhpals and received Signatures of two witnesses, including the signature of the owner of the plot, are taken on the office copy of number 8. If the interested person is not found in a case, then the forms are issued according to the rules and the signatures of two witnesses are also taken as evidence.
12. In respect of Abadi plots related to Government departments, a copy of its Survey Form VII, VIII and IX will be provided to the district level officer of the concerned department.
13. After receipt of the notice any person to whom the notice has been served, or any other person aggrieved by any entry of the record regarding the

entries number of the Form VII, shall submit his/her objections with the evidence, if any, to the Assistant Records Officer, on Form IX.

14. All objections or concurrence are given only on Survey Form IX at the Office of the Assistant Records Officer. Landlord's consent is considered if no objection is received.
15. The Assistant Records Officer will hear the parties on the objections related to the entries in the record and shall dispose the issues/disputes on the basis of conciliation or agreement. In the event of conciliation, a written agreement will be recorded between the concerned parties and the signatures/thumb marks of the respective parties will be obtained on it. The Assistant Records Officer will record his disposal of the issue on the same document and the recording of this disposal will be done on the portal in the relevant column of Form IX. The date of recording of the disposal of the settlement on the portal will also be mentioned in the hard copy of the agreement record.
16. If the disputes related to any plot are not resolved then the word "Disputed" will be recorded in the relevant column of Survey Form IX. Similarly, where objections related to clerical errors of, the word "Pending" will be recorded in the relevant column of Survey Form IX.
17. A person aggrieved by the order of Assistant Records Officer can submit his/her objections related to errors or settlement before the District Records Officer within 15 days. The District Records Officer shall settle the issues or objections received in the case of errors or disputes, only on the basis of reconciliation or agreement. All disposal of the District Record Officer will be recorded by the Assistant Records Officer in the relevant column of Rural Abadi Records, Abadi Survey Form IX.
18. In case of dispute regarding ownership of a plot, the word "Disputed" will be recorded in the relevant column in Form IX. When the concerned parties get the relief/order from the concerned Court, and submit a verified copy of the order, the recording of the revised entry will be done in the relevant column of Survey Form IX. All orders will be recorded by the Assistant Records Office.
19. In case of any clerical error, the related column in Form IX in respect of that error will be kept open on the portal till the time the error is not revised and agreed to by the owners of the concerned plot. Similarly, in respect of the errors of the map also, the errors will be marked "pending" in the column of Survey Form IX till corrected and agreed to.
20. In respect of the plots in which a entry of "disputed" or "pending" is marked in the relevant column of Survey Form IX, the Form X (Gharauni) of those plots will not be completely finalized. Form X will be fully finalized in other plots, in which no objection regarding dispute or clerical error is pending.

21. After inviting objections on Map 2 and recording any revisions the final Abadi Map 3 of each village or local area will be prepared by the Technical Agency.
22. The Abadi Records in Survey Form X will be finalised by making entries in the concerned columns of Survey Form IX, after the disposal of objections, if any about the entries recorded of each plot of Abadi for each village or local area by the Assistant Records Officer.
23. Recording of all types of disposals will be done only in Abadi Survey Form IX. No disposal will be, recorded in Abadi Survey Form X (Gharauni). In respect of the plots of land for which "disputed" or "pending" is recorded in the concerned column of Survey Form IX, the Words "disputed" or "pending" will be (recorded in the relevant column of Survey Form X.
24. The Assistant Records Officer (District Magistrate), after recording the disposals and corrections made by the competent level, shall verify the final rural Abadi records. Abadi Survey Form X (Gharauni) and Map 3, and shall inform the District Record Officer regarding such finalisation.
25. The District Record Officer (District Magistrate), on his satisfaction, shall send a proposal to the Government through Board to end Abadi Survey and Records Operations in the village or local area.

Benefit from the work of survey and record work of rural population through drones with modern technology under the ownership scheme:

1. Under Svamitva scheme, usage of modern technology such as drones ensure that the work of survey and record of the rural population is completed very quickly.
2. Human error is not possible as survey work is done with the help of modern technology which has ensured accuracy of the records.
3. Maps prepared using modern technology are more refined and accurate than maps prepared by manual technique.
4. Compilation of all data ownership is done on online portal rather than manual registers thus make corrections and maintaining these records is easier.

Epilogue

In the rural area (fields) usage of manual survey techniques for measurement faced challenges in the form of standing crop, population, water logging or uneven land, which led to errors in the record but usage of modern technology have eliminated these types of problem. Similarly, instead of time consuming and error ridden manual surveying, modern technology takes less time to survey, less human labour and accuracy in records is also higher.

The accuracy of records only ensures confidence of the public in the record preparation process but it reduces disputes and promises reduced number of cases in the courts.

In addition, records prepared online/computerized will reduce the risk of loss of records chronic, corroded, burnt, lost, destroyed records on one hand. And on the other hand, better maintenance of records, providing stability and publicity with ease and transparency will also be available.

In this way, it is clear that the use of modern technology in survey work is convenient for everyone and employees, as well as it is also need of the hour. Therefore, it is being considered by the Uttar Pradesh Revenue Board that the current rules should be amended to conduct surveys with modern technology for rural areas (agricultural land) and training revenue official to use modern techniques so that surveys of farms and rural population, etc. should be conducted with modern technology. This will ensure that survey work is done in quickly and less human labour, as well as more precise and permanent records can be prepared than before.

2.12

West Bengal

Chittaranjan Das

The State of West Bengal was a part of the Bengal Presidency where land revenue system was governed by the Permanent Settlement Regulation, imposed by the British rulers in 1793. It created a tenancy structure, which influenced the subsequent land laws and the land records prepared under the laws during the British Raj. However, in the North Indian Provinces, it was "Mahalwari" system, whereas in the Southern India, it was Ryotwari system. As such, the methodology of preparation of land records and cadastral maps in this State is different from most of the States in India even today. To appreciate the problems of preparation of land records and ways evolved to redress them for better citizen services, the methodology of preparation of land records and cadastral maps in the State is discussed first in the following paragraphs.

Revenue Survey: A Brief Background

At the time of promulgation of Permanent Settlement Regulation by Lord Cornwallis in 1793 in the Bengal Presidency, by which all Estates were permanently settled with the intermediaries or Zamindars, there was no accurate record of areas of the Estates available at that time. As such, assessment of revenue was also not based on any scientific basis. The Government decided to conduct "Revenue Survey" by scientific method to prepare accurate land map of all the Estates in the Bengal Presidency and thus make correct assessment of revenue to be paid by each Estate. The villages in an Estate were taken as units of survey. Big villages or cluster of small villages were taken as units of 'revenue villages' or mauzas. The boundaries of the mauzas were identified and delineated with earthen pillars and were given identification names.

To prepare accurate map of a mauza by scientific method, theodolite traverse survey was conducted around the boundary of the mauza, connecting the pillars by survey lines around the boundary, forming a polygon, with reference to the True North direction, by making astronomical observations. Rectangular coordinates of the pillar stations were calculated from the data consisting of observed angles, length of survey lines and bearings. Area of the closed polygon was calculated by using the rectangular coordinates and the areas of the land falling inside or outside the polygon within the boundary of the mauza, called offset areas, were calculated separately. By adding (outside offset areas) or subtracting (inside offset areas) the offset areas within the polygon area, accurate area of the mauza was found out. In the Revenue Survey, only the boundary of a mauza was surveyed and mapped to find out the accurate area of the mauza, but no internal details like plot boundaries were surveyed or plotted. The scale used for Revenue Survey mapping was 4 inch = 1 mile.

The Revenue Survey was conducted between 1835 and 1877 in Bengal Presidency by British Surveyors, many of whom were British Army engineers, assisted by native Amins. The mauzas created during the Revenue Survey, have been adopted as units of survey and mapping in all subsequent Survey and Settlement Operations in the State till date. All Revenue Survey maps have unique numbers, which are still noted in the corresponding current cadastral mauza maps as references.

Survey for Preparation of Cadastral Mauza Maps

The unique feature of the cadastral survey in this province was that the survey and mapping of the mauza included survey of the plots or fields held by tenants in the mauza in their true shape and relative position as internal details of the mauza, in a particular scale of mapping. Because of the accuracy of the mapping system, areas of individuals plots were extracted from the map itself, which was shown in the record of rights, no separate map for each plot, like Tippons or FMBs with the dimensions of the sides given, were prepared as part of cadastral mapping

For preparation of record of rights under the provisions of the Bengal Tenancy Act.[52] In 1885 for each class of tenant, including raiyats and under-raiyats, a Survey & Settlement Operation was conducted in the Bengal Province

[52] Bengal Tenancy Act, 1885 was the first Tenancy law in Bengal, which provided specific classification of tenancy or classes of tenants existing in Bengal at that time and had provisions for preparation of Record of Rights for each class of tenants. The tenants were classified as follows:

i) Tenure-holders, including under-tenure holders, who were mainly intermediaries with the right to hold land for the purpose of collecting rent or bringing it under cultivation by establishing tenants on it. Proprietors of Estates were tenure-holders under the Government.

ii) Raiyats, who held lands for the purpose of agriculture under a tenure holder or under tenure holder and paid rent to the landlord. There were also three classes of raiyats i.e. a) Raiyats holding at fixed rent or rate of rent, b) Occupancy raiyats, with right of occupancy on the land held, and c) Non-occupancy raiyats with no right of occupancy.

iii) Under-raiyats, holding land immediately or mediately under raiyats.

The statutes for the rights and obligations of each class of tenant were elaborately provided in the Act, including obligations to pay rent and grounds for ejection from tenancy. Cadastral maps and Record of Rights for all classes of tenants were prepared for the first time in the Province under sections 101 to 103A of this Act.

for the first time, which was known as District Survey and Operation. It was also called Cadastral Survey & Settlement Operation, because cadastral mauza maps were prepared for the first time by scientific survey method, taking a mauza as a unit of survey and preparation of land records.

The District Survey & Settlement Operation was started in the district of Chittagong (now in Bangladesh) in 1888 and was completed in the districts of Dinajpur and Howrah in 1940.

The successive stages of preparation of Cadastral maps by scientific survey method, followed by preparation of land records in a mauza by Survey & Settlement Operation are discussed here.

Control Survey by Theodolite Traverse

Control survey, preferably by theodolite traverse survey, is conducted for establishing control points in and around the unit of survey i.e. a mauza, basing on which cadastral survey is done for preparation of mauza map.

a) *Field work*: For theodolite traverse, a reconnaissance of the boundary of the unit is first made by the surveyor and stout wooden pegs are embedded flush on the selected points at or near each major bend along the boundary or as close to it as possible and deep inside the area, generally 5 to 20 chains apart. The linear distances between the successive pegs are measured by steel band chain (currently by EDM equipment) and the angles between the lines joining the successive pegs are measured by a theodolite. (Presently, the works of distance measurement and angle measurement are done by Electronic Total Station equipment). When the linear and angular measurements on all the pegs around the periphery of the unit (or mauza) are completed, a closed polygon of straight lines is formed on the ground, roughly corresponding to the boundary of the unit of survey. The polygon forms the main circuit of the traverse survey.

   To provide sufficient number of control points for facilitating detailed survey inside the unit or mauza, sub-traverse lines or sub-circuits are run connecting the traverse stations on the main circuit or other sub-circuits to divide the polygon into several blocks.

b) *Observations for Azimuth*: For computing Azimuths, i.e. the angle a traverse line makes with the True North (geographic north) direction, theodolite observations are made 15 to 20 pegs or stations apart, for determining the angular altitude of the Sun or Polaris or any major star, noting the time of observation, the data available from the Nautical Almanac and the latitude of the place. Then applying necessary formulae of spherical trigonometry, the angular value of the Azimuth of the survey line at the point of observation is deduced.

c) *Computations*: As the unit of cadastral survey is a small area on the Earth's surface, it is taken as a plane surface. As such, the Azimuth of the traverse line, which is the angle between the Meridian passing through the point of observation towards the True North direction and the traverse line is converted to Bearing, which is the angle between the traverse line and the North direction by a straight line at the point of observation (i.e. a peg). Bearing of the traverse line is required to deduce the rectangular co-ordinate of the point of observation. The Bearing of the traverse line is obtained by applying Correction for Convergency to the Azimuth of that reference traverse line. The Bearings of all traverse lines connecting successive pegs on the main circuit or sub-circuit of the traverse survey can be computed from the initial bearing deduced as above, with checks for accuracy from the Azimuth observations on the subsequent Azimuth Stations (pegs) at regular intervals.

For computation of coordinates of the traverse stations, the Traverse Survey is always connected to two or more nearest Great Trigonometric (GT) Survey stations. The geographical coordinates of the GT stations are converted into rectangular coordinates according to Cassini Projection. For this projection, one Origin of survey is adopted for the entire area under survey within a district. For every district in the State, one pair of geographical coordinates have been adopted as District Origin. For example:

	Origin	
District	*Latitude*	*Longitude*
Darjeeling	27d 00m 00s	88d 30m 00s
Jalpaiguri	26d 00m 00s	89d 00m 00s

Computations of the rectangular coordinates from spherical coordinates are done by using the "Table 8 Sur., Auxiliary Table" of the Survey of India.

Computation of the azimuth of the reference traverse line at each azimuth station is computed by using the "Auxiliary Tables Part III" of the Survey of India.

The Rectangular Coordinates of each Traverse Station (peg) in the form of northings, southings, easting and westings, are computed from the data consisting of lengths, observed angles and bearings of the Traverse lines at the respective Traverse Stations, after applying necessary corrections to keep the accumulated errors within the prescribed limit of error.

d) *Plotting*: The Traverse Stations are then plotted on a special graph paper, known as P-70 sheet (normally 1 inch square) of size 30" by 22". The Traverse Stations on the main circuit in or around the periphery of the unit of survey or mauza and the Traverse stations on the sub-circuit or sub-traverse lines inside the mauza on the ground are plotted on the P-70 sheet in their true relative position in respect to the North direction shown on the

P-70 sheet in the required scale of mapping. These networks of Traverse Stations are used as control points for detailed survey to maintain required degree of accuracy in survey work and mapping.

e) *Scale of Plotting*: The scales of plotting of the traverse stations or control points on P 70 sheets are ordinarily 1:3960 (in FPS) or 1:4000 (in CGS) in rural areas, 1:1980 or 1:990 in FPS or in corresponding 1:2000 or in 1:1000 in CGS in urban areas. In special cases, the scale may be 1:600 or in 1:500. The core area of the city of Calcutta (Kolkata) has been surveyed and mapped in 1:600 scale during 1905 to 1914, which is still being maintained and updated by the Kolkata Municipal Corporation (KMC).

Small Scale Maps

Basing on the geographical coordinates generated during the traverse survey for cadastral mapping, small scale maps like police station maps and district maps were prepared and published by the Directorate of Land Records and Surveys.

a) **Police Station Maps** – Maps of all police stations were prepared based on the survey during District Survey and Settlement operation. Congregating the cadastral maps of the mauzas in the jurisdiction of each police station, PS maps were prepared in two scales – i) 4" = 1 mile or 1:15,840 scale and ii) 1" = 1 mile or 1:63,360 scale with graticule lines, by using Lambert Projection system. The PS maps are updated, when new police stations are created by bifurcation or amalgamation.

b) **District Maps** – District maps of every district were prepared by congregating the maps of all police stations within a district in 1" =1 mile or 1= 63.360 scale with graticule lines. The district maps are also updated, when new districts are created by bifurcation or amalgamation.

c) **State Map** – The State Map of West Bengal has been prepared by congregating the district maps in 1" =16 mile or 1:1,013,760 (or nearly 1:1 million) scale.

Cadastral Survey (or Kistwar)

The P-70 sheets with control points plotted on them in relevant scale are then handed over to the Revenue Officer or Revenue Inspector for Cadastral Survey (or Kistwar) i.e. survey of details in the mauza by Chain Survey or Plane Table Survey method, following the survey principle "From whole to part". The survey team, led by a Revenue Officer or a Revenue Inspector, is composed of two Amins, who are trained in Chain Survey or Plane Table survey, and two Chain-peons. In cadastral survey, survey of boundaries of the fields or plots held by individuals is done to make an accurate plan of the fields in the mauza or area under survey in the required sale of mapping.

a) *Equipment*: In the Chain Survey method, the main equipment used are: i) a plane table with tripod, ii) a Gunter's Chain, and iii) an optical square, apart from other instruments like diagonal scale, offset scale, a pair of dividers, one pole of 20 links length, six poles with flags, ten iron pins (9") etc.

For plane table survey, the necessary instruments are: i) a plane table with tripod, ii) one sight vane with or without telescope, iii) a magnetic compass, iv) a plumb bob, v) Gunter's chain or 20 metres chain with 100 links etc.

Gunter's Chain – It is a 22 yards long steel chain with 100 links, each link being of 7.92 inch length. The chain is used for ground measurement of survey lines. The first series of cadastral surveys were conducted in the District Survey and settlement Operation in the State during 1888-1940, when all measurements were made in FPS units, as CGS was not in use at that time.

Optical square – The optical square is an instrument with two reflecting mirrors positioned at 45 degree angle, an incoming ray of light, after double reflection on the two reflecting mirrors, goes out at 90 degree angle; following a principle of physics. With this instrument, it can be ascertained the point on the chain line of advance from which any selected point off that line is exactly perpendicular. The length of the perpendicular on the ground, called "offset", is measured and by means of an offset scale and divider, the position of the point is shown and plotted on the sheet.

For maintaining the required limit of accuracy, the limits of offsets are: i) 1 chain (66') in 1:3960 scale or 20 metres in 1:4000, ii) 75 links (49.5') in 1:1980 scale or 15 metres in 1:2000 scale, and iii) 50 links (33feet) in 1:990 scale or 10 metres in 1:1000 scale.

b) *Checking of equipment*: Before the start of the field work and also regularly during the field work, all survey instruments like the gunter's chain, the optical square, the sight vane etc. are checked for desired accuracy by the prescribed methods for each equipment.

c) *Finding of Traverse pegs*: The first stage of detailed survey in a mauza starts with finding of the traverse pegs on the ground. Before start of the work, the Amin, who assists the Revenue Officer in the field work, is provided with a copy of the plotted P 70 sheet, called a *khaka.* The Amin starts finding the traverse pegs with the help of the *khaka,* from one of the village tri-junction pillars, or any other permanent mark on the ground, which has been selected as a traverse station. A village tri-junction pillar is the meeting point of the boundaries of three adjoining mauzas, which were established during the District Survey and Settlement operation and are very important fixed points for any subsequent revisional survey in the mauza. The Amin will first find out the traverse stations on the main circuit, and then those of the sub-circuit and sub-traverse lines. The Amin will also establish intermediate stations on the traverse lines, as required, to facilitate forming of quadrilaterals or *Morabbas* at the next stage of work. While finding out the traverse pegs, the ground distance of each pair of successive traverse stations are measured by actual chaining and checked with the sheet distance.

If there be any missing traverse peg, it is relocated on the ground by using the plotted P 70 sheet and chain and optical square or plane table and sight-vane, as required.

d) *Preparation of Quadrilaterals*: Following the principle "From whole to part", the traverse circuit along the mauza boundary forming a polygon, is cut up into a number of quadrilaterals, taking the traverse stations or intermediate stations as corner points of the quadrilaterals. The sides of the quadrilaterals on the sheet are kept at 2 inches to 3 inches (5 cm to 8 cm) in length i.e. 10 acres to 20 acres on the ground in 16" = 1 mile scale of mapping or smaller areas in larger scale of mapping. The quadrilateral lines are measured on the ground by the Amin and are plotted on the sheet by the Revenue Officer. Any discrepancy or error between the ground measurement and sheet measurement between two quadrilateral stations, if within the prescribed limit of error (1:200), is distributed along the quadrilateral line on the sheet by prescribed methods.

e) *Plotting of fields and other details*: For survey of fields and other details inside a quadrilateral, starting points of chain lines on one side of the quadrilateral and ending points of the chain lines on the opposite side of the quadrilateral are selected first in such a way that no offsets taken by using the optical square from the chain lines, exceed the prescribed limit of offset lengths. These tertiary chain lines are called *Shikmi* lines, which are chosen in such a way that they run along the general direction of the longer side of the fields in order to minimise the lengths of the offsets.

The Amin will first of all go along the boundaries of the quadrilateral, plotting the bends and corners of the adjacent fields (plots) and other details, if any, on both sides lying within the limit of offsets by taking linear measurements with the Gunter's Chain and offsets by optical square. Then he will follow the *shikmi* lines one by one, taking linear measurements along the chain line and taking offsets to bends and corners of the fields on both sides of the chain line, and plot them on the sheet to form the field configurations on the sheet by joining the appropriate offset points by using a fine pencil.

Survey of details is done taking one polygon at a time to contain errors within the polygon, as it is easier to identify and rectify errors in a small area by running adequate independent check lines. After completing detailed survey and plotting on the sheet in one polygon, detailed survey of next polygon is taken up. Cadastral mapping of the whole mauza is completed when all quadrilaterals are surveyed and plotted on the sheet.

Survey of details inside a mauza includes all plots enclosed by boundaries, roads, pathways, canals, channels, waterbodies, bridges, buildings, masonry structures, railway lines etc. Existence of different features in the plots of land in the mauza like huts, bamboo clumps, cluster of palm/Palmyra/coconut trees etc. are shown on the map by conventional signs or alamats. The List of Conventional Signs for use in cadastral maps, approved and issued by the Department of Land Records and Surveys, contain more than 90 (ninety) items.

When survey is done along the village boundary, if it is found that some part of the boundary is beyond the offset limit from the traverse line or quadrilateral line, then additional control points are fixed on the ground near the mauza boundary by chain triangulation. For survey in riverine areas, sight-vane survey is resorted to.

f) *Survey of particular objects 'in situ'*: The following objects of permanent nature on the field are carefully surveyed in their true position: GT Stations and Bench Marks, village tri-junction pillars, other masonry pillars, kilometre/mile stones, telegraph posts, electric posts and pylons, pucca wells, deep tube-wells, pucca buildings, pucca bridges, culverts, railway lines, large isolated trees or other conspicuous objects of permanent nature. In subsequent revisional survey works, these surveyed-in-situ objects can be adopted as fixed points to facilitate the survey work.

g) *Independent checks*: Apart from the important survey principle of "from whole to part" another important principle is "Independent Check". Check lines or *partal* lines are extensively run by inspecting officers over the completed part of the survey to verify the accuracy of the survey work following prescribed norms. Firstly, partal lines are run over every morabba or quadrilateral after completion of survey and plotting in the morabba and corrections are incorporated if any discrepancy is detected. After all morabbas are completed and checked, then longer partal lines are run over the different parts of the mauza to check the overall accuracy of the cadastral mapping. The map is finally passed after it meets the required degree of correctness.

h) *Boundary comparison*: Boundary comparison of cadastral maps means the comparison of the common boundary of adjoining villages or mauzas. After kistwar is completed in a mauza, boundary comparison is done by juxtaposing the maps of two adjoining villages on a glass table in such a way that common traverse stations along the boundary to be compared are exactly superimposed on one another. Then it is examined whether the boundaries as surveyed in the two sheets coincide.

   In case any discrepancies are detected, necessary ground verification is done for rectification of the same. Boundary comparison is done to ensure that there is no gap or overlap in the areas surveyed between the adjoining villages.

i) *Inking of the cadastral map*: The plotting of the mapping sheet is done by fine pencil and after the pencil map is fully checked and passed, it is inked up in cobalt blue, including all pencil lines, the alamats or conventional signs, some traverse stations near the village boundary and other items on the map as per the Technical Rules and Instructions. The map remains in cobalt blue till the map is finally published along with Record of Rights of the Mauza under the relevant provision of the statute. After final publication, the mauza map in cobalt blue is inked in Indian Black ink.

j) *Final Cadastral mauza map*: The cadastral map of a mauza is plotted on mapping sheet of size 30"x22". A margin of two inches is kept clear on all sides of the map. The main map of the mauza remains in the centre position of the mapping sheet. Other cartographic items are drawn as follows:
   i) On the left hand top corner i.e. the north-west corner, the North Point in the north direction is drawn.
   ii) Close to it, the sheet heading is written, which shows the name of the mauza, both in English and Bengali, with sheet number, jurisdiction list number, name of police station, name of district, revenue survey number, season of survey (from commencement of survey till final publication of the RoR of the mauza) and the scale of survey.
   iii) Below the sheet heading, two diagonal scales are drawn, one in FPS and another CGS, using which linear measurements of both units may be taken from the sheet.
   iv) On the southwest margin, a Reference Block is drawn, in which, a few conventional signs like pucca building, old and new traverse stations, railway lines etc., plot numbers of roads, paths, tanks, canals, rivers, total number of plots in the sheet, the first and the last plot number in the sheet, missing plot numbers, if any etc., are shown,
   v) Names of adjoining mauzas with their JL numbers, village tri-junction pillars, a few traverse stations near the village boundary are shown on the sheet.
   vi) A certificate block is drawn, normally on the right hand south-east side of the map, showing the period of preparation of the map, the Statute under which the map has been prepared and in case of a revised map, the period of the old map and the signature of the prescribed authority.
   vii) Normally a mauza of area up to 500 acres may be shown in one sheet in 1:3960 scale. For mauzas of larger areas, the number of sheets increase accordingly. For mapping in larger scales, the number of sheets also increase further.

Revisional Survey

To implement the provisions for preparation of RoRs under the West Bengal Estate acquisition Act,[53] 1953, a second Survey & Settlement Operation was

[53] West Bengal Estate acquisition Act, 1953: The WBEA Act, 1953 was passed in the West Bengal Legislative Assembly as West Bengal Act I of 1954. It was a landmark statute after Independence in West Bengal. The WBEA Act came into operation in the State on 12.2.1953. After issuance of notifications under this Act by the Government, the following effects took place:

i) All estates and rights of intermediaries, including sub-soil rights in mines and minerals, sairati interests i.e. rights to collect rents in hats (rural market places), bazaars, ferries, fisheries, tolls etc. stood vested to the State free from all incumbrances on the 1st Day of Baisakh of Bengali year 1362 (15.4.1955) conducted from 1954 to 1960 simultaneously in all districts, except the district of Purulia and Islampur Subdivision in Paschim Dinajpur District, lands of which were transferred from Bihar to West Bengal under the Bihar and West Bengal (Transfer of Territories) Act, 1956. The provisions of the WBEA Act were implemented in these transferred territories from 1964 onwards.

This Survey and Settlement Operation under the WBEA Act 1953 was conducted for preparation of RoRs and cadastral maps by revising the finally published RoRs and cadastral maps prepared under the Bengal Tenancy Act, 1885. As such this Operation was known as Revisional Survey & Settlement Operation.

In Revisional Survey, a limited survey is conducted for the purpose of revising an old map so as to update it by incorporating the changes that have taken place in the configurations of fields and the new ground features that have come up and at the same time by omitting those features from the old map, which has ceased to exist since the old map was prepared.

---

ii) All grants or confirmation of titles in favour of intermediaries in respect of their estates stood vested to the State.

iii) Rights in all types of forest land held by intermediaries, stood vested to the State

iv) All Raiyats or non-agricultural tenants, holding land under an intermediary, held such land directly under the State from the date of vesting, as if the State had been the intermediary, on the same terms and conditions immediately before the date of vesting and pay rent to the State.

v) Different ceilings for different classes of land, that could be held by an individual, was prescribed in the Act.

vi) Restrictions were imposed on transfers of land among close and near relations during a certain period, and were subject to scrutiny on the assumption that such transfers were made to avoid the ceiling provisions.

Out of the total land of an estate belonging to an intermediary, usually the intermediary used to keep a part of the land under his khas (personal) possession and on the rest, rent receiving interests or tenancies were created. After an estate was vested to the State: i) the intermediary was allowed to retain certain quantum of land out of the land he held in his khas possession, as per ceiling provisions of the Act and the ceiling-excess land was vested to the State, and ii) his rent receiving interest on the rest of his estate ceased to exist. The intermediary became a raiyat on the land he was allowed to retain under the Act. By WBEA (Amendment Act) 1955, raiyats and under-raiyats were treated as intermediaries to bring them under the different provisions of the Act, as mentioned in the preceding paragraphs, including land ceiling and vesting of ceiling excess land. The date of vesting was the first day of Baisakh of Bengali year 1363 (14.4.1956). There were provisions for an elaborate process of assessment of loss of annual net income of an intermediary due to the vesting of his estate or ceiling excess land of a raiyat or under-raiyat and payment of compensation was made under the Act. With the WBEA Act, 1953 coming into force in the State in 1954, the entire tenancy structure had undergone a complete change from that of the Bengal Tenancy Act, 1885. The complex structure of superior interests and subordinate tenancies under the BT Act was replaced by much simpler tenancy structure, where the State was the only landlord and all possessors of land were raiyats under the State.

There was statutory provision for preparation of cadastral maps and RoRs under the WBEA Act by revising the Maps and RoRs prepared under the BT Act, 1885.

Revisional survey is resorted to only if about 1/3rd of the mapped area has undergone changes. In case it is found that there have been extensive changes in mapped details in more than 1/3rd of the mapped area, then de-novo or new survey is done on the basis of theodolite traverse survey.

In revisional survey, where changes are found to be of stray nature, such as a new building has been erected or a plot boundary has changed, in the vicinity of which other plot boundaries have remained unchanged or some old points still exist fixed on the ground and also on the map, such points are adopted as fixed points, from which necessary measurements are taken and plotting of the new details or corrections on the old map is done on the basis of these measurements. However, before adopting the fixed points for taking measurements, the positional fixity of these adopted stations should be checked by comparing the ground measurement and sheet measurement from at least two other fixed points in the vicinity.

LR Survey and Settlement Operation

For preparation of cadastral maps and RoRs under the WBLR Act,[54] a third Survey and Settlement Operation was initiated in the State from 1974 in all districts. The same methodology is being followed in this operation also. Taking each mauza as a unit, new RoRs and cadastral maps are being prepared

---

[54] West Bengal Land Reforms Act, 1955: In the spirit of the principles of policy to be followed by the State as specified in clauses (b) and (c) of article 39 of the Constitution of India, the West Bengal Land Reforms Act, 1955 was enacted in the West Bengal Legislative Assembly as West Bengal Act 10 of 1956. The Act has since undergone several amendments.

The salient features of the WBLR Act, 1955 can be summarized as follows:

i) Rights and obligations of a Raiyat in respect of his land have been elaborately enunciated, keeping land reforms measures in view.
ii) Statutes for restrictions on alienation of land held by Scheduled Tribes for their protection.
iii) Individual land ceiling under the WBEA Act was changed to family ceiling, depending on the size of the family, for fresh vesting of ceiling surplus land.
iv) Family was specifically defined regarding constituent members.
v) Rights of Bargadars or sharecroppers were specially recognized, with statutory protection against their forcible eviction or denying their due share of the cultivated crop, by the Landowners
vi) The old definition of 'Land' as defined in the WBLR Act till 1981, which mainly included agricultural land, was changed by Amendment Act, 1981, in which all classes of land were included in the Definition of 'Land", to facilitate vesting of more land to the State, as per ceiling provisions of the Act.
vii) Principles of distribution of the lands at the disposal of the Government (State) among the landless or the marginal farmers, who own less than one acre of agricultural, for agricultural or homestead purposes, are laid down in the Act. Such lands, settled with the beneficiaries, are heritable but not transferable.
viii) There is provision for preparation of cadastral maps and RoRs under the WBLR Act, 1955 by revising the Maps and RoRs prepared under the WBEA Act, 1953.

by revising the Finally Published RoRs and cadastral maps prepared under the WBEA Act, 1953. The operation is still continuing and is known as LR Survey and Settlement Operation.

The special feature of the LR Operation is that, all plots of land belonging to each raiyat in one mauza, is being shown in one khatian (RoR), prepared in the name of the raiyat, following the principle of "one-man-one-khatian" or OMOK. If the raiyat has other lands in a different mauza, he will have separate OMOK for that mauza. The number of such OMOK RORs have exceeded 36 million till now and the number of cadastral maps, more than 68,000. The total number of mauzas are 42,042 in the State.

As stated earlier, the first series of cadastral maps were prepared in the District Survey and Settlement operation during 1888–1940, but in the next two settlement operations i.e., under the WBEA Act, 1953 during 1954–1960 and under the WBLR Act, 1955 from 1974 till date, are revisional survey and settlement operations, in which maps of previous survey were revised or updated. In the areas where old map does not fully represent the ground configuration due to extensive changes, new cadastral survey is done on the basis of traverse survey.

Methodology of Survey and Settlement Operations

It will be relevant to discuss about the methodology of a survey & settlement operation for preparation or revision of land records in a mauza, which is a revenue village. When an order has been made by the Government under the relevant provision of a concerned Land Law or Act for preparation or revision of record of rights (RoRs), the record of rights are prepared or revised by the following process:

i) Traverse Survey for establishing control points
ii) Cadastral Survey for survey of details in the mauja
iii) Preliminary record writing (Khanapuri)
iv) Local explanation (Bujharat)
v) Attestation of preliminary record of rights (RoR)
vi) Publication of draft record of rights (DP)
vii) Disposal of objections
viii) Preparation and publication of the final record of rights (FP)

The cadastral map of a mauza is prepared by the first two stages of survey work. After the cadastral mauza map is ready, it is handed over to the Revenue officer for preparation RoRs or *khatians* on the field from the Khanapuri stage.

The first two stages are technical part of the survey for cadastral mapping, which have already been discussed in the preceding paragraphs, the rest are discussed as under:

a) Khanapuri – At this stage, fields or plots on the cadastral map are numbered and draft RoRs are prepared by plot to plot survey in the mauja. Separate

Khatian (RoR) for each person interested or group of persons interested in the land is opened and all particulars of the rights and liabilities of each person or persons interested, classification of the land as per land use etc. are entered in the khatian.

b) Bujharat – Areas of all plots or fields are extracted from the map at this stage and are entered in the draft RoRs. Each khatian is examined by the Revenue Officer on the ground with reference to the mauza map or cadastral map. A copy of each khatian is handed over to the person or persons interested and is explained to him or them. The RoRs and the mauza map are also corrected, if required.

The stages (i) to (iv) are omitted in case of Revisional Survey and Settlement Operations in an area, in which plot to plot enquiry and survey are made where necessary, for incorporating changes in maps previously prepared and record names of current possessors of the plots in the unit, i.e. a mauza.

c) Attestation – The work of Attestation of the draft RoRs is taken up by the Revenue officer in his office by issuing general notice to all persons having possession or interest in the lands of a mauza to appear before him on the dates fixed with relevant papers and documents in support of their title and possession. All changes that may have occurred in any tenancy since last finally published RoR due to inheritance, succession, transfer or otherwise is taken into account by the Revenue Officer before finalizing the draft RoR for Attestation. After attesting a RoR with his seal and signature by the Revenue Officer, a copy of the attested RoR is handed over to the stakeholder.

d) Draft Publication – After preparation or revision of all record of rights (RoRs) of the mauza has been completed, a draft of the RoRs are placed for public inspection, free of charges, for one month at a convenient place, as decided by the Revenue Officer after issuing public notice for general information in the mauza. Objections to the draft RoR are invited and are filed by interested individuals within a notified date, after which all objections are disposed of by the Revenue Officer by quasi-judicial process as per extant land law and rules.

e) Final Publication – After disposal of all objections and changes incorporated in the concerned draft published RoRs, the Revenue Officer finally publishes the RoRs with the prescribed certification of final publication on each RoR.

There is also provision for correction of entries in Finally Published RoRs within a stipulated period.

It is evident from the above paragraphs that there is scope for correction of the RoRs at all the stages during the preparation of RoRs giving opportunity to all stakeholders of being heard or represented. As such, all Finally Published RoRs have "presumption of correctness" in judicial scrutiny.

Land Reforms Organization

a) *Land and Land Reforms Department*: Before independence, the Department was named as Land Revenue Department. After Independence, the Department was renamed as Land, Land Revenue and Land Utilization Department. After the Left Front Government coming into power in West Bengal in 1977, the Department was again renamed as Land and Land Reforms Department. It is the topmost policy making body in the Government regarding land matters in the State. The greatest achievement of the Department is the implementation of the main object of the West Bengal Land Reforms Act, 1955, i.e. the vesting of ceiling surplus land and distribution of the same among a huge number of landless and marginal farmers (more than 13 lakh), apart from other land related matters. The main implementing agency of all policies formulated by the Department is the Directorate of Land Records and Surveys.

b) *Board of Revenue*: The Board of Revenue of the Bengal Province was created by Governor General Warren Hastings in 1772. After Independence it functioned as a single member Board till 1995, when it was abolished by the West Bengal Board of Revenue (Repealing) Act, 1995.

c) *Directorate of Land Records and Surveys*: The Revenue and Agriculture Department of the Government of India sanctioned the creation of the Directorate of Land Records and Agriculture in the Bengal Province by letter no. 433A dated 20 May 1884 and Mr. M. Finucane CIS, ICS took over as the first Director of Land Records and Agriculture on 30 December 1884 and continued till 1892. He was instrumental in organising and initiating the first Survey and Settlement Operation under the Bengal Tenancy Act, 1885 in the Bengal Province in 1888. A separate Directorate of Agriculture was created in 1905, leaving the Director of Land Records to devote his whole attention for conduct of settlement operations for preparation of village-wise Record of Rights of tenants on the districts.

During pre-independence period, the biggest achievement of the Directorate was the successful completion of the District Survey and Settlement Operations in all the districts of undivided Bengal Province during 1888 to 1940. Post-Independence, the completion of the Revisional Survey and Settlement Operation under the WBEA Act, 1953 and then the Land Reforms Survey & Settlement Operation under the WBLR Act, 1955, which will be a continuous one in 42000+ no. of mauzas in the State, are the most notable achievements of the Directorate, apart from other functions like conducting General Elections, preparation of electoral rolls in the Calcutta South Parliamentary constituency for the last five decades etc.

Initially, cadastral survey part of the Survey & Settlement Operation was carried by the officers of the Survey of India till 1905. Cadastral maps being an integral part of RoRs, a separate Survey Department was created under a

Director of Survey by the Bengal Government. However, to prevent overlapping of jurisdiction, the two Directorates were merged under one Director of Land Records and Surveys in 1923. The Survey Wing of the Directorate was headed by an Officer-in-Charge, who was on deputation from the Survey of India. The settlement wing and the survey wing of the Directorate were at two different locations in Calcutta till 1923, when the two wings were shifted and located in a newly constructed building, named the "Survey Building" at Alipore, Calcutta. It is a landmark building in this metro city.

After Independence, the survey office of the Directorate is headed by the Deputy Director of Survey, West Bengal, who comes from the State Civil Services. It is comprised of two parts: i) West Bengal Drawing Office (WBDO), erstwhile Bengal Drawing Office, and ii) West Bengal Traverse Party (WBTP), erstwhile Bengal Traverse Party.

d) *West Bengal Drawing Office*: It is the cartographic wing of the survey office. It is manned by an Assistant Survey Officer, five Head Draftsmen and 30 Draftsmen, who are all technically qualified personnel. The functions of the WBDO include: i) preparation and updating of small scale maps like Police Station Maps in 4 inches = 1 mile, 1 inch = 1 mile and 1:25000 scale by proportional reduction and controlled mosaicking of cadastral mauza maps, ii) preparation and updating of District maps in 1inch=4 mile scale by proportional reduction and controlled mosaicking of PS maps, iii) preparation of draft notifications of new police stations and districts, iv) digital updating of cadastral mauza maps, v) preparation of certified copies of CS and RS mauza maps, etc. The office is equipped with two AO size Scanners, two AO size digital plotters, 30 desktop computers, necessary cartographic software, etc.

e) *West Bengal Traverse Party*: It is the theodolite traverse survey wing of the survey office. The WBTP has two wings: i) Traverse survey wing, and ii) Traverse Computation wing. The Traverse Survey wing is manned by one Survey Officer, one Assistant Survey Officer and 14 Surveyors, all of whom are technically qualified from Government Polytechnics. The function of the Traverse Survey parties is to conduct theodolite control survey for providing network of control points in the mauzas under cadastral survey.

The Traverse Computation wing is manned by one Assistant Survey Officers and 20 Computors, who are equally qualified like those of Traverse Surveyors. The function of the Computation wing is to make computations from the survey field data sent by the Traverse Surveyors to prepare mapping sheets with control points plotted on them in the required scale, including North Direction from data of astronomical observations. These mapping sheets with plotted control points are provided to the Land Revenue authorities in the districts for detailed survey in the mauzas under cadastral survey.

The WBTP is equipped with 18 pairs of DGPS, 36 Electronic Total Stations, 15 T2 one second Theodolites, one A0 size Scanner, three A0 size digital plotters, 20 desktop computers, necessary software etc. The digitized cadastral mauza maps are now being uploaded in the "Banglarbhumi" website from the WBTP for providing Citizen e-Services.

f) *District LR set-up*: At present there are 23 districts in the State. At the district level, the head of LR set-up is the District Land and Land Reforms Officer (DLLRO), who is also referred to as ADM (LR). At the Sub-division level there is the Sub-divisional Land and Land Reforms Officer, at the Block level, the Block Land and Land Reforms Officer and at the Gram Panchayat level, there is Revenue Inspector. The functionaries at the different levels in the districts have their respective functions for preparation, maintenance and updating or RoRs and cadastral maps in each mauza in the districts.

Apart for these institutional set-ups at state and district level, the Directorate has a large map printing press with flat-bed map printing machines, where cadastral maps were printed centrally also the Directorate has a large Map Record Room, preserving all original cadastral mauza maps of the three survey and settlement operations since 1888, each series having more than 66,000 sheets, there are original Revenue Survey maps (1835-1877), Calcutta Survey maps since 1784 and many other antique originals. The total number maps being preserved in the Map Record Room is more than 2.5 lakhs.

Problems in Revisional Survey

a) One of the problems faced for incorporating new objects like buildings, new walls or similar objects in the old map, is the lack of availability of old fixed points which exist both on the ground and the map, due to changes in the adjoining area. To overcome this problem, recce has to be made only in the areas of the adjoining sheets to find out surveyed-in-situ objects, which exist both on the ground and the map and use at least three of them as fixed points to extend the points by chain triangulations to establish fixed points near to the new object to take measurements for survey and plotting on the map.

b) Another problem is creating new plots by division of an old plot, which is small in size on the sheet. The minimum size of a plot on a sheet may be 3 mm by 2.5 mm, but when such plot is required to be further subdivided due to partition, then it is difficult to create a new plot. The only alternative is to make an 'inset' on the margin of the map and take measurements from the fixed points and plot the new map in the inset in a larger scale, with a reference kept on the margin.

Initiatives Taken for the Modernization in Survey and Mapping

a) *Change in Coordinate System for better accuracy in mapping*: As discussed earlier, all traverse control survey work in the State were connected with the local Great Trigonometric Survey Stations or GT Stations, which had Everest system of coordinates, so that the coordinates of the control points of the traverse survey could also be converted to Everest Coordinates. However, for introducing more accuracy in the survey work, the Survey of India has changed its coordinate system of its network of GT Stations and similar new stations to WGS 1984 (World Geodetic System), an US coordinate system being used universally now, from its old Everest coordinate system, which was a local Indian System of coordinates, introduced by George Everest in 1830.

For changing the coordinate systems in the control survey in this State, Coordinates of 76 Primary Control Stations, covering all districts in the State, have been procured from the Survey of India. Using the DGPS, ETS and Electronic theodolites, 140 more Secondary Control points have been established throughout the State. Now, work is going on for establishing at least four tertiary control points in each mauza, for accuracy in updating of the cadastral maps.

b) *Procurement of Modern Survey equipment*: Modern Survey equipment like GPS, Electronic Total Stations, Electronic Theodolites etc. were in limited use in the West Bengal Surveys under the Dept. of Land Records. However for control survey for digital mapping. Eighteen pairs of DGPS of 1 mm accuracy and for detailed mapping, 36 Electronic Total Stations (ETS) have been procured in the last five years.

c) *Digitization of Cadastral Maps*: The total number of cadastral sheets in the State is more than 68,000, the size of each sheet being 30"x22" (about A1 size). Each sheet contain about 750 plots on the average, apart from cartographic texts, conventional signs etc. As such, digitization of the cadastral maps, maintaining the required accuracy, was a very big challenge. After long experimentation and sustained efforts of the State Survey Department and the NIC, 95% of the cadastral maps have been vector-digitized and all digitized maps have been uploaded and available in the website Banglarbhumi for citizen services.

Additional Notes

- *Computerization of Land Records in West Bengal: At a Glance*

Computers were installed in all 341 Blocks in the State by 2001-2002. One-window service for supply of certified copies of computerized Khatians to raiyats from Block Land Reforms offices were started subsequently. Initially the Computers at the Blocks were functioning as independent servers with data storage but subsequently all the Blocks have been connected by WAN with the State Server for central storage and stringent data security.

The data of about 36 million Khatians (RoRs) (one khatian for each raiyat, containing all plots in a mauja) in 42,042 mauzas in the State have been computerized so far. The total volume of electronic data of RoRs already entered is more than 40 GB. All the Computerized RoRs have been uploaded and available at official website "Banglarbhumi" for citizen service.

The statutory provision for preparation of RoRs in the WBLR Act,1955 have been suitably amended to recognize Computerized RoRs to be legally valid documents

- *Area measurement units used in West Bengal:*
  - I. 1 Katha = 16 Chhataks = 720 sq. ft. = 80 sq. yards
  - II. 1 Chhatak = 720/16 = 45 Sq. ft. = 5 sq. yards
  - III. 1 Bigha = 20 Kathas =20 x 80 sq. yards = 1600 sq yards
  - IV. 1 Acre = 3 Bighas + 8 Chhataks = 4800 sq. yards + 40 sq. yards = 4840 sq. yards
  - V. 1 Acre = 100 Decimals = 4840 sq. yards = 4840 x 9 sq. ft. = 43560 sq. ft.
  - VI. 1 Decimal = 43560/ 100 = 435.60 sq. ft.
  - VII. 1 Hectare = 2.47 Acres
  - VIII. 1 Standard Hectare = 1 Hectare in irrigated area = 1.40 Hectares in non-irrigated area
- *E-Services to the citizens on land related services:*

The Land Reforms Department of Government of West launched a website portal Banglarbhumi.in to provide transparent and prompt e-services to the citizen for land related service requirements. The portal provides on-line services for most of the matters as listed below, except for those, which require field work.

For Certified copies of LR RoRs, Plot information of different types etc. are provided in response to on-line applications along with e-payment of prescribed charges. Similarly, certified copies of mauja maps or plot maps along with adjoining plots are also available on-line. Soft copies of all these certified copies are required to be downloaded for printing.

Monitoring and Analysis of Electronic Transactions on land related matters: e-Taal (Electronic Transaction Aggregation & Analysis Layer) is a website of the National Informatics Centre, under the Ministry of Electronics and Information Technology, Government of India. The website monitors and analyses the e-transactions made in different Government Departments in the States in Digital India.

The data shown on e-Taal on 06.03.2021, give the quantity of e-services rendered by the Land Revenue Department Government of West Bengal from 01.01.2021 to 05.03.2021. A few of the service outputs are shown below:

Name of e-Services	*Number of e-Transactions*	*Date*
Certified copy of Mauja Map (online) and Mauja Map view (online)	1,41,502	05.03.21
Certified copy of Plot Information (online)	61,46,609	-do-
Certified copy of Plot Map (online)	14,620	-do-
Certified copy of RoR (online)	77,89,132	-do-
Conversion Application (online)	39,899	-do-
Khatian (RoR) view	3,45,24,036	-do-
Mutation Application (online)	23,15,127	-do-
Plot Information	5,97,14,843	-do-
Plot Map view	1,46,02,807	-do-
RS-LR Plot Information	21,04,510	-do-
Total e-Transactions	12,73,93,085	-do-

It may be seen that such huge quantity of e-services on land related matters have been given in the State in just first 64 days of the year 2021. As the data is updated regularly on the e-Taal, updated current data may be checked for any State on any day. The above data shows the enormous public demand for services and information on land matters and prompt services can be provided due to the high quality of computerization and digitization of RoRs and maps and their acceptability by the citizens of the State for the accuracy and reliability of the RoRs and cadastral maps.

Annexure 1: *Copy of RoR*

Copy of LR Record of Right

জেলা — উত্তর ২৪-পরগনা খতিয়ান নং — ৭৪৫ [১৫০৭০২৪]

মৌজা — [illegible] জে.এল.নং — ২৪ থানা — রাজারহাট

(১) রাজস্ব — ০.০০ টাকা

(২) জমির মোট পরিমাণ — ২.২৬ একর (৩) মোট দাগের সংখ্যা — ৩৪

(৪) অত্রস্বত্বের দখলকারের বিবরণ (৫) স্বত্ব (৬) মন্তব্য

নাম পিতা/স্বামী ঠিকানা	[illegible] নাথ সরকার [illegible] সরকার নিজ	রায়ত	

(৭) অত্রস্বত্বের নিজ দখলীয় জমি ঃ

দাগ নম্বর	জমির শ্রেণী	মন্তব্য	দাগের মোট পরিমাণ	দাগের মধ্যে অত্র স্বত্বের	দাগের মধ্যে অত্র-স্বত্বের জমির অংশের পরিমাণ	
			একর	অংশ	একর	হেক্টর
১৪৫৮	শালি		০.১৭	০.২৫০০	০.০৪	
১৪৬৩	শালি		০.২৫	০.২৫০০	০.০৬	
১৪৯২	শালি		[illegible]	১.০০০০	০.৪০	
১৫০৪	শালি		[illegible]	০.২৫০০	০.০৪	
১৫০৬	শালি		০.১৬	[illegible]	০.০৪	
১৫০৭	শালি		০.২৫	[illegible]	০.০৭	
১৫০৮	শালি		০.২০	[illegible]	০.০৫	
১৫০৯	শালি		০.০৮	[illegible]	[illegible]	
১৫১০	শালি		০.১০	০.২৫০০	০.০৩	
১৫১২	শালি		০.৮৭	[illegible]	০.১৭	
১৬২৩	শালি		০.৬০	[illegible]	০.১৫	
১৬৭৭	শালি		০.৩৫	[illegible]	০.০৯	
১৬৭৮	শালি		০.০৬	[illegible]	০.০১	
১৬৭৯	শালি		[illegible]	০.২৫০০	০.২০	
১৬৮০	শালি		[illegible]	০.২৫০০	০.০২	
১৬৮১	শালি		[illegible]	০.২৫০০	০.০০	
১৬৮২	শালি		০.০৩	০.২৫০০	০.০১	
দাগের মোট সংখ্যা						

(7)

Annexure 2 *Copy of Mouza Map*

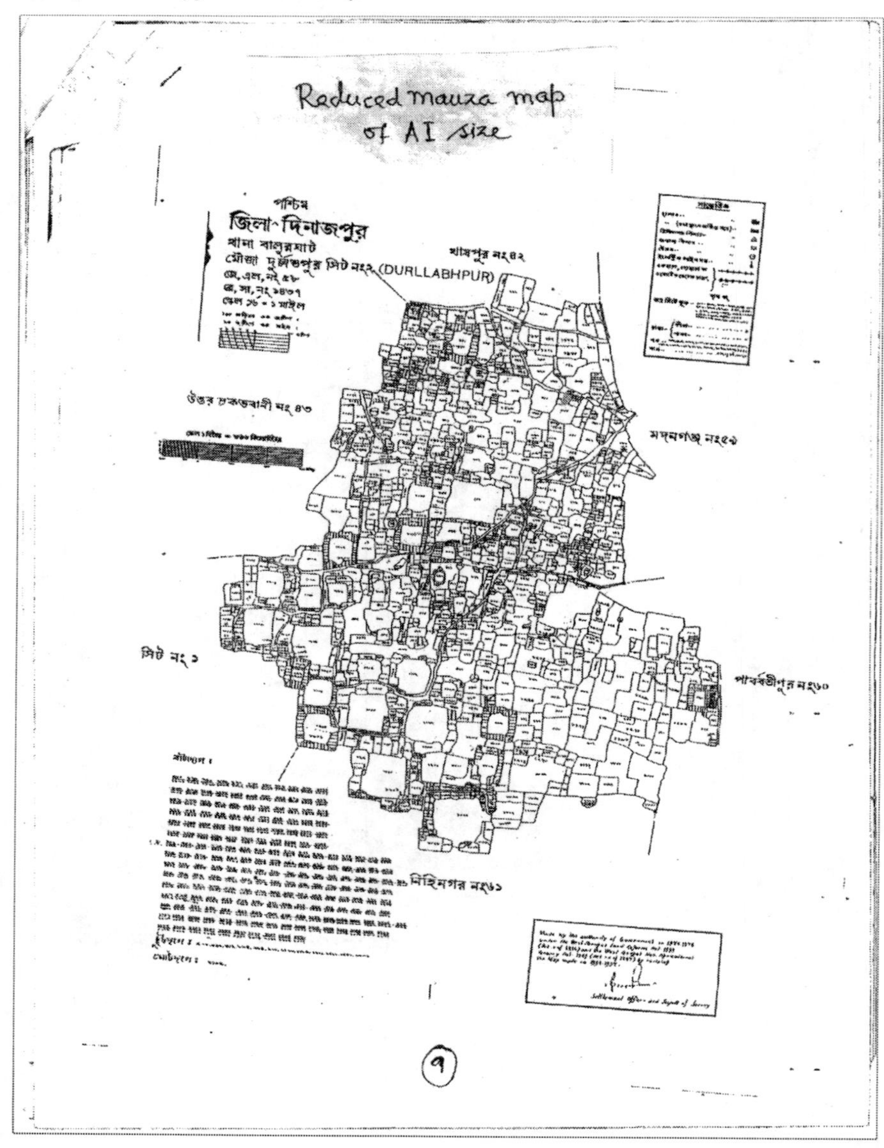

3

Modern Methods of Land Surveying: Models and Technologies

Lt. Gen Girish Kumar VSM (Retd.)

Introduction

The history of land surveying dates back to ancient times, with a recorded land register in Egypt in 3000 B.C., and re-establishment of farm boundaries following floods of the Nile River and construction of the Great Pyramid of Giza recorded about the same time. Under the Romans, land surveying was established as a profession and land surveyors established the basic measurements under which the Roman Empire was divided, such as a tax register of conquered lands. Our country also had robust land surveying mechanism from days of Raja Todarmal and great Trigonometric Arc Survey to till date. India has about 6.4 lakh revenue villages. Most of the villages were surveyed and corresponding village (cadastral) maps were prepared at 1:4,000 to 1:8,000 scales during late 19th and early 20th century. These cadastral maps were prepared using plane table survey and chain survey. These were prepared for assessing revenues on the basis of land parcel area, quality of land and output generated. However, there is a need to bring these old cadastral maps under standard projection/coordinate system for effective linkage of the developmental plans generated in the GIS environment.

With population explosion, sturdy and reliable infrastructure is one of the needs of the hour. It is imperative to perform land planning amid limited space available to build the level of settlements suitable for common citizen. Also, the Government and businesses invest heavily in infrastructure to scale and expand their infrastructure portfolio and provide for development. However, before making a real estate purchase, extensive land surveys are conducted and they form an integral part of an infrastructure development plan.

Land surveying has evolved rapidly with technology and eliminated the most primitive and persistent issues which existed almost thirty-five years ago. The previously available tools to conduct land surveys produced results which were adequate for the time and prevalent land surveying requirements. However, with the new age developments, the role of land surveying assumed a critical role to determine smooth infrastructure development. The Plane Table survey was initially devised to perform land surveys. It lost its charm to Theodolite which was updated to Electronic Theodolite, which evolved into Total Station. New technologies emerged with a focus on developing smarter solutions to reduce the processing time and increase effectiveness. The rise to the latest and most advanced tool in the field of land surveying are GPS/Rovers, CORS and Drone survey, which has simplified the entire process and produced good results.

Modern Technologies for Land Survey

Modern land surveying is done by three possible methods: (a) field survey, (b) aerial survey, and (c) satellite images. The first method comes under direct technique while the remaining two methods come within indirect technique. The selection of technology for land survey depends upon several factors, such as terrain conditions (hilly, undulating, plain), vegetative cover (dense, sparse), built-up areas (urban, settlements), size of survey area (state or region or project area), accuracy (required versus achievable), timeliness (short or normal), and cost (budget requirement versus available).[55]

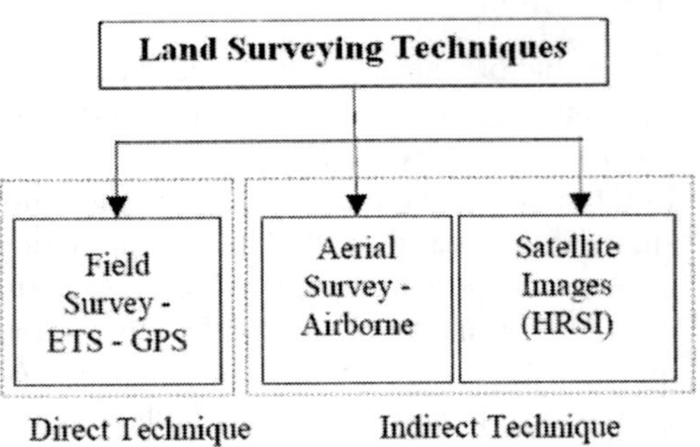

Figure 1 *Land Surveying Technique*

Field Surveys by Electronic Total Station and GPS

A total station consists of a theodolite with a built-in distance meter (distancer), and so it can measure angles and distances at the same time. Today's electronic total stations all have an opto-electronic distance meter (EDM) and electronic angle scanning. The coded scales of the horizontal and vertical circles are scanned electronically, and then the angles and distances are displayed digitally. The horizontal distance, the height difference and the coordinates are calculated automatically and all measurements and additional information can be recorded. Total stations are used wherever the positions and heights of points, or merely their positions, need to be determined.

Advantages of Total Station

(a) Quick setting of the instrument on the tripod using laser plummet.
(b) On-board area computation programme to compute the area of the field.
(c) Local language support.
(d) GIS layers creation.

[55] Ali et al, 2012

(e) Automation of old maps.
(f) Greater accuracy in area computation.
(g) Graphical view of plots and land for quick integration of data base.
(h) The area computation at any user required scale.

Disadvantages of Total Station

(a) It may be difficult for the surveyor to look over and check the work while surveying.
(b) The instrument is costly. And conducting surveys using total station, skilled personnel are required.
(c) For an over all check of the survey, it will be necessary to return to the office and prepare the drawings using appropriate software.
(d) **Time consuming.**[56]

High Resolution Satellite Imagery (HRSI)

HRSI based Land survey are used when the accuracy required is less like for a map of scale of 1:10000 and helps to keep the cost of project in check. It provides raw/direct deliverables of mono & stereo images with RPC information to process outputs for DTM (Terrain Model), Ortho Images, Contours, 2D & 3D Vector Data & Maps. The best Ground Sampling Distance (GSD)/spatial resolution currently available are in the range of 15 cms to 50 cms (mono/stereo).

It has varied applications in:

(a) Topographic Mapping
(b) Forestry
(c) Land use mapping and planning
(d) Change Detection application

Resurvey using HRSI: Procedures of resurvey using HRSI are as follows:[57]

(a) *Pre-processing of satellite data*: In order to make satellite data ready for parcel boundary extraction, a set of pre-processes are needed. Image processing techniques such as DEM generation, orthorectification and image enhancement are needed to eliminate distortions which were produced during the image acquisition by the sensor. Such corrected data can then be used for parcel boundary extraction
(b) *DEM Generation*: Digital Elevation Model (DEM) is a representation of ground surface topography in digital format. The raster generated from DEM contains elevation information of the terrain at each pixel.
(c) *Ortho-Rectification*: The raw satellite image has geometric distortions due to sensor orientation and varying terrain. The image displacements caused

[56] Er PraveshYagol, 2015
[57] S S Rao et al., 2014

by the above factors are geometrically corrected to match the projection of map co-ordinate system using transformation techniques.

(d) *Image Enhancement*: It is the process of enhancing the image information to produce the better look of the image. There are various image enhancement techniques, such as, contrast manipulation, histogram equalization, etc.

(e) *Parcel extraction from ortho-rectified satellite data*: Parcels are digitized over satellite images based on the visual interpretation using the ground surveyed vector layers.

Advantages of using HRSI vis-à-vis aerial imagery are:

(a) The satellite platform is operational as per tasking
(b) There are no restrictions and permissions
(c) No aircraft, cameras or otherwise expensive equipment's are required (by the end user) however as per HRSI policy of GoI, it will take minimum 8 to 12 week for acquisition
(d) Has more number of Spectral Bands for environmental monitoring.

Disadvantages of HRSI are:

(a) The imaging time is fixed. It cannot be optimized with respect to weather conditions and cloud coverage
(b) The image resolution is fixed for a particular sensor and low compared to most aerial imagery. Aerial images can be collected with the same resolution (in high altitude mode), if necessary
(c) The radiometric resolution is often too low (problems in shadows and saturation areas)
(d) The reliability of capture and delivery of imagery can be poor at times
(e) Strong possibilities of cloud cover and thus occlusions.

Aerial Photogrammetry Based Land Survey

Aerial photos are used when accuracy levels are very important for the survey. Sensors used for aerial imageries are primarily Digital Camera. They provide Raw/Direct Deliverables of Mono/Stereo Images with GPS/IMU data. And using the same we can process outputs for DTM (Digital Terrain Model), Ortho Images, Contours, 2D & 3D Vector Data & Maps. The best Ground sampling Distance/Spatial resolution currently available are based on the application and Mapping scale, Large Format Digital Cameras can acquire 5-10 cms GSD. The GSD Range can be from 25 cms to 5 cms based on the flying height (influenced by the application requirements). However, suitable overlapping aerial photography must be available to provide stereometric cover, that is, every part of the ground must appear on at least two adjoining photographs and some points must appear on three successive photographs in a strip of photography. The fore and aft overlap for photographs should be about 60 per cent while the lateral overlap between strips should be around 20 per cent. Having acquired such a block of photography and depending on its scale, the equipment used, the quality of the images of the coordinated points and the skill of the operators, then it is possible to measure the relative positions of points on the ground to within an accuracy of a few centimetres. Photogrammetry is essentially a mass production technique that becomes cost effective only when a sufficiently large number of points on the ground need to be fixed. The accuracy achievable with modern equipment is dependent on cost more than any other factor. An additional benefit that comes from using photogrammetry is that the techniques can be used not only for fixing control points but also for plotting detail and contour lines. Ground survey techniques are less suited to topographic mapping other than for relatively small areas.

It has varied applications in land survey as:

(a) Topographic Mapping
(b) 3-D City Modelling and visualization
(c) Land records/Cadastral Mapping
(d) Floodplain mapping and planning
(e) Agriculture/Crop Monitoring
(f) Airport mapping/aviation safety
(g) Urban Mapping and Planning
(h) Forestry
(i) Land use mapping and planning
(j) Electrical utilities/transmission line corridor mapping.

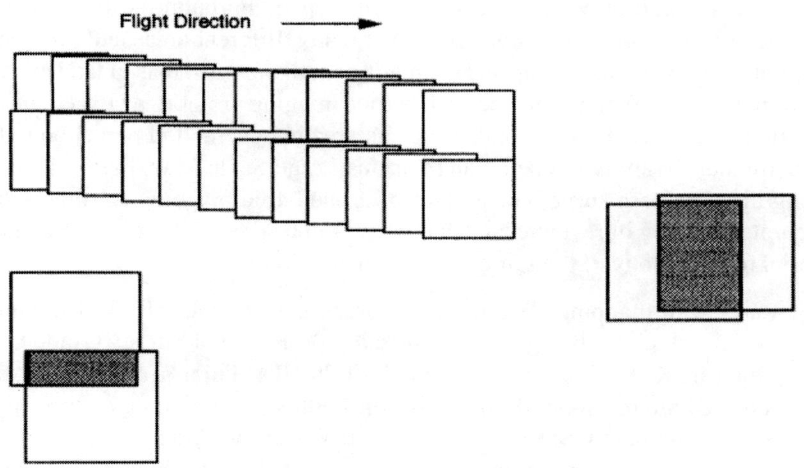

20% Lateral Overlap **60% Fore & Aft Overlap**

Figure 2 *Aerial Photogrammetry*

Procedure of feature extraction remains same for aerial imagery as that of HRSI except for mosaicking since the area of images are small in size.

Advantages of using aerial imagery vis-à-vis HRSI are:

(a) Only way to capture High Resolution imagery upto 5-10 cm GSD and opens up lots of application areas.
(b) Standalone Lidar (without camera) can penetrate through clouds and captures terrain data in night.
(c) Freedom to operate below cloud covers and low altitudes (Can be used post-disasters like floods, cyclones), so cloud free data delivery is guaranteed.
(d) Nowadays, Cameras are also capturing Infrared band along with RGB.

Disadvantages of Aerial imagery are

- Requires DGCA permissions to fly and capture data. It will take 2 to 4 week's time.

Current Survey Technologies for Land Parcel Survey

Drone Based Land Survey

Drone mapping is the process of surveying an area of land with a UAV. An operator flies the drone over an area of land, taking hundreds of pictures as it moves. Then, with the help of computer software, they stitch and layer the images, creating a model of the site. This process is also similar to how drone photogrammetry works and the end result is an accurate 2D and 3D representation of the area. However, the coverage of area is less compared to the earlier mentioned two methods. Drone survey can provide pixel up to 3 cm depending upon the flying height. The benefits of drone surveying cross over many different areas and provide an accurate method of inspecting and evaluating small or large areas of land creating their maps. From flatlands to deep pits, drone imaging provides an excellent way to safe and precise mapping and survey an area in general and parcel boundary in particular. Svamitva Scheme and various Large Scale Mapping projects are using these modern survey techniques of drone based mapping for precise and accurate mapping of revenue land and Abadi Land spread all across the country, a brief methodology of the same is enunciated as below:

(a) Large scale mapping of rural revenue areas using Drone or UAV (Unmanned Aerial Vehicle) is being carried out using Professional Survey Grade UAVs which are RTK (Real Time Kinematic)/PPK (Post Point Kinematic) enabled and use high resolution RGB sensor on 1:500 scale with image capturing of better than 5 cm GSD ± 12.5 cm or better planimetry accuracy to provide accurate projection centre and orientation of the images captured during the flying.
(b) Once Drone flying is complete over an AoI, Processing of data is done with Block Control and Adjustment – AT (Aerial Triangulation)/DEM (Digital

Elevation Model) generation and DTM (Digital Terrain Model) processing and finally ortho-rectified images (ORI) is created.

(c) ORI is used for extraction of all topographical features including property boundaries and other features or assets viz. open plots, government owned land, Gram Sabha owned properties, individual properties.

Land Survey Using Continuously Operating Reference System (CORS)

Requirement of Geodetic Control is most critical where intense development is taking place, particularly in urban and rural areas for land management, demarcation of individuals land boundaries, for development of smart cities, large scale cadastral mapping and the delineation of state boundaries where high accuracy surveys are required. Now, the surveying technology has seen remarkable developments during recent decades. Also, the requirements of the users have increased manifold. Users require precise spatial information instantly. Continuously Operating Reference System (CORS) is a geodetic infrastructure that will meet the evolving future economic, scientific and national security needs of the State and provide highly accurate spatial positions in real-time. GNSS (Global Navigation Satellite System), CORS (Continuously Operated Reference Station), which is Primarily GNSS augmentation system that facilitates, archive and distribution of GNSS data corrections for precise positioning in an automated manner, usually over an Internet connection. In this modern world, with the pervasive demand for high-precision and accuracy across a variety of applications, CORS technology is rapidly becoming the preferred method for accurate 2D and 3D positioning across the world and is in great demand among sectors that require greater positional accuracy repeatedly over a period of time.

CORS as Positioning Infrastructure: CORS is a geodetic and geo-positioning infrastructure that provides seamless consistent and uniform framework of the State/Country. It offers highly accurate DGPS service that also improves the speed, efficiency, and simplicity of in-house data-acquisition process. CORS takes the overall productivity to the next level by overcoming the limitations of the current Real Time Kinematic (RTK) technique. CORS Network has wide application in the development of India. It will help in the construction of large infrastructure projects and in generation and updating of revenue maps, which is one of the major problems being faced by the country today.

Concept of RTK: The conventional approach to RTK requires two base stations as well as a rover to accurately determine a position. Base stations are set up at the known points and a rover is used for observation for two hours. This observed data is processed later to determine the accurate new position. Using CORS this long duration observation is reduced considerably for providing accurate positional information.

Use and Benefits of CORS. A control Centre (CC) is established and all CORS stations are connected to the CC for real time corrections of their positions. Rovers are used in standalone mode to get the real time correct position from the Control Centre within 2-5 minutes of observations. Therefore the need to set-up reference station with all the related work like personal, power, and security in case of the RTK Network is eliminated once CORS infrastructure is in place. Constant communication of CC with the Rovers for providing positional corrections is maintained through Internet-based communication. With only one rover (GNSS receiver) required for calculating real time positioning data, ease of use, enhanced accuracy, productivity, cost of equipment, time and personnel is reduced significantly and can be used by any State agency/Department viz Revenue Department, Gram Panchayat (GP), Public Works Department, Rural Development Department, Agriculture, Drainage & Canal, Education, Electricity, Water, Health etc. for the survey and implementing/using GIS and Land survey based activities.

Conclusion

Land survey is essential not only for revenue administration but for planners and policy formulators from diverse fields like agriculture, urban and rural development, industry and mines and so on and so forth. Therefore, continuous updating of land records through revisional survey is must. In India, land revenue record has its old legacy of un-updated maps which do not match with the ground realities. India has a long traditional history of preparation of land records through survey, during British regime scientific land survey were undertaken using chain, cross-staff and plane table survey. Even after the independence, land records management through revisional survey was not implemented properly by many of the States, as the focus was only to implement land reforms. As a result, land records in most of the States are obsolete. However, some States have updated their records through revisional survey at an interval of 30-40 years.

Since 2000 onwards, many states started adopting modern technologies for survey of land parcels to update the age-old revenue records based on their suitability. Modern instruments like DGPS and ETS are being used in most of the states such as Gujarat, West Bengal, Madhya Pradesh, Kerala, Maharashtra, Haryana, and Karnataka. Rajasthan has adopted hybrid technology for updating of the land records whereas Bihar adopted Aerial Photography. However, in Uttar Pradesh manual process of surveying by using chain and plane-table are still in use. In Maharashtra, since 2000 onwards surveys were carried out by using DGPS/ETS, they have also tried Satellite Imagery for land survey on pilot basis.

Recently, Continuous Operating Reference Station (CORS) network has been installed by Maharashtra, Karnataka, Andhra Pradesh, Uttar Pradesh, Uttarakhand, Punjab, Himachal Pradesh and Rajasthan for updating their land records. Similarly, the CORS network has also been used by Haryana for updating their land records. The CORS network technology is very accurate, cost-effective and saves lot of time and resources in undertaking land surveys. CORS network is being extended in rest of the country under various Central/State supported schemes. Haryana, UT of A&N Islands and Andhra Pradesh have also started updating of their land records using high resolution images generated using professional survey grade drones in combination with CORS network which provide better technical solution in terms of accuracy, time and resource deployment for subject activity.

Technology has empowered the people dedicated to land survey and having the following benefits:

(a) *Accuracy*: Modern instruments used by land surveyors have an accuracy of distance measurements by +/- (2 mm + 2 ppm) x d. It is exceedingly accurate when compared to the results produced by the tools developed a decade ago. For a fundamental and complex process such as land surveying, accurate results have revolutionized the entire process.

(b) *Scope/Portfolio*: Previously, land surveying techniques were limited in scope as the technologies themselves. Fast forward to now, these methods have evolved extensively and are no longer limited to measuring land. They are now being used to survey the sea, and airspace to discover new infrastructure development opportunities and revolutionize land use.

(c) *Speed*: One of the areas which have been primarily impacted by the evolution of land surveying technologies is the speed of the process. With advanced technology, accurate results are presented in a few hours. Drones do not require much human effort and are designed and developed to deliver faster results.

(d) *Infrastructure Possibilities*: Land surveys are the core of infrastructure development. Smart cities, futuristic transportation, impressively designed buildings and much more are a result of the technological evolution in land surveys. Technologies like GPS and DGPS have brought about transparency in the infrastructure domain with its satellite mapping capabilities. Integration of high-level tech as such has been the main reason for our imagination coming true in the field of infrastructure.

As far as the modern technologies are concerned for land survey, any such instrument provides accurate and authentic data records but to use it for updating of revenue records, users should be more careful, ground truthing should be done in the presence of all stakeholders in the village itself so that final record preparation will be much more transparent, authentic and grievances, if any, would be redressed properly.

References

1. Ali, Z., 2012. Assessing Usefulness of High-Resolution Satellite Imagery (HRSI) in GIS-based Cadastral Land Information System. *Journal of Settlements and Spatial Planning*, 3(2), pp. 93-96.
2. S. S. Rao, J. R. Sharma, S. S. Rajasekhar, D. S. P. Rao, A. Arepalli, V. Arora, Kul-deep, R. P. Singh, M. Kanaparthi: ISPRS Annals of the Photogrammetry, Remote Sensing and Spatial Information Sciences, Volume II-8, 2014; ISPRS Technical Commission VIII Symposium, 09 – 12 December 2014, Hyderabad, India
3. Er PraveshYagol, comparative study on Cadastral surveying using Total station and High Resolution satellite image.pg 5-6. FIG- ISPRS workshop, 2015: international workshop on role of land professionals and SDI in disaster risk reduction.
4. Photogrammetry Survey: Chapter XII of Survey of India.

Contributors

The Editors

Anandhi, IAS officer of 2007 batch, Rajasthan cadre. She is currently serving as Deputy Director (Sr.) in Lal Bahadur Shastri National Academy of Administration, Musoorie since December, 2020. She has studied B.A, LL.B from Delhi University. She has served as District Collector in Bundi, Sawai Madhopur, Rajsamand, Udaipur and Alwar districts and given Best Collector Award in 2019 for work in Udaipur. She has also served as Managing Director, Rajasthan State Cooperative Marketing Federation Ltd. (Rajfed) and education sector as SPD, RMSA respectively and done a stint in Secretariat as Joint Secretary, Finance Tax.

Snehasis Mishra is working as Assistant Professor, B.N. Yugandhar Centre for Rural Studies, Lal Bahadur Shastri National Academy of Administration, Mussoorie. He is associated with various teaching and training programmes of IAS Officials during their professional courses. He has written research papers and co-authored/edited state-report on Land Records practices and implementation of Digital Indian Land Records Modernization Programme. He has co-edited (with Dr. A.A.A. Faizi) book on Conclusive Land Titling (2015) and *Journey Towards Land Titling in India* (2017 with Dr. Varsha Ganguly). He has participated and organised Seminars on land records and land titling related issues. His areas of interests cover e-governance, land records management, land governance, survey and mapping.

The Contributors

Ashok Nada, currently working as Deputy Director, (Inspection) in the office of Settlement Commissioner and Director of Land Records, Gujarat. He has dealing closely on land related matters, having more than 20 years of experience. He previously served as Superintendent of Land Records in Bharuch District.

Ashutosh Tiwari, currently working as Assistant Superintendent Land Record (ASLR) in the capacity of Junior Administrative Services, in the office of Commissioner Land Records Office, Gwalior, Madhya Pradesh. He possesses B. Tech and MBA degrees. He was previously engaged in Defence Accounts Dept., Ministry of Defence, Government of India. His areas of interests are Public Administration, Good Governance and Rural Development etc. He is presently supervising Land Management section at Commissioner Land Records Office, Gwalior.

Chandan Kumar, is a GIS Advisor in the Directorate of Land Records and Survey, Patna.

Chittaranjan Das, IAS (Retd.), an alumnus of the Presidency College, Calcutta and formerly belonging to the State Civil Services, retired from the IAS in 2010. He was associated with the training of IAS, IPS, State Civil Service and Judicial Service officers etc. in the Land Survey and Settlement Training programme for more than two decades, while he was in the Land and Land Reforms Dept. of the Government of West Bengal. Trained in the Survey of India, he was in charge of survey, mapping and map reproduction in the State for more than a decade. Later, he served as District Magistrate, Malda, DEO Calcutta North, Commissioner of Excise WB etc. and then as Member of the Land Reforms & Tenancy Tribunal, with powers of a Single Bench of the High Court of Calcutta for disposal of land related appeal cases. Presently, he is a regular guest faculty of the West Bengal Judicial Academy for training of Judicial Service Officers and also associated with the ATI, Kolkata. As a social activist, he acted as the Chairman of the Indian Red Cross Society, West Bengal for seven years, appointed by the Hon'ble Governor of West Bengal.

Dr. Anishia Jayadev is working as Assistant Professor at Institute of Management in Government, Kerala. She also functions as Nodal Officer, Gender. She holds her Ph.D. in Sociology from the University of Kerala. Research interests are in the fields of Health, Gender, Dalit (Indian Depressed Classes) studies and Issues of Governance. She is a Recognized Trainer for Direct Trainer Skills and Training Needs Analysis certified by the Thames Valley University, UK and the Department of Personnel and Training, Government of India. She is a Teacher for a M Phil level programme of Cochin University of Science and Technology conducted by Indian Institute of Technology And Management (ecological informatics) and Faculty for the PG Diploma programme on e-governance, Directorate of Technical Education, Government of Kerala. She has done the Training Needs Analysis of nearly 25 Government Departments. She is actively contributing to various policy-making initiatives for the State of Kerala.

Dr. Ashok Sanganal has been working as Senior Faculty and Head of Centre for Disaster Management, ATI, Mysuru. He had obtained B.E. (Civil-NITK Surathkal), M. Tech. (Structural Engg., NITK, Surathkal), PG Dip. (Housing-Institute for Housing Studies, Netherlands), Ph.D. (Urban Infr-IDS), PG Dip. (Training & Development-ISTD, New Delhi). He taught surveying & civil engineering subjects at NITK, Surathkal. Earlier worked as senior officer at HUDCO, GoI, New Delhi. His area of work includes teaching, training, research, practical and field experience in civil engineering, housing and infrastructure, disaster management, Public Private Partnership projects, appropriate technology. He has been recognized as national level master trainer for TDP programmes on DTS, DoT, MoT, TNA, NTP, master exercise design, Incident Response System and project management. He has written several books, case studies, research papers, handbooks and articles. Obtained National Award and First Prize from Ministry of Urban Development, GoI and UNCHS.

Dr. Shashi Jain is currently posted as Assistant Settlement Officer in the Commissionerate of Land Settlement, Government of Rajasthan, Jaipur. After having completed his B.Sc. (Hons.) in Agriculture from CCS, Haryana Agriculture University, Hisar, in the year 1991, he completed his M.Sc. in Soil Science and Ph.D. in Soil Science with special emphasis on Remote Sensing and GIS techniques from CCS, Haryana Agriculture University, Hisar. He joined the Rajasthan State Agriculture Department as Assistant Agriculture Research Officer in 1996 through Rajasthan Public Service Commission. Till date, Dr. Jain has served in many departments like Agriculture, Science & Technology and Settlement Department and has a vast experience of working at State Remote Sensing Application Centre, Jodhpur (Rajasthan). While at State Remote Sensing Application Centre, Dr. Jain was engaged in many Remote Sensing, GIS, Satellite Communication projects etc. in collaboration with ISRO and various line departments like Agriculture, Watershed, Forest, IT, Town Planning, Water Resources etc. of the State. At present, Dr. Jain is working as Assistant Settlement Officer and is engaged in preparation of digital land records under Survey Resurvey component of Digital Land Record Modernization Programme (DILRMP) of Government of India.

Indrajit Das is working as Assistant Director of Surveys in Assam, in the office of Joint Director of Surveys, Assam. He had obtained M.Sc. in Mathematics from Tezpur Central University, M.Sc. in Geo-informatics from Sikkim Manipal University, PG Diploma (Computer Application) from C-DAC. He had done Surveying course in Indian Institute of Surveying and Mapping, Hyderabad. He taught Surveying as a guest Lecturer in the Assam Survey and Settlement Training Centre, Guwahati, also worked in Survey of India. He looks after the planning, implementation, monitoring of survey of Non-cadastral villages of Assam and matters related to survey of international/district/village boundaries. He has been working as Charge Officer for the Joint field survey along the Assam (India) — Bangladesh International Boundary for Assam sector. And also looks after the administrative works of Assam Survey.

Jani Jyotinkumar Prahladbhai has retired as Deputy Director from Deendayal Institute of Survey & Revenue Administration, Gandhinagar. He had obtained B.Sc. in Chemistry. He served Government of Gujarat at various capacities, recruited as a Deputy Mamlatdar cadre in1983 and worked as Deputy Mamlatdar at Collectorate, Ahmedabad up to 1990, then became District Inspector of Land Records and promoted as a Deputy Director. His entire career moved around land and revenue administration. Apart from that, his specialization is to impart training on Survey Settlement & Revenue Administration, laws, rules, City Survey training etc. to Survey Settlement and Revenue Department officials.

Krishna Singh Shekhawat has a vast experience of more than 38 years in the field of settlement operations in the State of Rajasthan. After completing his Bachelor's degree in Science, Shri Shekhawat joined the Land Settlement Department, Rajasthan in 1980 as *Bhu-Mapak.* Since then, he has been associated with traditional land record/settlement operations. He was also actively involved in preparation of master plans, land acquisition plans and urban property surveys. He was engaged with many departments like Forest, Mining, JDA, Survey of India and was also a team member for studying the record operations of the States of Gujarat, Bihar, Haryana, Andhra Pradesh, Karnataka, Maharashtra. He attained software experience in Autocad, Micro station, Bentley, MGE, Intergraph, Arc-GIS, QGIS, Global Mapper etc. and also has worked on E.D.M., T2Theodolite, Total Station, DGPS (PPK&RTK) instruments. He has also worked as instructor for State Training Institute, Revenue Training Institute, Officers Training Academy etc. He also did a 2-month training course on Land Records in the United Kingdom. He is superannuated in the year 2018. After superannuation he is also rendering his services as a consultant to many organizations.

Lt. Gen Girish Kumar VSM (Retd.) has retired as Surveyor General of India (Oct. 2017-Jan. 2021), and has expertise in the geospatial domain with almost 39 years of service experience in wide ranging areas of Surveying, Mapping, Geospatial Policy, GIS applications, Digital data Generation, Geospatial Infrastructure, International boundary matters etc. He also served as Additional Director General Military Survey (GSGS), Military Survey, Army Headquarters.

As Civil Engineering Graduate of Punjab Engineering College (PEC), he joined Corps of Engineers of Indian Army in year 1980 and then seconded to Survey of India (SoI) in 1982. He has undergone various specialized courses in Surveying, Mapping and digital data generation in India and abroad including Production Photogrammetry PG course from ITC, Netherlands. He has wide ranging work experience in various positions and capacities covering Technical, Planning, Policy Making, Finance, Administration, Human Resource Management activities in SoI and Military Survey. He actively participated in National/International Seminars, Workshops, Forums and conferences as a speaker, member, presenter and an expert. He has led Indian delegations in International Bilateral and Multilateral forums in matters related to Surveying, Mapping and Geo-spatial data management.

He has played key role in formulating the National Map Policy (NMP) of the Government of India in 2005, pivotal work in preparing the design document and standards for National Land Record Modernization Programme (NLRMP) in year 2008, Modernization of Tidal Gauge network of the country, Digital Map Production in SoI, Finalization of India-Bangladesh Boundary Protocol-2011 as Advisor to MEA etc.

Presently his assignments are: Advisor (International Boundary), Ministry of External Affairs, Government of India, New Delhi, Mission Director, Large Scale Mapping Project of Governemt of Haryana, Vice Chairman, Drone Imaging and Information Services, Haryana (DRIISHYA) and Chairman, Monitoring, Implementation and Hand-Holding Committee under SVAMITVA Scheme of Ministry of Panchayati Raj, Government of India, New Delhi.

Manoj Kumar Jha is currently serving as Deputy Secretary, Revenue and Land Reforms Department, Government of Bihar. He is an Officer of Bihar Administrative Service of 42nd Batch. Since 2000, he has been serving Bihar Government in various capacities.

Manoranjan Ray is working as Assistant Director of Surveys, Assam. He has obtained M.Sc. from Guwahati University and completed the Surveying Course at Indian Institute and Surveying and Mapping, Hyderabad. Previously he worked in Survey of India. His area of work includes conducting and monitoring the field survey operations in Assam and also teaching and training at Assam Survey Settlement Training Centre on Modern Survey Techniques e.g. ETS, DGPS, GIS etc. and has field experience in the field of Surveying and Mapping.

Mohinder Kumar, IAS (Retd.), has worked in the field as SDM, ADC, DC in various districts of Haryana i.e. Ambala, Jhajjar, Bhiwani, Rewari and Panipat. He has been Divisional Commissioner, Ambala Division and Secretary to Governor of Haryana. He has served as Vice Chancellor in YMCA University of Science & Technology, Faridabad, Deenbandhu Chhoturam University of Science & Technology, Murthal, Sonipat and Indira Gandhi University, Meerpur, Rewari. His total experience of Vice Chancellor is about 4 years 5 months. At present, Sh. Mohinder Kumar is working as Consultant Revenue & Course Director of IAS & HCS in the Haryana Institute of Public Administration (HIPA), Gurugram.

Sham Khamkar, Retired Deputy Director of Land Records, has served the Government of Maharashtra for over 31 years and has manifested the vast experience gathered from multiple positions and postings as an author to write state chapter of Maharashtra in this handbook. While leading major projects as a Deputy Director, like computerisation and modernisation of land records and digitisation of cadastral maps, he helped pioneer the future of surveying by introducing modern techniques which were appreciated statewide. He has majorly contributed to the state in resurvey and studied the pros and cons of this complex subject. As a District and Divisional Head, he has also actively advocated training, workshops and seminars to help the newer generation become better problem solvers and critical thinkers. He enjoys mentoring aspirants and encourages everyone to carry a student mentality throughout life.

Siddharth Jain (IAS), Commissioner of Survey Settlements & Land Records, Andhra Pradesh.

Sunil Kumar Jha is a PCS officer of 2018 batch, posted as OSD Board of Revenue, Uttar Pradesh. He was selected as Naib Tahsildar in 1996 in Uttar Pradesh Revenue services. His first posting was in Kanpur (Rural) as Naib Tahsildar. He has worked in Kanpur (Rural), Kanpur Development Authority, Kanpur Nagar and Lucknow as Naib Tahsildar. As Tahsildar he has served in districts Lucknow, Barabanki, Lakhimpur Kheri and Board of Revenue. Graduated in 1990 in Physics and Mathematics from DBS Degree College, Kanpur and did his Post graduation in Electronics in 1992.